BARTHOLOMEW PAPERBACK
WORLD ATLAS

John Bartholomew & Son Ltd
Edinburgh

Printed in Scotland

Published by John Bartholomew & Son Ltd
Duncan Street, Edinburgh EH9 1TA

First Edition MCMLXXXIV

ISBN 0 7028 0700 1

BO49

Title page photograph courtesy of NASA

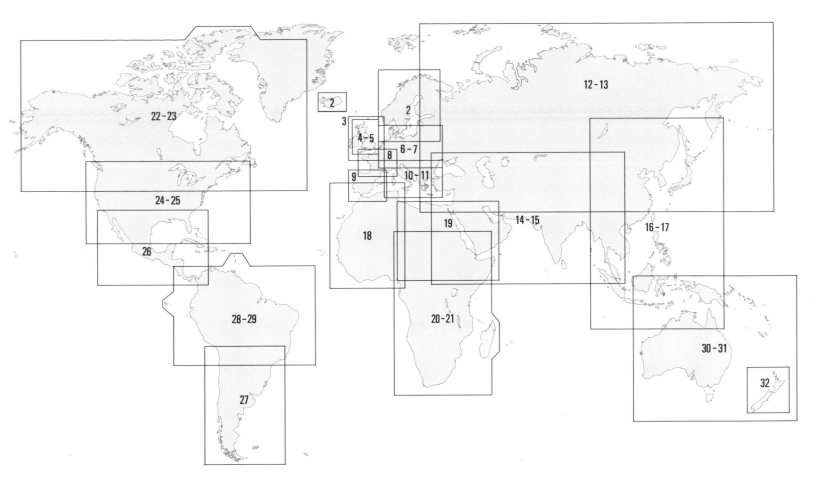

Contents

ARCTIC OCEAN

SVALBARD

Zemlya Frantsa Iosifa

Severnaya Zemlya

Novo Sibirskiye Ostrova

BARENTS SEA

KARA SEA

Os. Vrangelya (Wrangel I.)

UNION OF SOVIET SOCIALIST REPUBLICS

MONGOLIA
Ulaanbaatar

Manchuria

SINKIANG

Beijing

CHINA

TIBET

JAPAN
Tōkyō

INDIA

BURMA
THAILAND
Bangkok

PHILIPPINES

SRI LANKA

MALAYSIA
Singapore

BORNEO

INDONESIA

PAPUA NEW GUINEA

AUSTRALIA

INDIAN OCEAN

NEW ZEALAND

INTERNATIONAL DATE LINE

Longitude East 135° of Greenwich

v

THE WORLD IN FIGURES

MOUNTAIN HEIGHTS

Metres	Feet		Metres	Feet	
8848	29 028	Everest (Qomolangma Feng) *Nepal-Tibet*	6908	22 664	Ojos del Salado *Chile-Argentina*
8611	28 250	K2 (Godwin Austen) *Kashmir-Singkiang*	6870	22 541	Bonete *Bolivia*
8586	28 168	Kangchenjunga *Nepal-India*	6800	22 310	Tupungato *Argentina-Chile*
8475	27 805	Makalu *Tibet-Nepal*	6770	22 211	Mercedario *Argentina*
8172	26 810	Dhaulagiri *Nepal*	6768	22 205	Huascarán *Peru*
8126	26 660	Nanga Parbat *Kashmir*	6723	22 057	Llullaillaco *Argentina-Chile*
8078	26 504	Annapurna *Nepal*	6714	22 028	Kangrinboqê Feng (Kailas) *Tibet*
8068	26 470	Gasherbrum *Kashmir*	6634	21 765	Yerupaja *Peru*
8013	26 291	Xixabangma Feng (Gosainthan) *Tibet*	6542	21 463	Sajama *Bolivia*
7890	25 885	Distaghil Sar *Kashmir*	6485	21 276	Illampu *Bolivia*
7820	25 656	Masherbrum *Kashmir*	6425	21 079	Coropuna *Peru*
7817	25 645	Nanda Devi *India*	6402	21 004	Illimani *Bolivia*
7780	25 550	Rakaposhi *Kashmir*	6310	20 702	Chimborazo *Ecuador*
7756	25 447	Kamet *India-Tibet*	6194	20 320	McKinley *USA*
7756	25 447	Namcha Barwa *Tibet*	6050	19 850	Logan *Canada*
7728	25 355	Gurla Mandhata *Tibet*	5895	19 340	Kilimanjaro *Tanzania*
7723	25 338	Muztag (Ulugh Muztagh) *Sinkiang*	5700	18 700	Citlaltepetl *Mexico*
7719	25 325	Kongur Shan (Kungur) *Sinkiang*	5642	18 510	El'bruz *USSR*
7690	25 230	Tirich Mir *Pakistan*	5452	17 887	Popocatepetl *Mexico*
7590	24 903	Gongga Shan (Minya Konka) *China*	5200	17 058	Kenya *Kenya*
7546	24 757	Muztagata (Muztagh Ata) *Sinkiang*	5165	16 946	Ararat *Turkey*
7495	24 590	Pik Kommunizma *USSR*	5140	16 864	Vinson Massif *Antarctica*
7439	24 407	Pik Pobedy (Tomur Feng) *USSR-Sinkiang*	5110	16 763	Stanley *Zaire-Uganda*
7313	23 993	Chomo Lhari *Bhutan-Tibet*	5030	16 500	Jaya (Carstensz) *Indonesia*
7134	23 406	Pik Lenina *USSR*	4810	15 781	Mont Blanc *France*
7010	23 000	Ancohuma *Bolivia*	4508	14 790	Wilhelm *Papua New Guinea*
6960	22 834	Aconcagua *Argentina*	4201	13 784	Mauna Kea *USA*

RIVER LENGTHS

Km	Miles		Km	Miles	
6695	4160	Nile *Africa*	2850	1770	Danube *Europe*
6570	4080	Amazon *South America*	2820	1750	Salween *Asia*
6380	3964	Yangtze *Asia*	2780	1730	São Francisco *South America*
6020	3740	Mississippi-Missouri *North America*	2655	1650	Zambezi *Africa*
5410	3360	Ob-Irtysh *Asia*	2570	1600	Nelson-Saskatchewan *North America*
4840	3010	Huang He (Yellow River) *Asia*	2510	1560	Ganges *Asia*
4630	2880	Zaïre (Congo) *Africa*	2430	1510	Euphrates *Asia*
4500	2796	Paraná *South America*	2330	1450	Arkansas *North America*
4440	2760	Irtysh *Asia*	2330	1450	Colorado *North America*
4416	2745	Amur *Asia*	2285	1420	Dnepr *Europe*
4400	2730	Lena *Asia*	2090	1300	Irrawaddy *Asia*
4240	2630	Mackenzie *North America*	2060	1280	Orinoco *South America*
4180	2600	Mekong *Asia*	2000	1240	Negro *South America*
4100	2550	Niger *Africa*	1870	1160	Don *Europe*
4090	2540	Yenisey *Asia*	1859	1155	Orange *Africa*
3969	2466	Missouri *North America*	1799	1118	Pechora *Europe*
3779	2348	Mississippi *North America*	1609	1000	Marañón *South America*
3750	2330	Murray-Darling *Australia*	1410	876	Dnestr *Europe*
3688	2292	Volga *Europe*	1320	820	Rhine *Europe*
3240	2013	Madeira *South America*	1183	735	Donets *Europe*
3058	1900	St. Lawrence *North America*	1159	720	Elbe *Europe*
3030	1880	Rio Grande *North America*	1094	680	Gambia *Africa*
3020	1870	Yukon *North America*	1080	671	Yellowstone *North America*
2960	1840	Brahmaputra *Asia*	1014	630	Vistula *Europe*
2896	1800	Indus *Asia*	1006	625	Tagus *Europe*

LAKE AND INLAND SEA AREAS

Areas are average and some are subject to seasonal variations.

Sq. Km	Sq. Miles		Sq. Km	Sq. Miles	
371 000	142 240	Caspian *USSR-Iran (salt)*	22 490	8680	Nyasa (Malawi) *Malawi-Mozambique*
82 900	32 010	Superior *USA-Canada*	19 400	7490	Ontario *USA-Canada*
68 800	26 560	Victoria *Kenya-Uganda-Tanzania*	18 390	7100	Ladoga *USSR*
65 500	25 300	Aral *USSR (salt)*	17 400	6700	Balkhash *USSR*
59 580	23 000	Huron *USA-Canada*	10-26 000	4-10 000	Chad *Nigeria-Niger-Chad-Cameroon*
58 020	22 480	Michigan *USA*	9600	3710	Onega *USSR*
32 900	12 700	Tanganyika *Tanzania-Zambia-Zaire-Burundi*	0-8900	0-3430	Eyre *Australia*
31 330	12 100	Great Bear *Canada*	8340	3220	Titicaca *Peru-Bolivia*
30 500	11 800	Baykal *USSR*	8270	3190	Nicaragua *Nicaragua*
28 570	11 030	Great Slave *Canada*	6410	2470	Turkana (Rudolf) *Kenya-Ethiopia*
25 680	9910	Erie *USA-Canada*	5780	2230	Torrens *Australia (salt)*
24 390	9420	Winnipeg *Canada*	5580	2160	Vänern *Sweden*

GREATEST OCEAN DEPTHS

Metres	Feet	Location	Metres	Feet	Location
		PACIFIC OCEAN			**ATLANTIC OCEAN**
11 022	36 160	Marianas Trench	9220	30 249	Puerto Rico Trench
10 882	35 702	Tonga Trench	8264	27 113	South Sandwich Trench
10 542	34 586	Kuril Trench	7856	25 774	Romanche Gap
10 497	34 439	Philippine Trench	7500	24 600	Cayman Trench
10 047	32 962	Kermadec Trench			
9810	32 185	Izu-Bonin Trench			**INDIAN OCEAN**
9165	30 069	New Hebrides Trench	7450	24 442	Java Trench
9140	29 987	South Solomon Trench	7440	24 409	Weber Basin
8412	27 598	Japan Trench	7102	23 300	Diamantina Trench
8066	26 463	Peru-Chile Trench			
7822	25 662	Aleutian Trench			**ARCTIC OCEAN**
6662	21 857	Middle America	5570	18 274	Nansen Fracture Zone

STATES AND DEPENDENCIES

COUNTRY	Area (sq. km)	Population ('000)	Capital
North and Central America			
Anguilla (UK)	91	6	—
Antigua and Barbuda	442	75	St. John's
The Bahamas	13 864	210	Nassau
Barbados	430	249	Bridgetown
Belize	22 965	145	Belmopan
Bermuda (UK)	53	60	Hamilton
Canada	9 976 147	23 937	Ottawa
Cayman Is. (UK)	259	17	George Town
Costa Rica	50 899	2213	San José
Cuba	114 524	9859	La Habana (Havana)
Dominica	751	83	Roseau
Dominican Republic	48 441	5437	Santo Domingo
El Salvador	20 865	4540	San Salvador
Grenada	344	110	St. George's
Guadeloupe (Fr.)	1779	329	Basse Terre
Guatemala	108 888	7007	Guatemala
Haiti	27 749	5009	Port-au-Prince
Honduras	112 087	3691	Tegucigalpa
Jamaica	11 425	2188	Kingston
Martinique (Fr.)	1101	325	Fort-de-France
Mexico	1 967 180	67 458	México
Montserrat (UK)	102	12	Plymouth
Netherlands Antilles (Neth.)	993	257	Willemstad
Nicaragua	139 000	2672	Managua
Panama	75 648	1939	Panamá
Puerto Rico (USA)	8897	3675	San Juan
St Kitts-Nevis (UK)	260	50	Basseterre
St. Lucia	616	120	Castries
St. Vincent	389	124	Kingstown
Trinidad and Tobago	5128	1060	Port of Spain
United States of America	9 363 130	228 959	Washington
South America			
Argentina	2 777 815	27 740	Buenos Aires
Bolivia	1 098 575	5570	La Paz
Brazil	8 511 968	119 025	Brasília
Chile	756 943	11 487	Santiago
Colombia	1 138 907	26 670	Bogotá
Ecuador	455 502	8357	Quito
French Guiana (Fr.)	91 000	66	Cayenne
Guyana	214 969	865	George Town
Paraguay	406 750	3062	Asunción
Peru	1 285 215	17 625	Lima
Surinam	163 820	441	Paramaribo
Uruguay	186 925	2924	Montevideo
Venezuela	912 047	14 602	Caracas
Europe			
Albania	28 752	2732	Tiranë (Tirana)
Andorra	453	35	Andorra-la-Vella
Austria	83 848	7559	Wien (Vienna)
Belgium	30 512	9833	Bruxelles (Brussels)
Bulgaria	110 911	9007	Sofiya (Sofia)
Cyprus	9251	629	Nicosia
Czechoslovakia	127 870	15 282	Praha (Prague)
Denmark	43 030	5122	København (Copenhagen)
Faroes (Den.)	1399	41	Tórshavn
Finland	337 032	4863	Helsinki
France	551 000	54 085	Paris
Germany, East	107 860	16 854	Berlin (East)
Germany, West	248 528	60 931	Bonn
Gibraltar (UK)	6	30	Gibraltar
Great Britain and N. Ireland, see United Kingdom			
Greece	131 955	9329	Athínai (Athens)
Greenland (Den.)	2 175 600	52	Godthåb
Hungary	93 030	10 754	Budapest
Iceland	102 828	231	Reykjavík
Ireland	70 282	3308	Dublin
Italy	301 245	56 940	Roma (Rome)
Liechtenstein	161	25	Vaduz
Luxembourg	2587	364	Luxembourg
Malta	316	315	Valletta
Monaco	1·8	28	Monaco
Netherlands	33 940	14 284	Amsterdam/'s-Gravenhage
Norway	324 218	4079	Oslo
Poland	312 683	35 805	Warszawa (Warsaw)
Portugal	91 671	9836	Lisboa (Lisbon)
Romania	237 500	22 268	Bucuresti (Bucharest)
San Marino	61	22	San Marino
Soviet Union, see USSR			
Spain	504 745	37 746	Madrid
Sweden	449 791	8322	Stockholm
Switzerland	41 287	6466	Bern
United Kingdom	244 104	55 886	London
USSR	22 402 000	266 674	Moskva (Moscow)
Vatican City	·4	1	Vatican City
Yugoslavia	255 803	22 328	Beograd (Belgrade)
Asia			
Afghanistan	674 500	15 940	Kabul
Bahrain	660	422	Al Manāmah
Bangladesh	144 020	90 199	Dhaka (Dacca)
Bhutan	46 620	1296	Thimbu
Brunei	5765	220	Bandar Seri Begawan
Burma	678 031	35 289	Rangoon
Cambodia	181 035	5760	Phnom Penh
China	9 561 000	1 008 000	Beijing (Peking)
Hong Kong (UK)	1062	5106	Victoria
India	3 287 593	683 810	New Delhi
Indonesia	1 919 263	146 243	Jakarta
Iran	1 648 184	38 126	Tehrän
Iraq	434 924	13 072	Baghdäd
Israel	20 770	3876	Jerusalem
Japan	371 000	116 551	Tōkyō
Jordan	97 740	3244	Amman
Korea, North	121 248	17 892	P'yŏngyang
Korea, South	98 447	38 455	Sŏul (Seoul)
Kuwait	24 300	1353	Kuwait
Laos	236 798	3426	Vientiane
Lebanon	10 399	2658	Beirut
Macau (Port.)	16	315	Macau
Malaysia	330 669	13 436	Kuala Lumpur
Maldives	298	154	Malé
Mongolia	1 565 000	1669	Ulaanbaatar (Ulan Bator)
Nepal	141 414	14 288	Kathmandu
Oman	212 379	891	Masqaṭ (Muscat)
Pakistan	803 941	83 782	Islamabad
Philippines	299 765	48 098	Manila
Qatar	11 437	231	Doha
Saudi Arabia	2 400 930	8960	Riyadh
Singapore	616	2414	Singapore
Sri Lanka	65 610	14 815	Colombo
Syria	185 179	8977	Dimashq (Damascus)
Taiwan	35 980	17 480	T'ai-pei
Thailand	513 517	46 961	Bangkok
Turkey	780 576	45 358	Ankara
United Arab Emirates	83 600	1040	Abū Dhabi
Vietnam	329 566	54 175	Hanoi
Yemen	195 000	5812	San'ä'
Yemen, South	333 038	1903	Aden ('Adan)
Africa			
Algeria	2 381 731	18 919	Alger (El Djezair)
Angola	1 246 694	7078	Luanda
Benin	112 622	3530	Porto Novo
Botswana	582 000	800	Gaborone
Burundi	27 834	4110	Bujumbura
Cameroon	475 499	8444	Yaoundé
Cape Verde	4033	324	Praia
Central African Republic	622 996	2294	Bangui
Chad	1 284 000	4455	N'Djamena
Comoros	1862	353	Moroni
Congo	342 000	1537	Brazzaville
Djibouti	21 699	352	Djibouti
Egypt	1 000 250	39 773	Cairo
Equatorial Guinea	28 051	363	Malabo
Ethiopia	1 221 918	31 468	Addis Ababa
Gabon	267 667	657	Libreville
The Gambia	10 688	603	Banjul
Ghana	238 538	12 244	Accra
Guinea	245 855	5425	Conakry
Guinea-Bissau	36 125	793	Bissau
Ivory Coast	322 463	8637	Abidjan
Kenya	582 644	15 865	Nairobi
Lesotho	30 344	1396	Maseru
Liberia	111 370	1858	Monrovia
Libya	1 759 530	3100	Tripoli
Madagascar	587 042	8714	Antananarivo
Malawi	94 100	5951	Lilongwe
Mali	1 240 142	6940	Bamako
Mauritania	1 030 700	1634	Nouakchott
Mauritius	1865	958	Port Louis
Morocco	459 000	20 182	Rabat
Mozambique	784 961	10 473	Maputo
Namibia	824 293	1009	Windhoek
Niger	1 267 000	5318	Niamey
Nigeria	923 769	84 732	Lagos
Réunion (Fr.)	2510	525	Saint-Denis
Rwanda	26 338	5098	Kigali
São Tomé and Principé	964	113	São Tomé
Senegal	196 722	5661	Dakar
Seychelles	443	66	Victoria
Sierra Leone	71 740	2735	Freetown
Somalia	637 539	3914	Muqdisho (Mogadishu)
South Africa	1 221 038	29 285	Pretoria
Sudan	2 505 792	18 371	Khartoum
Swaziland	17 366	557	Mbabane
Tanzania	942 000	18 141	Dar es Salaam
Togo	56 785	2476	Lomé
Tunisia	164 148	6354	Tunis
Uganda	236 036	13 201	Kampala
Upper Volta	274 122	6040	Ouagadougou
Western Sahara	266 000	165	—
Zaire	2 344 885	29 270	Kinshasa
Zambia	752 617	5680	Lusaka
Zimbabwe	390 308	7730	Harare
Oceania			
American Samoa (USA)	197	32	Fagatogo
Australia	7 682 300	14 927	Canberra
Fiji	18 272	615	Suva
French Polynesia (Fr.)	4198	148	Papeete
Guam (USA)	549	106	Agaña
Kiribati	800	59	Tarawa
Nauru	21	7	Yaren
New Caledonia (Fr.)	19 104	140	Nouméa
New Zealand	268 675	3268	Wellington
Niue (NZ)	259	4	Alofi
Pacific Is., Trust Terr. (USA)	1300	121	Kolonia
Papua New Guinea	461 692	3200	Port Moresby
Solomon Islands	29 785	229	Honiara
Tonga	699	97	Nuku'alofa
Tuvalu	25	8	Funafuti
Vanuatu	14 763	117	Vila
Western Samoa	2831	156	Apia

URBAN POPULATIONS

North and Central America	'000
New York USA	16 120
México Mexico	14 750
Los Angeles USA	11 496
Chicago USA	7868
Philadelphia USA	5549
San Francisco USA	5182
Detroit USA	4618
Boston USA	3448
Houston USA	3102
Washington USA	3060
Toronto Canada	2999
Dallas USA	2975
Cleveland USA	2834
Montréal Canada	2828
Miami USA	2640
Guadalajara Mexico	2468
St. Louis USA	2355
Pittsburgh USA	2264
Baltimore USA	2174
Minneapolis USA	2114
Seattle USA	2092
Atlanta USA	2030
Monterrey Mexico	2019
San Diego USA	1862
La Habana Cuba	1861
Cincinnati USA	1660
Denver USA	1620
Milwaukee USA	1570
Tampa USA	1569
Phoenix USA	1508
Kansas City USA	1327
Vancouver Canada	1268
Buffalo USA	1242
Portland USA	1242
New Orleans USA	1187
Indianapolis USA	1167
Columbus USA	1093
San Juan Puerto Rico	1084
San Antonio USA	1072
Sacramento USA	1014
Rochester USA	972
Salt Lake City USA	936
Providence USA	919
Memphis USA	913
Louisville USA	906
Nashville-Davidson USA	851
Birmingham USA	847
Oklahoma City USA	834
Dayton USA	830
Greensboro USA	827
Santo Domingo Dominican Rep.	818
Norfolk USA	807
Albany USA	795
Guatemala Guatemala	793
Toledo USA	792
Honolulu USA	763
Jacksonville USA	738
Hartford USA	726
Ottawa Canada	718
Port-au-Prince Haiti	703
Orlando USA	701
Tulsa USA	690
Puebla Mexico	678
Edmonton Canada	657
Panamá Panama	655
Kingston Jamaica	655
Syracuse USA	642
Scranton USA	640
Charlotte USA	637
Allentown USA	637
Richmond USA	632
Grand Rapids USA	602
Ciudad Juárez Mexico	597
Calgary Canada	593
León Mexico	590
Winnipeg Canada	585
Québec Canada	576
West Palm Beach USA	573
Omaha USA	570
Greenville USA	569
Hamilton Canada	542
Austin USA	536
Tijuana Mexico	535
Youngstown USA	531
Tucson USA	531
Raleigh USA	531
Springfield USA	531

South America	'000
Buenos Aires Argentina	9910
São Paulo Brazil	8584
Rio de Janeiro Brazil	5184
Santiago Chile	4039
Lima Peru	3969
Bogotá Colombia	3831
Caracas Venezuela	2576
Belo Horizonte Brazil	1815
Salvador Brazil	1526
Medellín Colombia	1442
Fortaleza Brazil	1339
Montevideo Uruguay	1314
Recife Brazil	1241
Brasília Brazil	1203
Pôrto Alegre Brazil	1159

	'000
Nova Iguaçu Brazil	1094
Curitiba Brazil	1054
Cali Colombia	990
Belém Brazil	949
Barranquilla Colombia	825
Guayaquil Ecuador	823
Rosario Argentina	807
Maracaibo Venezuela	792
Córdoba Argentina	791
Campinas Brazil	663
La Paz Bolivia	655
Manaus Brazil	635
Valparaíso Chile	620
São Gonçalo Brazil	615
Quito Ecuador	600
Duque de Caxias Brazil	576
Asunción Paraguay	565
Santo André Brazil	553
Goiânia Brazil	516
Concepción Chile	513
La Plata Argentina	479

Europe	'000
London UK	12 075
Paris France	8613
Moskva USSR	8099
Leningrad USSR	4638
Madrid Spain	3188
Berlin E Ger.-W Ger.	3056
Roma Italy	2830
Birmingham UK	2748
Manchester UK	2687
Kiyev USSR	2144
Athínai Greece	2101
Budapest Hungary	2064
Bucureşti Romania	1934
Tashkent USSR	1779
Barcelona Spain	1755
Glasgow UK	1728
Hamburg W Germany	1664
Milano Italy	1634
Lisboa Portugal	1612
Warszawa Poland	1596
Wien Austria	1590
Baku USSR	1550
Khar'kov USSR	1444
København Denmark	1396
Stockholm Sweden	1393
Gor'kiy USSR	1344
Porto Portugal	1315
Novosibirsk USSR	1312
München W Germany	1297
Minsk USSR	1276
Kuybyshev USSR	1216
Sverdlovsk USSR	1211
Napoli Italy	1210
Lyon France	1186
Praha Czechoslovakia	1182
Torino Italy	1103
Marseille France	1077
Dnepropetrovsk USSR	1066
Tbilisi USSR	1066
Odessa USSR	1046
Chelyabinsk USSR	1031
Donetsk USSR	1021
Yerevan USSR	1019
Rotterdam Netherlands	1017
Bruxelles Belgium	1016
Omsk USSR	1014
Sofiya Bulgaria	1014
Perm' USSR	999
Kazan' USSR	993
Köln W Germany	977
Ufa USSR	969
Amsterdam Netherlands	965
Lille France	944
Rostov-na-Donu USSR	934
Volgograd USSR	929
Alma Ata USSR	910
Helsinki Finland	882
Saratov USSR	856
Łódź Poland	836
Riga USSR	835
Krasnoyarsk USSR	796
Voronezh USSR	783
Zaporozh'ye USSR	781
Beograd Yugoslavia	774
Genova Italy	760
Valencia Spain	752
Kraków Poland	716
Zürich Switzerland	707
Palermo Italy	699
Göteborg Sweden	694
's-Gravenhage Netherlands	672
L'vov USSR	667
Antwerpen Belgium	659
Essen W. Germany	658
Sevilla Spain	654
Krivoy Rog USSR	650
Oslo Norway	645
Frankfurt W Germany	631
Bordeaux France	622
Wrocław Poland	618
Dortmund W Germany	613
Düsseldorf W Germany	600

	'000
Yaroslavl USSR	597
Zaragoza Spain	591
Stuttgart W Germany	584
Karaganda USSR	572
Zagreb Yugoslavia	566
Leipzig E Germany	563
Duisburg W Germany	563
Krasnodar USSR	560
Bremen W Germany	559
Thessaloníki Greece	557
Poznań Poland	553
Irkutsk USSR	550
Vladivostok USSR	550
Izhevsk USSR	549
Sheffield UK	547
Dublin Ireland	544
Novokuznetsk USSR	541
Hannover W Germany	538
Liverpool UK	537
Barnaul USSR	533
Frunze USSR	533
Khabarovsk USSR	528
Toulouse France	521
Dresden E Germany	516
Tula USSR	514
Kishinev USSR	503
Zhdanov USSR	503
Tol'yatti USSR	502
Dushanbe USSR	493
Nürnberg W Germany	486
Penza USSR	483
Bologna Italy	481
Vilnius USSR	481
Samarkand USSR	476

Asia	'000
Tōkyō Japan	11 696
Shanghai China	10 820
Calcutta India	9166
Beijing China	8626
Bombay India	8203
Sŏul South Korea	6879
Manila Philippines	5901
Jakarta Indonesia	5849
Delhi India	5277
Bangkok Thailand	5154
Tehrān Iran	4496
Tianjin China	4280
Madras India	4277
Karachi Pakistan	4000
Shenyang China	3600
Dhaka Bangladesh	3459
Saigon Vietnam	3420
Baghdād Iraq	3206
T'ai-pei Taiwan	3050
Bangalore India	2914
İstanbul Turkey	2773
Yokohama Japan	2729
Osaka Japan	2700
Ankara Turkey	2624
Hanoi Vietnam	2570
Hyderabad India	2566
Ahmadabad India	2515
Pusan South Korea	2450
Singapore Singapore	2414
Chongqing China	2400
Kowloon Hong Kong	2378
Lahore Pakistan	2148
Wuhan China	2146
Nagoya Japan	2086
Phnom Penh Cambodia	2000
Guangzhou China	1840
Nanjing China	1750
Kanpur India	1685
Pune India	1685
Harbin China	1670
Lüda China	1650
Xi'an China	1600
Rangoon Burma	1586
Surabaya Indonesia	1556
P'yŏngyang North Korea	1500
Kyōto Japan	1467
Lanzhou China	1450
Chittagong Bangladesh	1388
Kobe Japan	1371
Taiyuan China	1350
Sapporo Japan	1337
Taegu South Korea	1309
Qingdao China	1300
Nagpur India	1298
Haiphong Vietnam	1279
Chengdu China	1250
Tel Aviv-Yafo Israel	1220
Bandung Indonesia	1202
Changchun China	1200
Damascus Syria	1142
Kao-hsiung Taiwan	1115
Kunming China	1100
Jinan China	1100
Fushun China	1080
Kita-Kyūshū Japan	1068
Fukuoka Japan	1055
Anshan China	1050
Zhengzhou China	1050
Kawasaki Japan	1041

	'000
Lucknow India	1007
Jaipur India	1005
Hangzhou China	960
Tangshan China	950
Beirut Lebanon	939
Baotou China	920
Aleppo Syria	878
Hiroshima Japan	859
Zibo China	850
Victoria Hong Kong	849
Changsha China	825
Faisalabad Pakistan	822
Shijiazhuang China	800
Inch'on South Korea	797
Sakai Japan	783
Qiqihar China	760
İzmir Turkey	758
Coimbatore India	736
Suzhou China	730
Jilin China	720
Chiba Japan	712
Madurai India	711
Xuzhou China	700
Hyderabad Pakistan	700
Fuzhou China	680
Nanchang China	675
Rawalpindi Pakistan	673
Esfahān Iran	672
Ammān Jordan	672
Mashhad Iran	670
Riyadh Saudi Arabia	667
Guiyang China	660
Wuxi China	650
Semarang Indonesia	647
Medan Indonesia	636
Agra India	635
Hefei China	630
Sendai Japan	628
Khulna Bangladesh	623
Colombo Sri Lanka	616
Davao Philippines	611
Varanasi India	607
Kwangju South Korea	606
Huainan China	600
Benxi China	600
Tabriz Iran	599
Kabul Afghanistan	588
Palembang Indonesia	583
Luoyang China	580
Adana Turkey	575
Jiddah Saudi Arabia	561
Indore India	561
Nanning China	550
Multan Pakistan	542
Okayama Japan	536
Jabalpur India	535
Hohhot China	530
Amagasaki Japan	528
T'ai-nan Taiwan	513
Allahabad India	513
Taejŏn South Korea	506
Higashiosaka Japan	501
Hsining China	500
Ürümqi China	500
Kumamoto Japan	498
Surat India	493
Patna India	491
Kagoshima Japan	490
Hamamatsu Japan	485

Africa	'000
Cairo Egypt	6588
Alexandria Egypt	2320
Kinshasa Zaire	2008
Casablanca Morocco	1753
Johannesburg South Africa	1536
Alger Algeria	1503
Lagos Nigeria	1477
El Gîza Egypt	1247
Addis Ababa Ethiopia	1133
Cape Town South Africa	1108
Dar es Salaam Tanzania	870
Durban South Africa	851
Abidjan Ivory Coast	850
Ibadan Nigeria	847
Nairobi Kenya	835
Dakar Senegal	799
Accra Ghana	738
Kananga Zaire	704
Harare Zimbabwe	686
Tunis Tunisia	648
Lusaka Zambia	599
Rabat Morocco	597
Pretoria South Africa	563
Tripoli Libya	551
Conakry Guinea	526
Port Elizabeth South Africa	476

Oceania	'000
Sydney Australia	2874
Melbourne Australia	2578
Brisbane Australia	943
Adelaide Australia	883
Perth Australia	809
Auckland New Zealand	766

This page explains the main symbols, lettering style and height/depth colours used on the reference maps on pages 2 to 32. The scale of each map is indicated at the top of each page. Abbreviations used on the maps appear at the beginning of the index.

BOUNDARIES

	International
	International under Dispute
	Cease Fire Line
	Autonomous or State
	Administrative
	Maritime (National)
	International Date Line

COMMUNICATIONS

	Motorway/Express Highway
	Under Construction
	Major Highway
	Other Roads
	Under Construction
	Track
	Road Tunnel
	Car Ferry
	Main Railway
	Other Railway
	Under Construction
	Rail Tunnel
	Rail Ferry
	Canal
⊕	International Airport
✈	Other Airport

LAKE FEATURES

	Freshwater
	Saltwater
	Seasonal
	Salt Pan

LANDSCAPE FEATURES

	Glacier, Ice Cap
	Marsh, Swamp
	Sand Desert, Dunes

OTHER FEATURES

	River
	Seasonal River
	Pass, Gorge
	Dam, Barrage
	Waterfall, Rapid
	Aqueduct
	Reef
▲4231	Summit, Peak
.217	Spot Height, Depth
	Well
▵	Oil Field
▲	Gas Field
Gas / Oil	Oil/Natural Gas Pipeline
Gemsbok Nat. Pk	National Park
∴UR	Historic Site

LETTERING STYLES

CANADA	Independent Nation
FLORIDA	State, Province or Autonomous Region
Gibraltar (U.K.)	Sovereignty of Dependent Territory
Lothian	Administrative Area
LANGUEDOC	Historic Region
Loire **Vosges**	Physical Feature or Physical Region

TOWNS AND CITIES

Square symbols denote capital cities

			Population
▣	●	**New York**	over 5 000 000
▪	●	**Montréal**	over 1 000 000
▫	○	Ottawa	over 500 000
▪	●	**Québec**	over 100 000
▫	○	St John's	over 50 000
▫	○	Yorkton	over 10 000
▫	○	Jasper	under 10 000

Built-up-area

Height

	6000m
	5000m
	4000m
	3000m
	2000m
	1000m
	500m
	200m
0	0 Sea Level
	200m
	2000m
	4000m
	6000m
	8000m

Depth

1:5M

50 100 150 200 km
50 100 mls

A 10 B 5 C D E

① Nordhordland Dalen
Bergen
NORWAY
Herma Ness
Unst
Isbister Fetlar
Yell *Shetland*
St Magnus B. Whalsay
Foula Lerwick
Sumburgh Hd

Sotra
Sunnhordland Stord
Leirvik
Bømlo Skjold
Haugesund
Karmøy
② Stavanger
Sandnes

Fair Isle

Westray
Rousay Sanday
N. Rona Stromness Stronsay
Sula Sgeir Stack Skerry Kirkwall
Flannan Is. Scapa Flow
St Kilda Hoy *Orkney*

C. Wrath
Butt of Lewis Thurso Duncansby Hd
Stornoway Ben Hope Wick
Outer Hebrides Lewis 927
Ben More Helmsdale
Assynt
998
Harris Ullapool Dornoch
N. Uist The Minch Dingwall Moray Firth Dornoch Firth
Portree Elgin Banff Fraserburgh
Skye Kyle Inverness Peterhead
S. Uist of Lochalsh L. Ness Spey Buchan Ness
Barra Fort Ben Macdui Aberdeen
Rum Augustus 1309 Dee
SCOTLAND Braemar Stonehaven
Mallaig
Coll Fort William Ben Nevis Mts
1344 Pitlochry Montrose
Tiree Ben
Mull Lawers Perth Dundee Arbroath
1214 F. of Tay St Andrews
Oban L. Awe
F. of Lorn L. Lomond Kirkcaldy
Colonsay Jura Stirling F. of Forth
Islay Greenock **Glasgow** Edinburgh St Abbs Hd
Paisley Motherwell Berwick-upon-Tweed
Arran Irvine Holy I.
Kilmarnock Galashiels
Campbeltown Ayr White
Coomb
Tory I. Malin Hd 822
Rathlin I. Moffat Hawick Alnwick
⑤ Aran I. Merrick Cheviots
Errigal L. Foyle Coleraine Girvan 843 Morpeth Blyth
752 Stranraer Dumfries Newcastle-upon-Tyne
Londonderry N. IRELAND Larne S. Shields
Rossan Pt Ballymena Kirkcudbright Carlisle Pennines Gateshead Sunderland
Donegal Bangor Solway Firth Durham Hartlepool
Donegal B. Omagh Belfast Luce B. Penrith Darlington Middlesbrough
Erris Hd Enniskillen Portadown Scafell Pike Yorkshire Moors Scarborough
L. Neagh Armagh 977
Achill I. Sligo L. Erne Newry Isle of Man Kendal Flamborough Hd
Ballina Monaghan Douglas Barrow Lancaster
L. Conn Castlebar Dundalk -in-Furness Morecambe Harrogate York
Crew B. Boyle Cavan Blackpool Ouse Hull
L. Allen IRISH SEA Preston Bradford Leeds Spurn Hd
L. Mask Roscommon Longford Huddersfield Grimsby
Tyne Hd Galway L. Ree Mullingar Bolton **Manchester** Doncaster Humber
Galway B. Athlone Drogheda Liverpool Sheffield
L. Corrib Dublin Birkenhead Warrington Lincoln
Aran Is. Shannon (Baile Atha Cliath) Holyhead Chester
Dun Laoghaire Anglesey Crewe Stoke Nottingham
Ennis L. Derg Nenagh **REP. OF** Bray Bangor on-Trent The Wash King's Lynn
Port Snowdon Derby Norwich Great Yarmouth
Kilrush **IRELAND** Laoise Carlow Wicklow 1085 Trent Nene Lowestoft
Limerick Kilkenny Arklow Dee Leicester Ouse
Tralee Tipperary Shrewsbury Peterborough
Clonmel Cardigan Aberystwyth Wolverhampton Coventry Newmarket
Carrauntoohill Waterford **WALES** **Birmingham** **ENGLAND** Cambridge
1041 Dungarvan Worcester Northampton Ipswich
Killarney Youghal Builth Wye Bedford Colchester Felixstowe
Bantry B. Cork Wells Gloucester Luton Harwich
Brecon Severn Chelmsford
C. Clear Fishguard Carmarthen Oxford London Southend
St David's Swindon Windsor on-Sea
Hd Pembroke Newport Reading Maidstone Thames
St George's Chan. Swansea Cardiff Bristol Canterbury
Bath Dover
Lundy I. Weston- Crawley Folkestone
super-Mare Guildford Hastings
Barnstaple Winchester Eastbourne Str.
Bude Taunton Salisbury Southampton Brighton
Exeter Bournemouth Portsmouth
Newquay Dartmoor Weymouth Isle of Wight
Truro Plymouth Torbay
Penzance Land's End
Falmouth Prawle Pt
Isles of Scilly Lizard Pt **English Channel**

③ Vlieland
Texel
Den Helder
Alkmaar
Haarlem NETHERLANDS
's-Gravenhage Leiden
(Den Haag)
Rotterdam
Dordrecht

Zeebrugge
Oostende Antwerpen
Brugge
Calais Dunkerque Gent BELGIUM
St-Omer Kortrijk Bruxelles
Boulogne Tourcoing (Brüssel)
Roubaix Soignies
Bethune Lille Tournai Mons
Montreuil Douai Valenciennes
Abbeville Arras Denain Maubeuge
Le Tréport Cambrai Fourmies
Dieppe St-Quentin
Amiens PICARDIE
C. de la Hague Neufchâtel Montdidier Laon
pte de Barfleur Fécamp Oise
Alderney Bolbec Beauvais Compiègne Aisne
Cherbourg Le Havre Soissons Reims
Guernsey Sark Valognes Deauville Seine Rouen Senlis Château-
Channel Is. St-Lô Bayeaux Lisieux Elbeuf Cergy- Thierry
(U.K.) Jersey St Helier Caen Louviers Pontoise Meaux Epernay
Golfe de St-Malo Coutances Evreux Mantes Paris
Granville Argentan Dreux Versailles Provins Romilly-s-S.
Roscoff FRANCE Eure Sèzanne
Morlaix St-Malo Mont- Domfront Rambouillet Etampes Melun
St-Brieuc St-Michel NORMANDIE Orne Alençon Chartres Fontainebleau Troyes
Brest Dinan Mayenne Provins
Carhaix- Fougères Sens
I. d'Ouessant Plouguer

NORTH SEA

Esbjerg

① ② ⑤ ③ ④ 50

B C D

1:2.5M

Scale markers: 25 50 75 100 km / 25 50 mls

Shetland — Unst, Herma Ness, The Faither, Fetlar, Yell, Whalsay, Isbister, Hillswick, St Magnus Bay, Bressay, Noss, Lerwick, Scalloway, Papa Stour, Foula, Fitful Hd, Sumburgh Hd, Fair Isle

at the same scale

NORTH SEA — Dogger Bank, Long Forties, Forties, Buchan Deep, Devil's Hole, Farne Deep

Norway, U.K., Esbjerg, Edda, Lomond, Dod, Albuskjell, Argyll, Josephine, Auk, Montrose, Piper, Tartan, Claymore, Buchan, Beatrice, Forties

Orkney — Papa Westray, N. Ronaldsay, Westray, Sanday, Rousay, Eday, Stronsay, Shapinsay, Mainland, Kirkwall, Stromness, Hoy, Scapa Flow, S. Ronaldsay, Burray, Duncansby Hd, Pentland Firth, John o' Groats, Dunnet Hd

N. Rona, Sule Skerry, Stack Skerry, Sula Sgeir, Butt of Lewis, Flannan Is., Scarp, Taransay, Pabbay, Monach Is., N. Rona

Western Isles / **Outer Hebrides** — Lewis, Stornoway, Loch Roag, Harris, Tarbert, Sd of Harris, North Uist, Benbecula, Lochmaddy, South Uist, Lochboisdale, Barra, Castlebay, Barra Hd, St Kilda

SCOTLAND / HIGHLAND — C. Wrath, Durness, Tongue, Loch Hope, Ben Hope 927, Ben Loyal, Loch Naver, Ben More Assynt 998, Bdn Kilbreck 961, Lochinver, Ullapool, Ben Dearg 1067, Ben Wyvis 1043, Loch Maree, Gairloch, Loch Torridon, Rubha Reidh, Raasay, Portree, Uig, L. Shizort, Cuillin Hills, Isle of Skye, Rum, Eigg, Muck, Coll, Tiree, Staffa, Iona, Colonsay, Jura, Islay, Port Ellen, Port Askaig, Mull of Kintyre

Thurso, Wick, Lybster, Helmsdale, Brora, Golspie, Dornoch, Tain, Dornoch Firth, Tarbat Ness, Cromarty Firth, Black Isle, Beauly, Dingwall, Inverness, Moray Firth, Nairn, Forres, Elgin, Lossiemouth, Buckie, Keith, Dufftown, Huntly, Banff, Fraserburgh, Peterhead, Buchan Ness, Kinnairds Hd

Fort Augustus, Loch Ness, Invergarry, Loch Lochy, Ben Nevis 1344, Fort William, Kyle of Lochalsh, Mallaig, Arisaig, Loch Shiel, L. Morar, Ardnamurchan Pt, Tobermory, Mull, Oban, Morvern, L. Sunart, Ardrishaig, Inveraray, Loch Fyne, Crianlarich, Killin, Loch Lomond, Dumbarton

GRAMPIAN — Aberdeen, Girdle Ness, Stonehaven, Inverurie, Ythan, Don, Dee, Banchory, Ballater, Braemar, Ben Macdui 1310, Lochnagar 1155, Cairngorms, Aviemore, Kingussie, Monadhliath Mts, Grantown-on-Spey, Spey

TAYSIDE — Montrose, Arbroath, Brechin, Forfar, Blairgowrie, Blair Atholl, Pitlochry, Dundee, Perth, Aberfeldy, Loch Tay, Loch Rannoch, Loch Ericht, Loch Katrine, Callander, Aberfoyle

FIFE — St Andrews, Fife Ness, Firth of Forth, Cupar, Methil, Kirkcaldy, Dunfermline, Kinross, Loch Leven

CENTRAL — Stirling, Falkirk, Grangemouth

STRATHCLYDE — Glasgow, Paisley, Hamilton, Motherwell, Coatbridge, Greenock, Helensburgh, Gourock, Largs, Ardrossan, Irvine, Troon, Ayr, Maybole, Girvan, Kilmarnock, Cumnock, Arran, Brodick, Bute, Campbeltown, Ballantrae, Firth of Clyde, Kintyre

LOTHIAN — Edinburgh, Haddington, Pentland Hills, Moorfoot Hills, Lammermuir Hills

BORDERS — Galashiels, Peebles, Selkirk, Hawick, Jedburgh, Kelso, Duns, Berwick-upon-Tweed, St Abb's Hd, Eyemouth, North Berwick, Holy I., Tweed, Tweedsmuir Hills

DUMFRIES and GALLOWAY — Dumfries, Stranraer, Newton Stewart, Wigtown, Kirkcudbright, Castle Douglas, Annan, Lockerbie, Moffat, Gretna, Merrick 843, Galloway, Mull of Galloway, Corsewall Pt, Loch Ryan, Luce Bay, Wigtown Bay

Co. DURHAM / NORTHUMBERLAND — Newcastle upon Tyne, Tynemouth, Sth Shields, Gateshead, Sunderland, Tyne and Wear, Blyth, Morpeth, Alnwick, Hexham, Haltwhistle, Alston, Carlisle, Langtown, The Cheviot 816, Cheviot Hills, Nat. Park, Solway Firth, Eden

NORTHERN IRELAND — Londonderry, Coleraine, Portrush, Ballymoney, Ballycastle, Rathlin I., Antrim Hills, Ballymena, Limavady, Magherafelt, Strabane, Omagh, Sperrin Mts, L. Neagh

Donegal — Errigal 752, Bloody Foreland, Sheep Haven, Gweedore, Blue Stack Mts, Lifford, Inishowen, Malin Hd, L. Swilly, Fanad Hd

North Channel, Stanton Banks

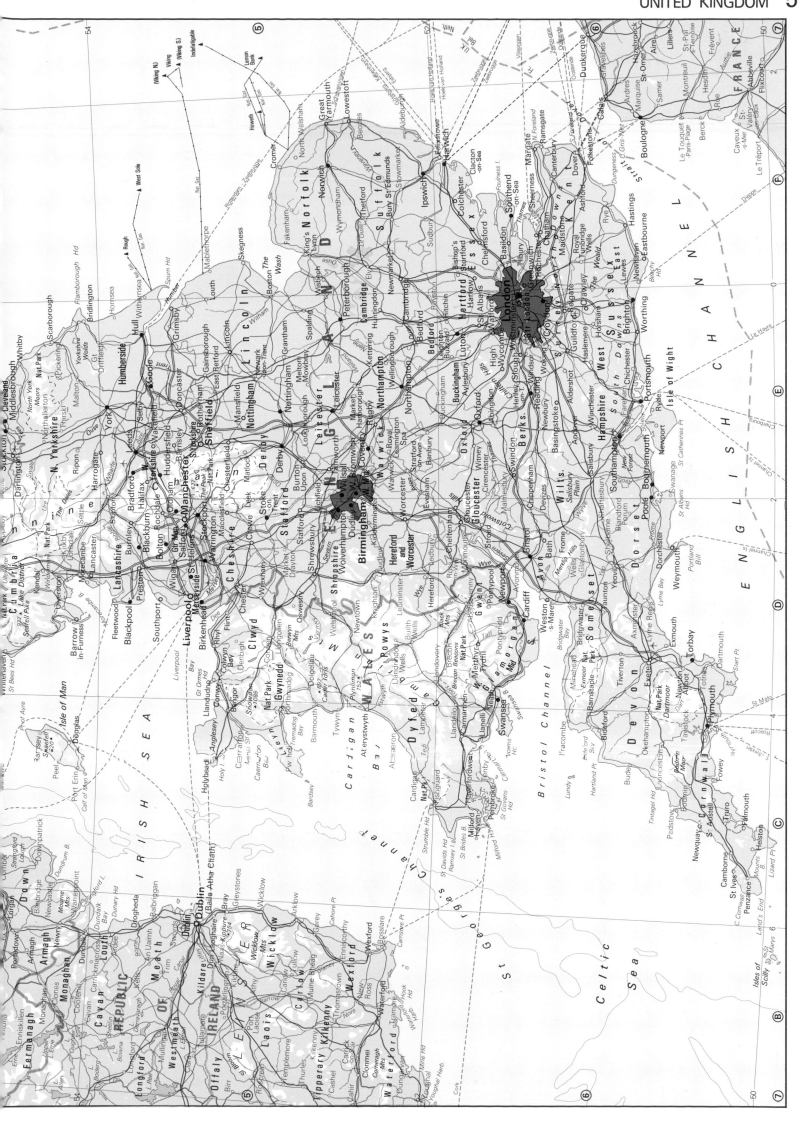

1:5M

50 100 150 200 km
50 100 mls

NORTH SEA

BALTIC

Countries / Regions: DENMARK, SWEDEN, EAST GERMANY, WEST GERMANY, FRANCE, BELGIUM, LUXEMBOURG, NORTH SEA, SWITZERLAND, AUSTRIA, ITALY, YUGOSLAVIA, ČESKÉ ZEMĚ, NIEDERSACHSEN, SCHLESWIG-HOLSTEIN, NORDRHEIN-WESTFALEN, HESSEN, RHEINLAND-PFALZ, SAARLAND, BADEN-WÜRTTEMBERG, BAYERN, LORRAINE, BOURGOGNE, FRANCHE-COMTÉ, SAVOIE, DAUPHINÉ, ARDENNES, LIECHTENSTEIN, Kattegat, Jylland (Jutland), Sjælland, Fyn, Lolland, Falster, Rügen, Bornholm

Major cities:
København (Copenhagen), Malmö, Lund, Helsingborg, Göteborg, Jönköping, Ålborg, Århus, Odense, Esbjerg, Kolding, Kiel, Lübeck, Hamburg, Bremen, Bremerhaven, Wilhelmshaven, Hannover, Braunschweig, Wolfsburg, Magdeburg, Berlin, Potsdam, Rostock, Schwerin, Stralsund, Szczecin, Poznań, Frankfurt an-der-O, Cottbus, Dresden, Leipzig, Halle, Erfurt, Jena, Gera, Karl Marx Stadt, Görlitz, Wrocław, Wałbrzych, Legnica, Zielona Góra, Gorzów Wlkp., Koszalin, Kołobrzeg, Białogard, Ustka

Amsterdam, Rotterdam, 's-Gravenhage (Den Haag), Utrecht, Leiden, Haarlem, Groningen, Leeuwarden, Zwolle, Arnhem, Nijmegen, Eindhoven, Tilburg, Breda, Antwerpen (Anvers), Bruxelles (Brüssel), Gent, Brugge, Oostende, Liège, Namur, Charleroi, Mons, Maastricht, Aachen, Köln, Bonn, Düsseldorf, Essen, Dortmund, Duisburg, Wuppertal, Mönchengladbach, Krefeld, Münster, Bielefeld, Osnabrück, Paderborn, Kassel, Siegen, Marburg, Giessen, Fulda, Koblenz, Wiesbaden, Mainz, Frankfurt, Offenbach, Darmstadt, Mannheim, Ludwigshafen, Heidelberg, Karlsruhe, Pforzheim, Stuttgart, Heilbronn, Würzburg, Schweinfurt, Bamberg, Bayreuth, Nürnberg, Fürth, Erlangen, Regensburg, Ingolstadt, München (Munich), Augsburg, Ulm, Freiburg, Konstanz, Friedrichshafen

Lille, Roubaix, Tourcoing, Valenciennes, Dunkerque, Reims, Metz, Nancy, Strasbourg, Mulhouse, Belfort, Besançon, Dijon, Lyon, St-Étienne, Chambéry, Grenoble, Annecy, Genève, Lausanne, Bern, Basel, Zürich, Luzern, St Gallen, Winterthur, Schaffhausen, Innsbruck, Salzburg, Linz, Wien (Vienna), Bratislava, Graz, Klagenfurt, Ljubljana, Zagreb, Trieste, Udine, Venezia (Venice), Padova, Verona, Vicenza, Brescia, Bergamo, Milano (Milan), Monza, Como, Novara, Torino (Turin), Trento, Bolzano

Physical features: Mont Blanc 4807, Mt Cenis 2803, Gran Paradiso, Matterhorn, Jungfrau, Gotthard, Simplon, St Bernard, Ortles 3899, Wildspitze 3772, Grossglockner 3798, Brenner, Dachstein 2996, Hochkönig 2938, Rachel 1452, Brd Y, Böhmerwald, Erzgebirge, Thüringer Wald, Schwäbische Alb, Schwarzwald, Rhein, Elbe, Oder (Odra), Weser, Ems, Donau, Main, Mosel, Saône, Rhône

FRANCE

GERMANY
WEST

BELGIUM
LUXEMBOURG
SWITZERLAND
LIECHTENSTEIN
ITALIA (ITALY)
CORSE (CORSICA)

ENGLAND

Paris
London
Bruxelles (Brussel)
Antwerpen (Anvers)
Amsterdam
Frankfurt
Köln
Düsseldorf
Duisburg
Essen
München
Stuttgart
Nürnberg
Zürich
Bern
Genève
Lyon
Marseille
Bordeaux
Toulouse
Nantes
Rennes
Brest
Lille
Strasbourg
Nancy
Metz
Dijon
Besançon
Grenoble
Nice
Monaco
Torino (Turin)
Milano (Milan)
Genova (Genoa)
Bologna
Firenze (Florence)
Bilbao
Pamplona

BAY OF BISCAY
(GOLFE DE GASCOGNE)

English Channel

Ligurian Sea

1:5M

1:5M

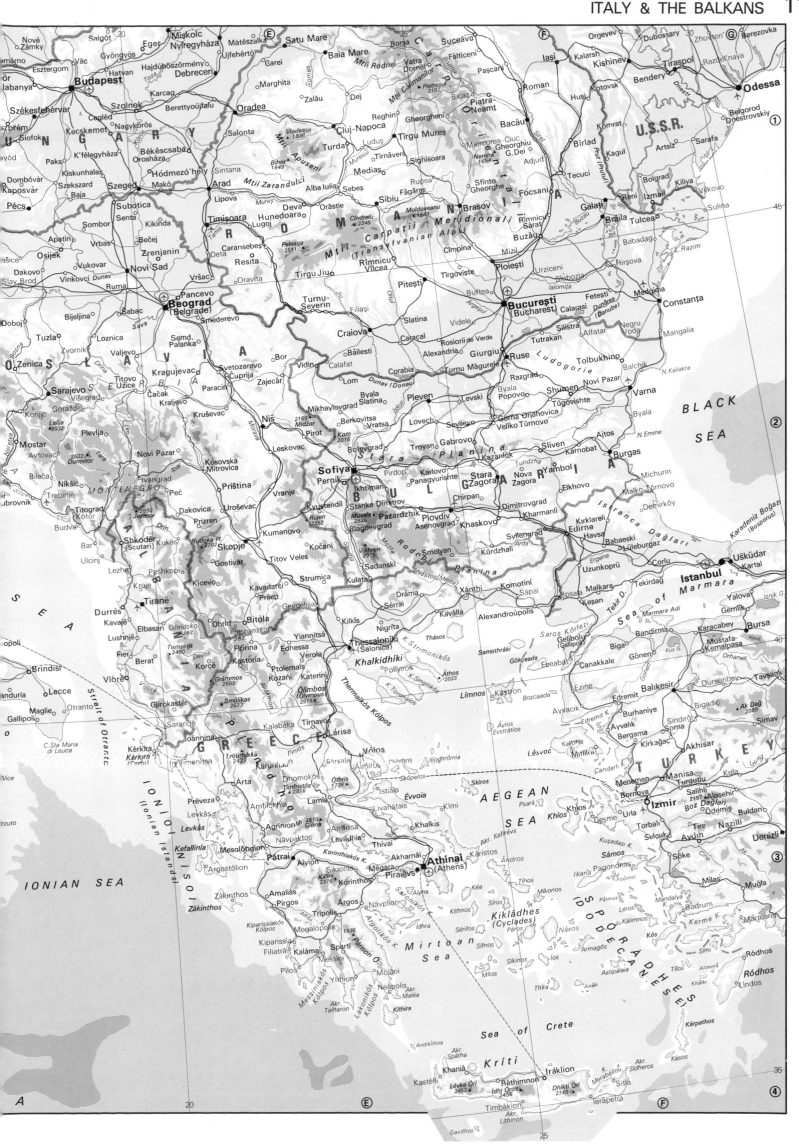

1:20M

200   400   600   800 km
0
200   400 mls
0

Legend

R.S.F.S.R.
1 Chuvashskaya A.S.S.R.
2 Checheno-Ingushskaya A.S.S.R.
3 Severo-Osetinskaya A.S.S.R.
4 Kabardino-Balkarskaya A.S.S.R.
GRUZINSKAYA S.S.R.
5 Abkhazskaya A.S.S.R.
6 Adzharskaya A.S.S.R.
AZERBAYDZHANSKAYA S.S.R.
7 Nakhichevanskaya A.S.S.R.

(Map of the USSR and surrounding regions. Principal labelled features include:)

Arctic Circle · NORWEGIAN SEA · BARENTS SEA · KARA SEA · NORTH SEA · BALTIC SEA · BLACK SEA · CASPIAN SEA

SVALBARD (SPITSBERGEN) (Nor.) · ZEMLYA FRANTSA JOSIFA (FRANZ-JOSEF-LAND) · NOVAYA ZEMLYA

SCOTLAND · UK · DENMARK · GERMANY · POLAND · SWEDEN · NORWAY · FINLAND · IRAQ · IRAN · AFGHANISTAN · SINKIANG

ROSSIYSKAYA · Zapadno Sibirskaya · KAZAKHSKAYA S.S.R. · TURKMENSKAYA S.S.R. · UZBEKSKAYA S.S.R. · KIRGIZSKAYA S.S.R. · TADZHIKSKAYA S.S.R.

Cities: Glasgow, Edinburgh, Aberdeen, Inverness, Bremen, Hamburg, Berlin, København, Kiel, Gdańsk, Warszawa, Kraków, Lublin, Stockholm, Oslo, Bergen, Trondheim, Leningrad, Moskva, Minsk, Kiev, Kharkov, Odessa, Rostov-na-Donu, Volgograd, Saratov, Kuybyshev, Kazan, Gorkiy, Sverdlovsk, Chelyabinsk, Omsk, Novosibirsk, Tbilisi, Yerevan, Baku, Tashkent, Frunze, Alma Ata, Karaganda, Tehrān

USSR

ARCTIC OCEAN

SEVERNAYA ZEMLYA (NORTH LAND)
Ostrov Komsomolets
Ostrov Oktyabrskoy Revolyutsii
Ostrov Bol'shevik

NOVOSIBIRSKYE OSTROVA (NEW SIBERIAN ISLANDS)
Ostrova De Longa
O. Bennetta
O. Novaya Sibir
Ostrov Faddeyevskiy
O. Kotel'nyy

LAPTEV SEA

EAST SIBERIAN SEA

CHUKCHI SEA

Bering Str.

BERING SEA

Poluostrov Taymyr
Gory Byrranga
Ozero Taymyr
Gory Putorana

Mys Chelyuskin
Mys Shalaurova

KAMCHATKA
Poluostrov Kamchatka
Petropavlovsk-Kamchatskiy
Sredinnyy Khrebet

Kolymskoye Nagor'ye
Koryakskoye Nagor'ye

Anadyrskiy Zaliv

Khrebet Cherskogo
Verkhoyanskiy Khrebet
Khrebet Orulgan

YAKUT A.S.S.R.
Yakutsk
Verkhoyansk
Oymyakon
Vilyuysk
Zhigansk

R.S.F.S.R.

Sredne Sibirskoye Ploskogor'ye

SEA OF OKHOTSK

SAKHALIN
Yuzhno-Sakhalinsk
Aleksandrovsk-Sakhalinskiy
Komsomol'sk-na-Amure

Kuril'skiye Ostrova (Kuril Islands)

Magadan
Okhotsk

Ust'-Kut
Bratsk
Kansk
Krasnoyarsk
Achinsk
Abakan
Minusinsk
Irkutsk
Angarsk
Ulan-Ude
Chita

Buryatskaya A.S.S.R.
Tuvinskaya A.S.S.R.
Kyzyl

Stanovoy Khrebet
Aldanskoye Nagor'ye
Patomskoye Nagor'ye

Khabarovsk
Blagoveshchensk
Birobidzhan
Svobodnyy
Belogorsk

Vladivostok
Nakhodka
Ussuriysk

HOKKAIDO
Sapporo
Otaru
Hakodate

HONSHU
JAPAN
TOKYO
Yokohama
Osaka
Kyoto
Nagoya
Sendai
Niigata
Akita
Morioka

Fukuoka
KYUSHU
SHIKOKU
Nagasaki
Kagoshima

MONGOLIA
Ulaanbaatar
Darhan

MANCHURIA
Harbin
Changchun
Qiqihar
Mudanjiang
Jilin

Shenyang
Beijing (Peking)
Tianjin (Tientsin)
Baotou
Hohhot
Datong
Taiyuan
Shijiazhuang
Jinan
Qingdao

INNER MONGOLIA

NORTH KOREA
P'yŏngyang
Hamhŭng
Ch'ŏngjin

SOUTH KOREA
Seoul
Inch'ŏn
Taejŏn
Taegu
Pusan
Kwangju
Mokpo

SEA OF JAPAN

YELLOW SEA

Bo Hai

CHINA

Qilian Shan
Yinchuan
Lanzhou

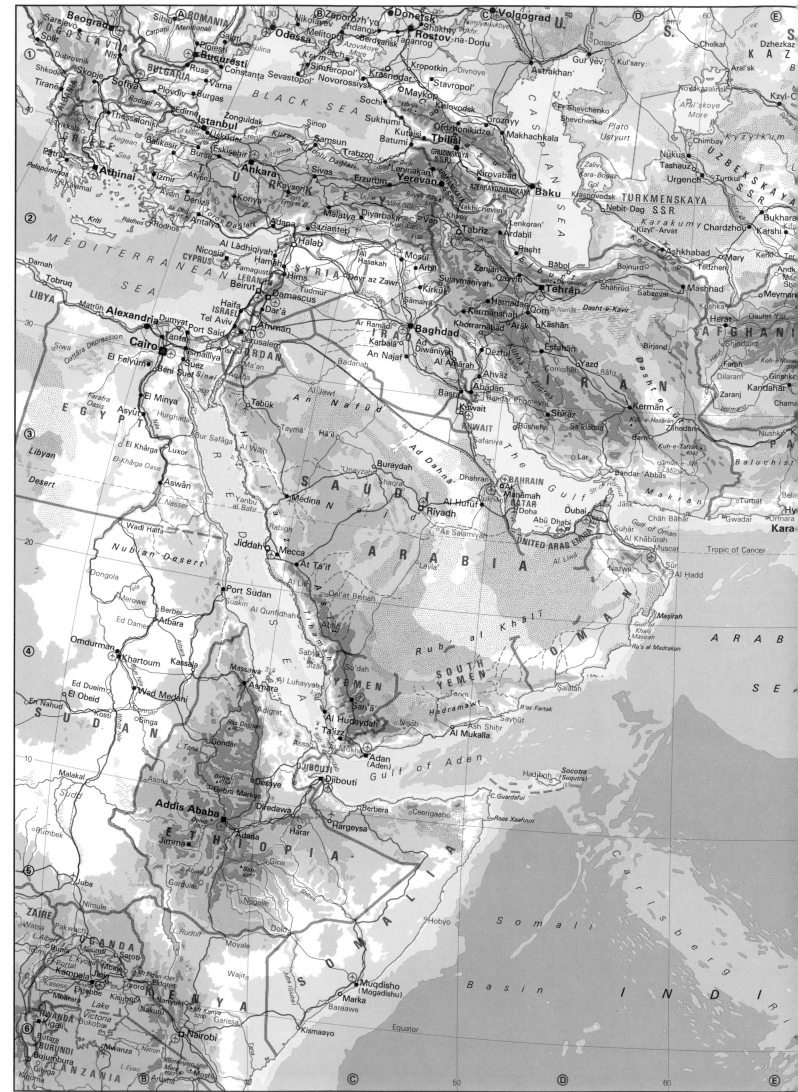

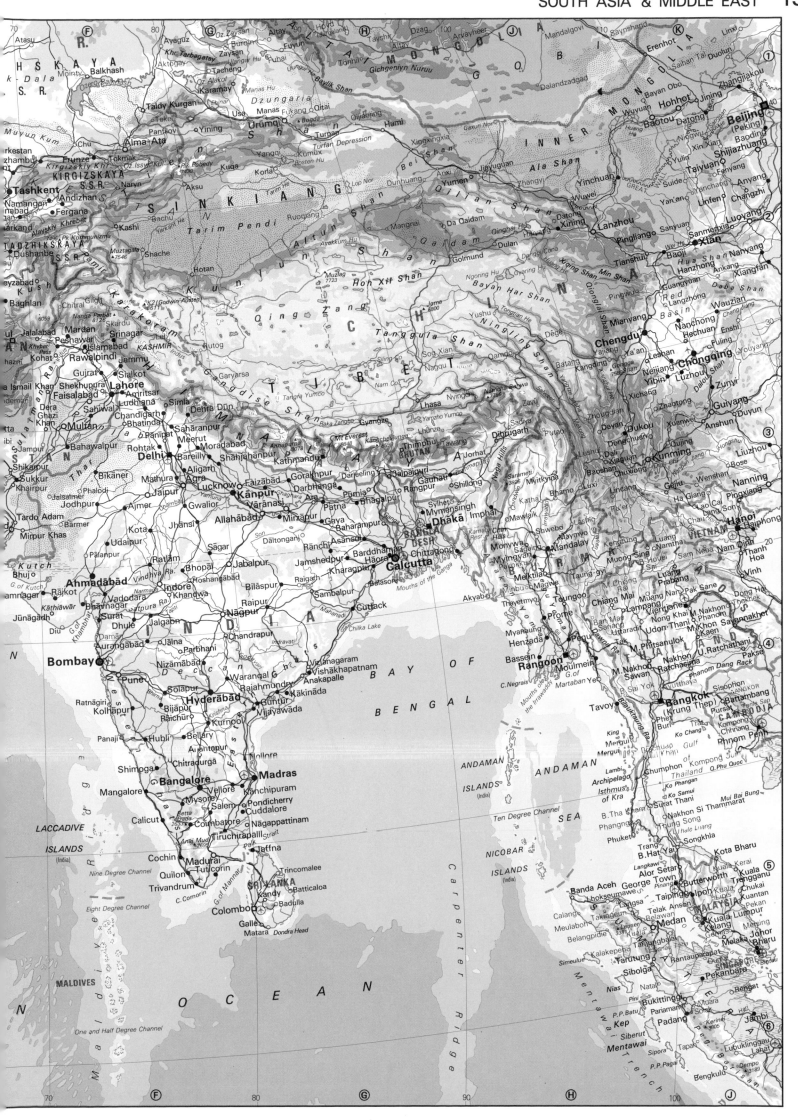

1:20M

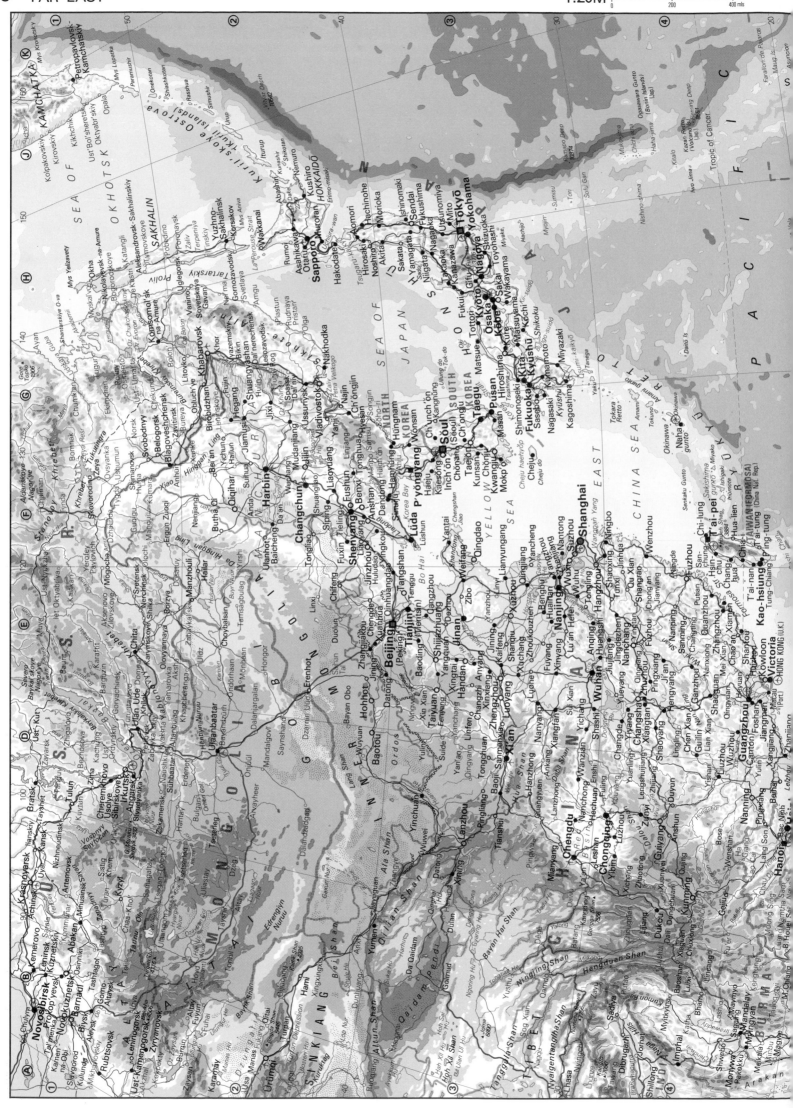

PAPUA NEW GUINEA

IRIAN JAYA

CORAL SEA

AUSTRALIA

Arnhem Land

Gulf of Carpentaria

ARAFURA SEA

TIMOR SEA

BANDA SEA

CERAM SEA

MOLUCCAS

CELEBES SEA

SULAWESI

FLORES SEA

JAVA SEA

BORNEO

INDONESIA

KALIMANTAN

SULU SEA

PHILIPPINES

LUZON

MINDANAO

Manila

Quezon City

SOUTH CHINA SEA

Spratly Islands

MALAYSIA

SABAH

SARAWAK

BRUNEI

SINGAPORE

PENINSULA MALAYSIA

Kuala Lumpur

THAILAND

CAMBODIA

INDO-CHINA

VIETNAM

Bangkok

Saigon (Ho Chi Minh)

Da Nang

Phnom Penh

Vientiane

LAOS

Rangoon

ANDAMAN SEA

Jakarta

Bandung

Semarang

Surabaya

JAWA

Bali

INDIAN OCEAN

PACIFIC OCEAN

Northern Marianas

MARIANA

Trust Terr. of the PACIFIC ISLANDS (USA)

CAROLINE ISLANDS

Fed. States of Micronesia

Rep. of Belau

Palau Islands

Port Moresby

Darwin

Equator

Scale: 200   400   600 km / 100   200   300 mls

Inset — Açores (Azores)

Corvo
Flores
São Jorge
Faial · Terceira · Angra Do Heroismo
Pico
Graciosa
São Miguel
Santa Maria · Ponta Delgada · Formigas
Açores (Azores) (Portugal)
at the same scale

Main map

PORTUGAL · Lisboa (Lisbon)
SPAIN · Badajoz · Beja · Albacete · Ibiza · Islas Baleares (Balearic Is) · Sardegna (Sardinia) · Cagliari
Sierra Morena · Ciudad Real · Murcia · Alicante · Cartagena
Faro · Huelva · Sevilla (Seville) · Córdoba · Linares · Granada · Almería
Cádiz · Málaga · Gibraltar (U.K.) · Alger · Algiers · Tizi Ouzou · Bejaïa (Bougie) · Skikda (Philippeville) · Annaba (Bône) · Bizerte · La Galite · Tunis
MEDITERRANEAN SEA
Tanger (Tangier) · Ceuta (Sp) · Tetouan · Melilla (Sp) · Oran · Mostaganem · Cherchell · Constantine · Souk Ahras · El Kef · Kairouan · Sousse · Sfax
Casablanca (El-Dar-El-Beida) · Rabat · Kenitra · Meknès · Fès · Oujda · Tlemcen · Sidi-bel-Abbès · Mascara · Sétif · Batna · Tébessa · Gafsa
El Jadida · Settat · Oued Zem · Azrou · Taza · Bou Saâda · M'sila · Djelfa · Biskra · Touggourt
Safi · Marrakech · Beni Mellal · Midelt · Ghardaïa · Laghouat · El Oued · Nalût
Essaouira · Haut Atlas · Toubkal 4165 · Ouarzazate · Béchar · Ouargla · Hassi-Messaoud
Agadir · Tiznit · Tata · Zagora · Abadla · El Golea · El Gassi · Ghadames · Daraj
SAHARA

MOROCCO · WESTERN SAHARA
La Palma · Santa Cruz De La Palma · Islas Canarias (Canary Islands) (Spain) · Lanzarote · Arrecife · Fuerteventura
Gomera · Hierro · Santa Cruz De Tenerife · Gran Canaria · Las Palmas De Gran Canaria
Tan-Tan · Tarfaya · La youn · Smara · El Farsia · Tindouf
Dakhla · Guelta Zemmur · Bir Moghrein · Zouerate · F'dérik · Tourine

ALGERIA
Tabelbala · Timimoun · Reggane · In Salah · Aoulef · Arak · Idelès · Djanet · Ghat
Chegga · Troudenni · Bidon 5 (Ruins) · Tamanrasset · Hoggar (Ahaggar) · Tahat 2918

MAURITANIA
Nouadhibou · Ras Nouadhibou · Atar · Chinguetti · Ouadâne · Tichla · Akjoujt
Nouakchott · Boutilimit · Tidjikja · Tichitt · Néma · Tombouctou · Gao · Bourem
St-Louis · Rosso · Dagana · Kaédi · Kiffa · Aioun El Atrouss · Goundam · Ansongo · Ménaka
Louga · Linguère · Nioro · Nara · Niafounké · Agadez · Ingal

NIGER
Tahoua · Madaoua · Zinder · Goudoumaria · Diffa · Gouré · Maradi · Tessaoua

MALI
L. Faguibine · Niamey · Sokoto · Katsina · Kano · Zaria · Kaduna · Bauchi · Gombe

SENEGAL
Dakar · Thiès · Diourbel · Kaolack · Touba · Tambacounda · Kayes · Bakel
THE GAMBIA · Banjul · Georgetown
GUINEA-BISSAU · Bissau
GUINEA · Conakry · Labé · Kankan · Siguiri · Kindia · Mamou
SIERRA LEONE · Freetown · Makeni · Bo · Kenema
LIBERIA · Monrovia · Buchanan · Greenville · Harper
IVORY COAST · Abidjan · Bouaké · Man · Daloa · Korhogo
UPPER VOLTA · Ouagadougou · Bobo Dioulasso · Koudougou
GHANA · Accra · Kumasi · Tamale · Bolgatanga · Cape Coast · Takoradi · Sekondi
TOGO · Lomé
BENIN / DAHOMEY · Cotonou · Porto Novo · Parakou
NIGERIA · Lagos · Ibadan · Ife · Ilorin · Oshogbo · Ogbomosho · Abeokuta · Benin City · Enugu · Onitsha · Calabar · Aba · Port Harcourt · Minna · Jos · Makurdi
CAMEROON · Douala · Yaoundé · Buéa · Mt Cameroun 4095
EQUATORIAL GUINEA · Malabo · Bioko (Fernando Poo) · Bata · Libreville
S.TOME & PRINCIPE · São Tomé · Príncipe
Bight of Benin · Bight of Biafra · GULF OF GUINEA
Mouths of the R. Niger

Inset — Cape Verde

25W · Sto Antão · S Vicente · S Luzia · S Nicolau · Sal · Boa Vista
S Tiago · Fogo · Maio · Praia · Brava
CAPE VERDE
at the same scale · 15 N

Inset — Madeira

Madeira (Portugal) · Funchal · Porto Santo · Ilhas Selvegens (Port.)

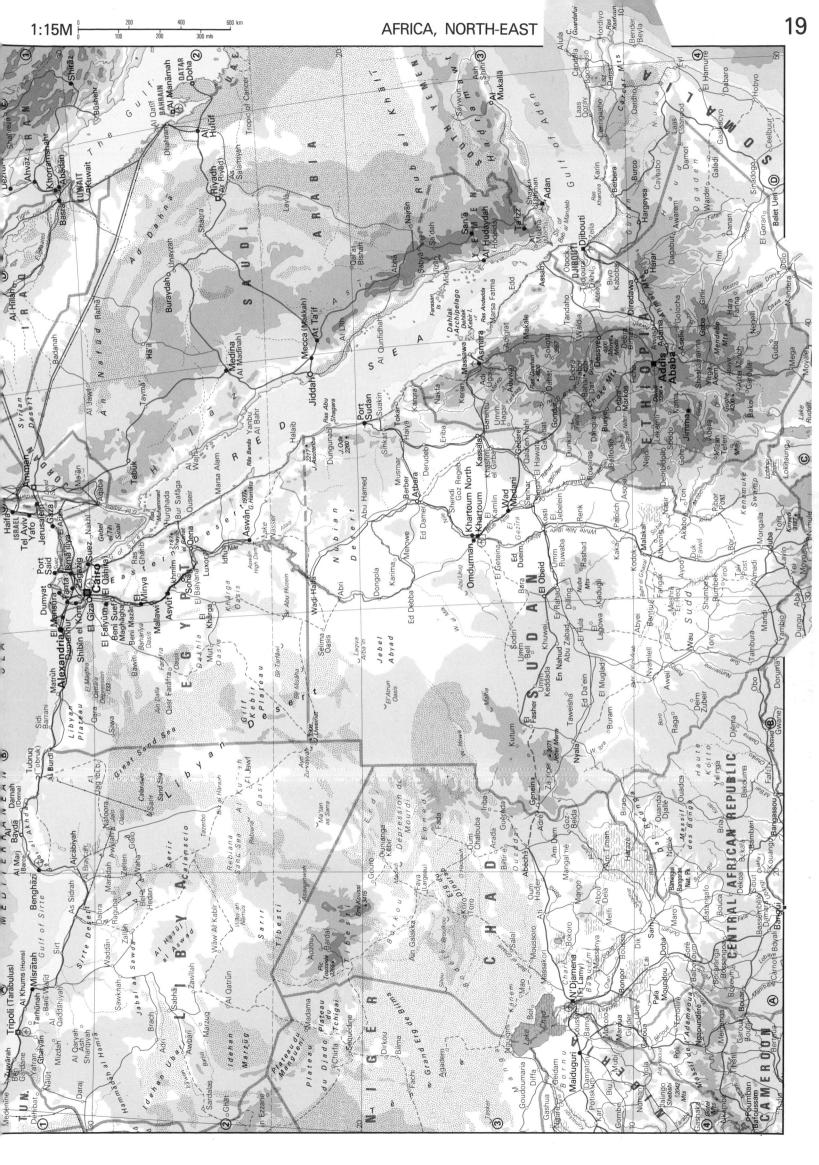

Scale bar: 200 400 600 km / 100 200 300 mls

Countries: SAUDI ARABIA, YEMEN, LIBYA, CHAD, NIGER, NIGERIA, CAMEROON, EQUATORIAL GUINEA, S.TOME & PRINCIPE, GABON, CONGO, ZAIRE, CENTRAL AFRICAN REPUBLIC, SUDAN, ETHIOPIA, SOMALIA, KENYA, UGANDA, RWANDA, BURUNDI, TANZANIA

Water bodies: RED SEA, Gulf of Aden, INDIAN OCEAN, Lake Victoria, Bight of Biafra

Selected cities/features: Mecca (Makkah), At Ta'if, Jiddah, San'a, Aden, Djibouti, Addis Ababa, Asmara, Massawa, Port Sudan, Khartoum, Omdurman, Kassala, El Obeid, Nyala, Muqdisho (Mogadishu), Nairobi, Mombasa, Kampala, Entebbe, Kigali, Bujumbura, Kisangani (Stanleyville), Mbandaka (Coquihatville), Kinshasa (Léopoldville), Brazzaville, Libreville, Yaoundé, Douala, Bangui, N'Djamena (Ft Lamy), Maiduguri, Kano, Zinder, Mt Kenya, Kilimanjaro

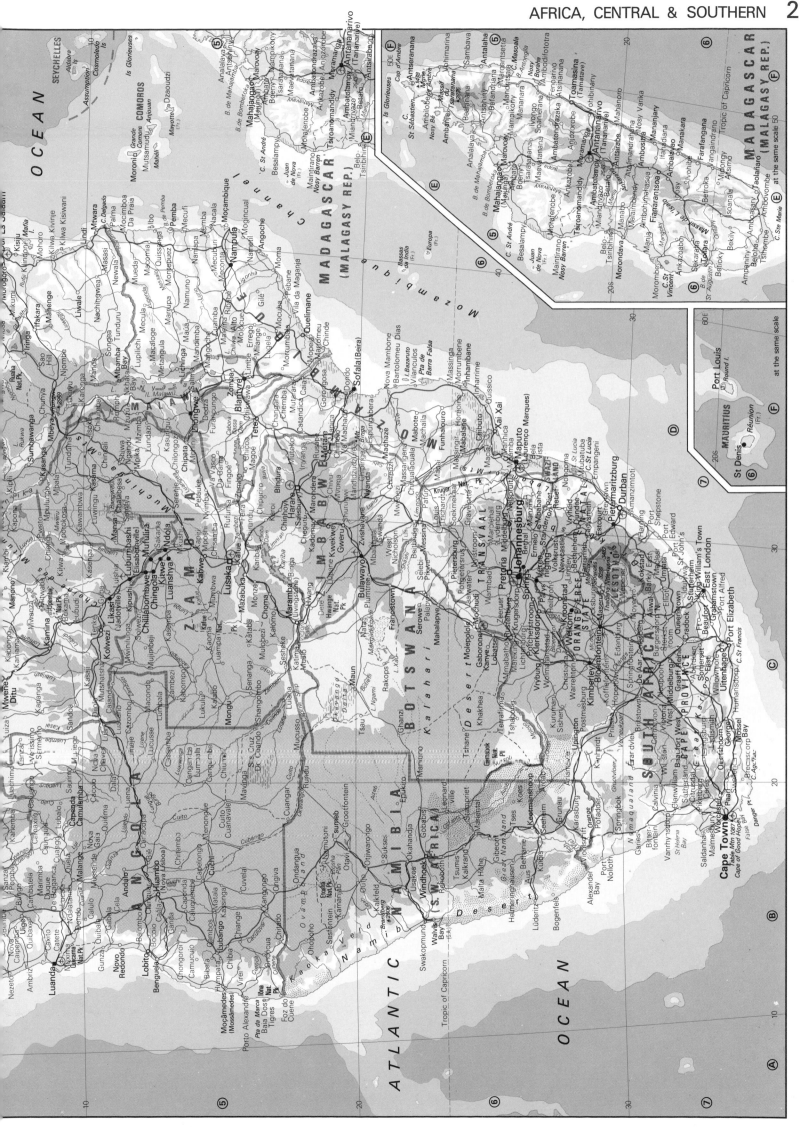

1:15M

200 400 600 km
100 200 300 mls

ARCTIC OCEAN

BEAUFORT SEA

U.S.S.R.

Bering Str.

BERING SEA

St. Lawrence I.

Gulf of Alaska

PACIFIC OCEAN

ALASKA

Brooks Range

Endicott Mts

Alaska Range

Mt McKinley

Aleutian Ra.

Kodiak Island

Kenai Pen.

YUKON TERRITORY

Ogilvie Mts

Mackenzie Mountains

Selwyn Mountains

Whitehorse

Dawson

BRITISH COLUMBIA

COAST MOUNTAINS

ROCKY MOUNTAINS

Queen Charlotte Islands

Prince Rupert

Vancouver Island

Vancouver

Victoria

Prince George

NORTHWEST TERRITORIES

CANADA

Great Bear Lake

Great Slave Lake

Yellowknife

Banks Island

Victoria Island

Prince of Wales Island

PARRY Island

Melville Island

ALBERTA

Edmonton

Calgary

Red Deer

Lethbridge

Lake Athabasca

Wood Buffalo Nat. Pk

Caribou Mountains

Peace River

Fort McMurray

SASKATCHEWAN

Saskatoon

Regina

Prince Albert

Reindeer Lake

Wollaston Lake

MANITOBA

Winnipeg

Lake Winnipeg

The Pas

Lake Winnipegosis

Lake Manitoba

WASHINGTON

Seattle

Tacoma

Olympia

Spokane

OREGON

Portland

Salem

Eugene

Bend

IDAHO

Boise

Twin Falls

Pocatello

MONTANA

Helena

Butte

Billings

Great Falls

Missoula

WYOMING

Yellowstone Nat. Pk

Casper

NORTH DAKOTA

Bismarck

Fargo

Grand Forks

Minot

SOUTH DAKOTA

Pierre

Rapid City

Black Hills

GREENLAND (Denmark)

ICELAND

BAFFIN BAY

DAVIS STRAIT

DENMARK STRAIT

Labrador Sea

NEWFOUNDLAND

Lancaster Sound

Devon Island

Baffin Island

Foxe Basin

Foxe Channel

HUDSON STRAIT

Ungava Bay

HUDSON BAY

James Bay

QUEBEC

ONTARIO

LABRADOR

Newfoundland

Gulf of Saint Lawrence

Anticosti Island

Cape Breton I.

NOVA SCOTIA

NEW BRUNSWICK

PRINCE EDWARD ISLAND

MAINE

NEW HAMPSHIRE

VERMONT

NEW YORK

MASS.

CONN.

MICHIGAN

WISCONSIN

MINNESOTA

LAKE SUPERIOR

L. Huron

L. Michigan

L. Erie

L. Ontario

ATLANTIC OCEAN

Churchill

Thunder Bay

Duluth

St Paul

Milwaukee

Detroit

Toronto

Hamilton

Buffalo

Montreal

Ottawa

Québec

Boston

Providence

Hartford

New Haven

Halifax

Sydney

St John's

Corner Brook

Gander

Goose Bay

Schefferville

Sept-Îles

Baie-Comeau

Chicoutimi

Gaspé

Sault Ste Marie

Sudbury

Timmins

Kapuskasing

Kirkland Lake

North Bay

Pembroke

Kingston

Syracuse

Rochester

Albany

Springfield

Worcester

Portland

Bangor

Fredericton

Saint John

Moncton

Charlottetown

Truro

New Glasgow

Glace Bay

Yarmouth

200 400 600 km
100 200 300 mls

UNITED STATES

NORTH CAROLINA
Wilmington
C. Fear
SOUTH CAROLINA
Charleston
Columbia
Rock Hill
Florence
Greenville
Spartanburg
Augusta
GEORGIA
Savannah
Brunswick
Waycross
Jacksonville
St. Augustine
Gainesville
Ocala
FLORIDA
Orlando
C. Canaveral
Melbourne
Ft. Pierce
W. Palm Beach
Ft. Lauderdale
Hollywood
Miami
Miami Beach
Key West
Marquesas Keys
The Everglades
L. Okeechobee
Tampa
St. Petersburg
Clearwater
Tampa Bay
Apalachee B.
Tallahassee
Panama City
Pensacola
Mobile
Biloxi
New Orleans
Lake Charles
Orange
Pt. Arthur
Beaumont
Galveston
Houston
Port Lavaca
Victoria
Corpus Christi
Kingsville
Padre I.
McAllen
Brownsville
Matamoros

TENNESSEE
Chattanooga
Huntsville
Gadsden
Birmingham
ALABAMA
Tuscaloosa
Montgomery
Columbus
Phenix City
Dothan
Meridian
MISSISSIPPI
Jackson
Hattiesburg
Laurel
Vicksburg
Natchez
Baton Rouge
LOUISIANA
Lafayette
Alexandria
Monroe
Shreveport

ARKANSAS
Little Rock
Pine Bluff
Hot Springs
Texarkana
Ft. Smith
Fayetteville
Boston Mts
OKLAHOMA
Oklahoma City
Tulsa
Muskogee
McAlester
Durant

TEXAS
Dallas
Fort Worth
Waco
Austin
San Antonio
Abilene
San Angelo
Odessa
Midland
Big Spring
El Paso
Edwards Plateau
Del Rio
Eagle Pass
Laredo
Nuevo Laredo

NEW MEXICO
Albuquerque
Las Cruces
Roswell
Carlsbad
Artesia
Santa Fe
Sacramento Mts
ARIZONA
Phoenix
Tucson
Nogales
Douglas
Yuma

CALIFORNIA
San Diego
Tijuana
Mexicali
Ensenada

MEXICO
Chihuahua
Ciudad Juárez
Monterrey
Saltillo
Torreón
Gómez Palacio
Durango
Mazatlán
Culiacán
Los Mochis
Ciudad Obregón
Hermosillo
Guaymas
La Paz
San José del Cabo
Cabo San Lucas
Baja California
Golfo de California
Guadalajara
Aguascalientes
Zacatecas
San Luis Potosí
León
Guanajuato
Irapuato
Celaya
Querétaro
Morelia
México
Toluca
Cuernavaca
Puebla
Acapulco
Oaxaca
Veracruz
Jalapa
Orizaba
Córdoba
Villahermosa
Coatzacoalcos
Minatitlán
Tuxtla Gutiérrez
Tehuantepec
Golfo de Tehuantepec
Tapachula
Quezaltenango
Mérida
Progreso
Campeche
Ciudad del Carmen
Chetumal
Cancún
Cozumel
Yucatán
Bahía de Campeche

Sierra Madre Oriental
Sierra Madre Occidental
Sierra Madre del Sur
Tropic of Cancer

GULF OF MEXICO

THE BAHAMAS
Nassau
Andros
Great Bahama Bank
Great Abaco
Eleuthera
Exuma
Long I.
Cat I.
San Salvador
Crooked I.

CUBA
Habana (Havana)
Matanzas
Cárdenas
Santa Clara
Cienfuegos
Sancti Spíritus
Ciego de Ávila
Camagüey
Holguín
Bayamo
Santiago de Cuba
Guantánamo
Pinar del Río
Isla de la Juventud
Straits of Florida

JAMAICA
Montego Bay
Kingston
Spanish Town
Grand Cayman (U.K.)
Little Cayman
Cayman Brac

CARIBBEAN SEA

BELIZE
Belmopan
Belize

GUATEMALA
Guatemala
Flores

EL SALVADOR
San Salvador
Santa Ana
Sonsonate

HONDURAS
Tegucigalpa
San Pedro Sula
La Ceiba
Puerto Cortés

NICARAGUA
Managua
León
Granada
Matagalpa
Bluefields
Lago de Nicaragua
Lago de Managua

COSTA RICA
San José
Puntarenas
Limón
Alajuela
Cartago
Pen. de Nicoya

PANAMÁ
Panamá
Colón
David
Golfo de Panamá
Archipiélago de las Perlas

PACIFIC OCEAN

Clipperton I. (France)
Revillagigedo
Isla Socorro
Isla Clarión
I. del Maíz

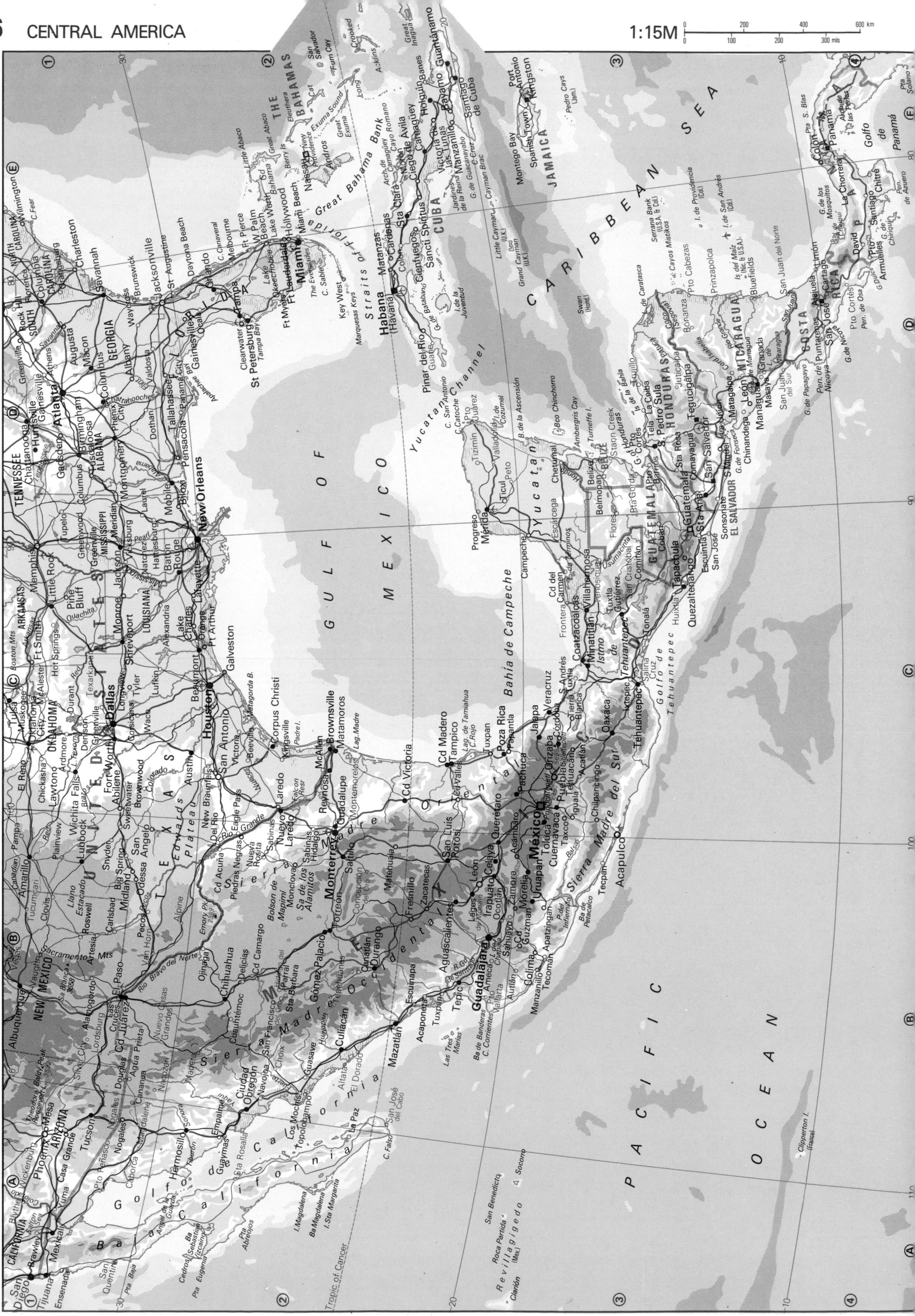

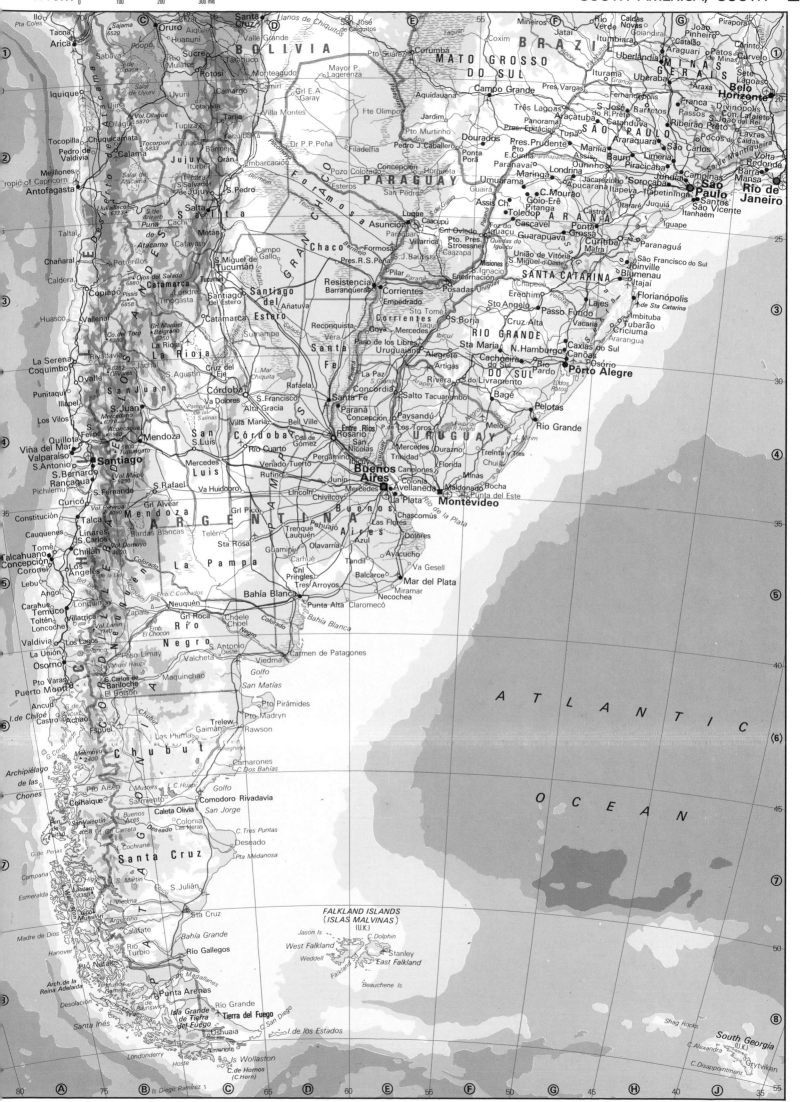

1:15M

PANAMA
COSTA RICA
NICARAGUA
COLOMBIA
VENEZUELA
ECUADOR
PERU
BOLIVIA
CHILE
ARGENTINA
RORAIM
AMAZONAS
ACRE
RONDÔNIA

PACIFIC OCEAN

Tegucigalpa
Comayagua
Siguatepeque
San Miguel
La Unión
Somoto
Choluteca
Chinandega
Estelí
Matagalpa
León
Managua
Masaya
Granada
L. de Nicaragua
S. Carlos
Rivas
Puntarenas
San José
Cartago
Chirripó Grande 3486
David
Pto Armuelles
Chitré
Santiago
La Palma
La Chorrera
Panamá
Colón
Pto Cabezas
I. de Providencia (Col.)
I. de San Andrés (Col.)
Bluefields
Pen. de Nicoya
G. de Nicoya
B. de Coronado
G. de Chiriquí
Pta Mariato
Arch. de las Perlas
G. de Panamá
I. Coiba

Sta Marta
Ciénaga
Barranquilla
Cartagena
Riohacha
Maicao
Valledupar
Sincelejo
S. Jacinto
El Banco
Magangué
Montería
Turbo
Quibdó
Caucasia
Barrancabermeja
Yarumal
Bello
Itagüí
Medellín
Manizales
Pereira
Cartago
Armenia
Ibagué
Tuluá
Buga
Palmira
Cali
Buenaventura
Santander
Popayán
Neiva
Pasto
Ipiales
Tulcán
Mocoa
Pto Asís
Florencia
Belén
Pitalito
Pto Rico
Calamar
Girardot
Bogotá
Villavicencio
Granada
Tunja
Sogamoso
Chocontá
Orocué
Pto Carreño
Pto Ayacucho
Mitú
Leguízamo

Cúcuta
Pamplona
Bucaramanga
Ocaña
Málaga
Barbosa
Chiquinquirá

Maracaibo
Cabimas
Cd Ojeda
Machiques
L. de Maracaibo
Mérida
Valera
Trujillo
Barinas
San Cristóbal
Pto Fijo
Coro
Pto Cabello
Maiquetía
Caracas
Valencia
Maracay
Barquisimeto
Acarigua
Guanare
Barcelona
Anaco
Zárara
El Tigre
Cumaná
Pto la Cruz
Carúpano
Güiria
Maturín
Tucupita
San Fernando
Cd Bolívar
Cd Guayana
Upata
El Dorado
Sta Elena
Boa Vista
Caracaraí

Willemstad
Curaçao
Aruba
Bonaire
Is Los Roques
I. de Margarita
La Asunción
G. de Paria
Pta Gallinas
G. de Venezuela

Quito
Cotopaxi
Ambato
Chimborazo 6267
Riobamba
Guaranda
Babahoyo
Guayaquil
La Libertad
Playas
I. Puná
G. de Guayaquil
Tumbes
Machala
Zaruma
Loja
Zamora
Cuenca
Azogues
Gualaceo
Macas
Manta
Chone
Jipijapa
C. San Lorenzo
Esmeraldas
S. Lorenzo
Ibarra
Otavalo
Cojimíes
Jama
Tumaco
El Divisor
Cayambe
Coca
Lago Agrio
Tena
Napo
Putumayo

Iquitos
Leticia
Tabatinga
Caxias
Elvira
Cruzeiro do Sul
Feijó
Sena Madureira
Rio Branco
Brasiléia
Cobija
Porvenir
Riberalta
Guajará-Mirim
Abunã
Porto Velho
Humaitá
Lábrea
Manacapuru
Tefé

Talara
Negritos
Sullana
Paita
Piura
Catacaos
Chulucanas
Huancabamba
Jaén
Chachapoyas
Moyobamba
Tarapoto
Yurimaguas
Lambayeque
Chiclayo
Chepén
Ferreñafe
Cajamarca
Celendín
Pacasmayo
Huamachuco
Otuzco
Trujillo
Chimbote
Huaraz
Huascarán 6768
Casma
Pomabamba
Pucallpa
Tingo María
Huánuco
La Unión
Huarmey
Oxapampa
Cerro de Pasco
La Merced
Pativilca
Barranca
Huacho
Ancón
Callao
Lima
Huancavelica
Huancayo
Jauja
Tarma
La Oroya
Acobamba
Ayacucho
Andahuaylas
Abancay
Cuzco
Machu Picchu
Quillabamba
Pto Maldonado
Pto Heath
Chincha Alta
Pisco
Ica
Pen. de Paracas
Nazca
Coropuna 6425
Majes
Chala
Camaná
Arequipa
Mollendo
Matarani
Moquegua
Ilo
Tacna
Arica
Puno
Juliaca
Sicuani
Ayaviri
L. Titicaca
La Paz
Oruro
Cochabamba
Quillacollo
Santa Cruz
Sucre
Potosí
Uyuni
Salar de Uyuni
Sajama 6520
Tupiza
Tarija
Iquique
Tocopilla
Pedro de Valdivia
Calama
Chuquicamata
Antofagasta
Mejillones
Tropic of Capricorn

ISLAS GALÁPAGOS (ARCHIPIÉLAGO DO COLÓN) (Equ.)
Culpepper (Wenman)
Pinta (Marchena)
Genovesa
Fernandina
Isabela
San Salvador
Santa Cruz
San Cristóbal
Baquerizo Moreno
Santa María
Española

ISLAS JUAN FERNÁNDEZ (Chile)
Alejandro Selkirk
Robinson Crusoe
Sta Clara

200 400 600 800 km
200 400 mils

BORNEO

MOLUCCAS

Manado
Minahassa Peninsula
Gorontalo
Tolitoli
Belang Sea
Ternate
Weda
Teluk Weda
Halmahera
Morotai
Tubelo
Kep. Asia
Kep. Ayu
P.P. Mapia

SULAWESI (CELEBES)

Samarinda
Balikpapan
Samboja
Banjarmasin
Kintap
Tg. Selatan
Laut

Makassar Strait

Donggala
Palu
Toboli
Poso
Teluk Tomini
Kep. Togian
Peleng
Taliabu
Banggai
Kep. Sula

Parepare
Majene
Watampone
Teluk Bone
Kabaena
Kep. Tukangbesi
Buton
Bau-Bau
Kendari
Butung

Ujung Pandang (Makassar)

Namlea
Buru
Ambon
Piru
Seram
Ceram Sea

Waigeo
Sorong
Salawati
Misool
Faktak
Teluk Berau

IRIAN JAYA

Manokwari
Biak
Cendrawasih
Numfoor
Yapen
Teluk Cendrawasih
Sarmi

NEW GUINEA

Jayapura
Aitape
Wewak
Schouten Is

PAPUA NEW GUINEA

Admiralty Is
Manus
Bismarck Archipelago
Kavieng
New Hanover
New Ireland

Bismarck Sea

Mt Wilhelm
Mt Hagen
Mendi
Goroka
Madang
Manam
Long
Umboi
New Britain

Bulolo
Kerema
Lae
Morobe

Gulf of Papua

Kikori
Digul

Merauke
Dolak

Arafura Sea

Port Moresby
Kupiano
Owen Stanley Ra.

Torres Strait
C. York
Somerset
Pr. of Wales I.

Banda Sea

Kep. Banda
Kep. Kai
Kep. Aru
Dobo

Kep. Barat Daya
Damar
Romang
Babar
Kep. Sermata
Kep. Leti

Tanimbar
Wetar
Alor

Flores Sea

Timor Sea

Dili
Kupang
Roti
Sawu

Bali
Denpasar
Lombok
Sumbawa
Mataram
Raba
Ruteng
Flores
Ende
Lombien
Waingapu
Sumba

INDIAN OCEAN

Java Trench

Melville I.
Bathurst I.
Van Diemen G.
Coburg Pen.
Croker I.

Darwin
Clarence Str.
Rum Jungle
Adelaide River
Burrundie
Pine Creek
Katherine
Daly
Roper

Arnhem Land

C. Arnhem
Nhulunbuy
Groote Eylandt

Gulf of Carpentaria

Weipa
Cape York
Iron Range
Coen
Cape York Peninsula

Wessel Is
Sir Edward Pellew Group
Mornington
Wellesley Is

Borroloola
Daly Waters
Newcastle Waters
Powell Creek
Barkly Tableland
Burketown
Normanton
Croydon
Georgetown
Forsayth

Cooktown
Laura
Mitchell River
Mitchell
Princess Charlotte B.

NORTHERN TERRITORY

Wave Hill
Tennant Creek
Barrow Creek
Camooweal
Cloncurry
Mount Isa
Richmond
Hughenden
Winton

QUEENSLAND

Mt Bartle Frere
Cairns
Innisfail
Ravenshoe
Ingham
Palm Is.
Townsville
Charters Towers
Bowen
Proserpine
Collinsville
Mackay

Great Dividing Range

Clermont
Emerald
Rockhampton
Longreach
Barcaldine
Mount Morgan
Blackall

WESTERN AUSTRALIA

Port Hedland
Shay Gap
Marble Bar
Monte Bello Is
Barrow I.
Dampier
Roebourne
Nullagine
Wittenoom
Hamersley Ra.
Mt Bruce
Paraburdoo
Newman
Ashburton
Onslow
North West C.
Fortescue

Shark B.
Dirk Hartog I.
Carnarvon
Gascoyne
Mt Augustus
Barlee Ra.
McLeod
Lyons

Great Sandy Desert
Gibson Desert
L. Disappointment
Lake Mackay
Macdonnell Ranges
Mt Ziel

Alice Springs
Mt Woodroffe
Musgrave Ra.
Petermann Ra.
Mt Aloysius
Tomkinson Ra.
L. Carnegie
L. Wells

Simpson Desert
Birdsville
Windorah
Diamantina

Great Victoria Desert

SOUTH AUSTRALIA

Coober Pedy
Oodnadatta
Marree
Lake Eyre Basin
L. Eyre
Milparinka

Woomera
L. Torrens
Leigh Ck
L. Frome
Wilcannia
Menindee
Ivanhoe

Carnegie
Wiluna
Meekatharra
Cue
Sandstone
Leonora
L. Barlee
Mt Magnet
Northampton
Mullewa

Geraldton
Dongara
Houtman Abrolhos
Moora
Bullfinch
Southern Cross
Merredin
Corrigin
Kalgoorlie
Coolgardie
Norseman
Ooldea
Tarcoola
Penong
Ceduna
Eucla

Nullarbor Plain
Rawlinna
Forrest
Eyre

Great Australian Bight

L. Gairdner
Gawler Ranges
Iron Knob
Port Augusta
Whyalla
Port Pirie
Iron Baron
Peterborough
Quorn
St Mary Pk

Port Lincoln
Eyre Pen.
Spencer Gulf
Investigator Str.
Kangaroo I.
Gulf St Vincent
Elizabeth
Adelaide
Murray Bridge
Victor Harbour
Kingston

Perth
Fremantle
Pinjarra
Bunbury
Collie
Wagin
Narrogin
Katanning
C. Naturaliste
Busselton
Manjimup
Augusta
C. Leeuwin
Bluff Knoll
Mt Knob
Albany
C. Pasley
Esperance
Arch. of the Recherche

NEW SOUTH WALES

Broken Hill
Cobar
Nyngan
Bourke
Walgett
Narrabri
Tamworth
Armidale
Moree
St George
Cunnamulla
Charleville
Quilpie
Roma
Miles
Toowoomba
Goondiwindi

Balranald
Mildura
Hay
Griffith
Deniliquin
Narrandera
Wagga Wagga
Cootamundra
Young
Bathurst
Orange
Dubbo
Gilgandra
Forbes
Condobolin
Albury
Shepparton
Wangaratta

Sydney
Wollongong
Newcastle
Maitland
Cessnock
Lithgow
Katoomba
Canberra
A.C.T.
Mt Kosciusko

VICTORIA

Melbourne
Geelong
Ballarat
Bendigo
Ararat
Horsham
Hamilton
Naracoorte
Mount Gambier
Portland
Port Fairy
Warrnambool
Colac
Morwell
Sale
Bairnsdale
Orbost
Wonthaggi
Wilson's Prom.

Bass Strait
King I.
Furneaux Group
Flinders
C. Barren

TASMANIA

Smithton
Burnie
Devonport
Launceston
St Mary's
Queenstown
Mt Ossa
Hobart
Geeveston
South West C.
South East C.

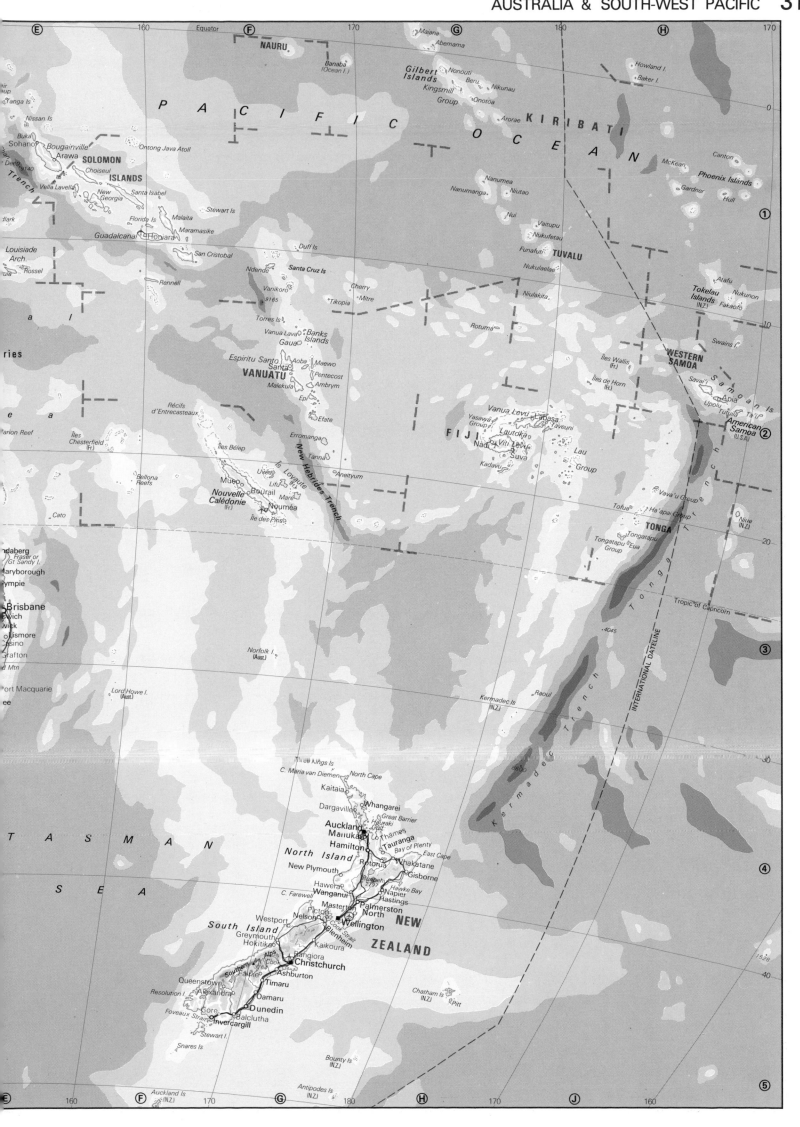

E   160   Equator   F   170   G   180   H   170

PACIFIC   OCEAN

NAURU
Banaba
(Ocean I.)

Maiana
Abemama

Gilbert
Islands
Kingsmill
Group

Nonouti
Beru
Nikunau
Onotoa

Howland I.
Baker I.

KIRIBATI

Tanga Is

Nissan Is

Buka
Sohano
Bougainville
Arawa

SOLOMON
ISLANDS

Choiseul

Vella Lavella
New
Georgia

Santa Isabel

Ontong Java Atoll

Arorae

Nanumea
Niutao

Nanumanga

McKean
Gardner
Canton
Hull

Phoenix Islands

Louisiade
Arch.
Rossel

Guadalcanal
Honiara

Florida Is
Malaita
Maramasike

San Cristobal

Stewart Is

Duff Is

Nui

Vaitupu
Nukufetau

Funafuti   TUVALU

Nukulaelae

Niulakita

Atafu
Nukunon
Tokelau
Islands
(N.Z.)
Fakaofo

Swains I.

Rennell

Ndende
Santa Cruz Is

Vanikoro
9165

Cherry
Tikopia
Mitre

Rotuma

WESTERN
SAMOA

Savai'i
Upolu
Apia
Tutuila
Tau

American
Samoa
(U.S.A)

Torres Is

Vanua Lava
Gaua

Banks
Islands

Îles Wallis
(Fr.)

Îles de Horn
(Fr.)

Espiritu Santo
Santa
VANUATU
Malekula

Aoba
Maewo
Pentecost
Ambrym
Epi

Récifs
d'Entrecasteaux

Efate

Vanua Levu
Labasa
Taveuni

Yasawa
Group
Lautoka
Nadi
Viti Levu
Suva

FIJI

Lau
Group

Kadavu

Vava'u Group

Îles Chesterfield
(Fr.)

Bellona
Reefs

Îles Bélep

Erromanga
Tanna

Aneityum

Marion Reef

Cato

Îles Loyauté
Uvéa
Muéo
Bourail
Nouvelle
Calédonie
(Fr.)
Nouméa
Lifu
Maré
Île des Pins

New Habrides Trench

Tofua
Ha'apai Group

Tongatapu
Group

Tongatapu
'Eua

Niue
(N.Z.)

TONGA

Bundaberg
Fraser or
Gt Sandy I.
Maryborough
Gympie
Brisbane
Ipswich
Warwick
Lismore
Casino
Grafton
d Mtn
Port Macquarie
ee

Norfolk I.
(Aust.)

Lord Howe I.
(Aust.)

4045

Tropic of Capricorn

INTERNATIONAL DATELINE

Tonga Trench

Kermadec Is
(N.Z.)

Raoul

Karmadec Trench

TASMAN
SEA

Three Kings Is
C. Maria van Diemen
North Cape

Kaitaia

Dargaville
Whangarei
Great Barrier
Hauraki
Gulf
Auckland
Manukau
Thames
Hamilton
Tauranga
Bay of Plenty
East Cape
North Island
Rotorua
Whakatane
New Plymouth
Gisborne
Hawera
Ruapehu
2797
Wanganui
Hawke Bay
Napier
Hastings
Masterton
Palmerston
North

C. Farewell

Westport
Nelson
Picton
Blenheim

Greymouth
Hokitika
South Island
Alps
Cook

Kaikoura

Rangiora
Christchurch
Ashburton
Timaru

NEW
ZEALAND

Chatham Is
(N.Z.)
Pitt

Queenstown
Resolution I.
Alexandra
Foveaux Strait
Gore
Balclutha
Invercargill

Southern
Fairlie
Oamaru
Dunedin

Snares Is

Stewart I.

1528

Auckland Is
(N.Z.)

Antipodes Is
(N.Z.)

Bounty Is
(N.Z.)

E   160   F   170   G   180   H   170   J   160

0 50 100 150 200 km
0 50 100 mls

A 170 B 175

Three Kings Is
C. Maria van Diemen
North Cape
Rangaunu B.
Ninety Mile Beach
Doubtless B.
Ahipara B.
Kaitaia
Tauroa Pt
Kaikohe
Kawakawa
Bay of Islands
C. Brett
Russell
Hokianga Har.
Hikurangi
Whangarei
Dargaville
Bream B.
Hen & Chickens Is
Little Barrier I.
Wellsford
Great Barrier I.
C. Colville
Mangawhai
Kaipara Har.
Hauraki Gulf
C. Colville
Mercury Is
Mercury Bay
Auckland
Takapuna
Papatoetoe
Manukau
Papakura
Coromandel Peninsula
Pukekohe
Waiuku
Thames
Mayor I.
Waihi
Paeroa
Te Puke
White I.
C. Runaway
Hicks Bay

NORTH

Huntly
Te Aroha
Matakana I.
Tauranga
Bay of Plenty
Glen Afton
Morrinsville
Tauragga Har.
Ngaruawahia
Whakatane
Hamilton
Cambridge
Opotiki
Te Awamutu
Putaruru
Rotorua
Kawerau
Tangatua
Kawhia
Raukumara Ra.
Otorohanga
Rotorua
Tokoma Bay
Waitomo
Te Kuiti
Taupo
Tolaga Bay

ISLAND

Mangakino
Murupara
Gisborne
N. Taranaki Bight
Ohura
Taumarunui
L. Taupo
Poverty Bay
Waitara
New Plymouth
Inglewood
Mt Ngauruhoe
Kaimanawa Mts
Makorako
Tarawera
Wairoa
C. Egmont
Mt Egmont
Stratford
Mt Ruapehu
Wahiki Mts
Hawke
Opunake
Eltham
Raetihi
Ohakune
Waiouru
Eskdale
Napier
Taradale
Hawera
Ohakune
Taihape
Hastings
Patea
Havelock North
S. Taranaki Bight
C. Kidnappers
Wanganui
Waipukurau
Marton
Rangitikei Ra.
Feilding
Dannevirke
Palmerston N.
Woodville
Pahiatua
Foxton
C. Turnagain
Levin
Herbertville
Otaki
Eketahuna

C. Farewell
Farewell Spit
Golden Bay
Separation Pt
C. Stephens
Collingwood
Rocks Pt
Takaka
Masterton
Carterton
Tasman Mts
The Twins 1826
D'Urville I.
Paraparaumu
Hector
Martinborough
Tasman Bay
Motueka
Porirua
Upper Hutt
Wairarapa
Karamea
Motueka
Nelson
Picton
Tawa
Lower Hutt
Bight
Richmond
Wellington
Mt Ross 983
Seddonville
Richmond Ra.
Wairau
Blenheim
Palliser Bay
C. Palliser
Westport
Murchison
C. Foulwind
Rotoiti
Awatere
C. Campbell
Buller
Victoria Ra.
L. Rotoiti
Ra.
Reefton
Spenser Mts
Mt Travers 2338
Tapuaenuku 2885
Runanga
Grey
Kaikoura Ra.
Greymouth
Lewis Pass
Hanmer Springs
Clarence
Hokitika
L. Brunner
Waiau
Kaikoura
Kaikoura Pen.
Ross
L. Sumner
Waiau
Culverden
Arthurs Pass
Hurunui
Cheviot

SOUTH

Abut Hd
Waipara
Pegasus Bay
Franz Josef Gl.
Rangiora
SOUTHERN ALPS
Puketeraki Ra.
Kaiapoi
Coleridge
Waimakariri
ISLAND
Mt Cook
Methven
Christchurch
Mt Sefton 3157
Hermitage
Rakaia
Lyttelton
L. Tekapo
Geraldine
Lincoln
Banks Peninsula
Jackson Hd
Pukaki
Fairlie
Ashburton
Akaroa
Cascade Pt
Pollux
Temuka
Ellesmere
Canterbury Bight
Awarua Pt
Young Ra.
L. Benmore
Timaru
Mt Aspiring 3027
Ohau
Milford Sd
Wanaka
Waimate
Homer Tunnel
Omarama
Mt Pyramid 2326
Wanaka
L. Aviemore
George Sd
Hawea
Kurow
Waitaki
Caswell Sd
Arrowtown
Waimate
Queenstown
Ranfurly
Oamaru
Fiordland
Secretary I.
Cromwell
Clyde
Hampden
Nat. Park
L. Te Anau
Kingston
Alexandra
Palmerston
Doubtful Sd
Manapouri
Roxburgh
Waikouaiti
Breaksea Sd
Mt Ward
Lumsden
Waikouaiti
Resolution I.
Riversdale
Port Chalmers
Dusky Sd
Ohai
Clutha
Otago Peninsula
Puysegur Pt
Te Waewae Bay
Heriot
Mosgiel
Dunedin
Cameron Mts
Winton
Milton
Waitapere
Gore
Balclutha
Riverton
Mataura
Kaitangata
Edendale
Invercargill
Owaka

TASMAN SEA
SEA

PACIFIC OCEAN

COOK STRAIT

Foveaux Strait
Bluff
Solander I.
Codfish I.
Oban
Paterson Inlet
Stewart Island
Mt Allen 730
Shelter Pt
Port Pegasus

35
40
45

Index

Introduction to the index

In the index, the first number refers to the page, and the following letter and number to the section of the map in which the index entry can be found. For example, Cairo 19C1 means that Cairo can be found on page 19 where column C and row 1 meet.

Abbreviations used in the index

Afghan	Afghanistan	Hung	Hungary	Pol	Poland	Arch	Archipelago
Alb	Albania	Ind	Indonesia	Port	Portugal	B	Bay
Alg	Algeria	Irish Rep	Ireland	Rom	Romania	C	Cape
Ant	Antarctica	N Ire	Ireland, Northern	S Arabia	Saudi Arabia	Chan	Channel
Arg	Argentina	Leb	Lebanon	Scot	Scotland	Gl	Glacier
Aust	Australia	Lib	Liberia	Sen	Senegal	I(s)	Island(s)
Bang	Bangladesh	Liech	Liechtenstein	S Africa	South Africa	Lg	Lagoon
Belg	Belgium	Lux	Luxembourg	S Yemen	South Yemen	L	Lake
Bol	Bolivia	Madag	Madagascar	Switz	Switzerland	Mt(s)	Mountain(s)
Bulg	Bulgaria	Malay	Malaysia	Tanz	Tanzania	O	Ocean
Camb	Cambodia	Maur	Mauritania	Thai	Thailand	P	Pass
Can	Canada	Mor	Morocco	Turk	Turkey	Pass	Passage
CAR	Central African Republic	Mozam	Mozambique	USSR	Union of Soviet Socialist	Pen	Peninsula
Czech	Czechoslovakia	Neth	Netherlands		Republics	Plat	Plateau
Den	Denmark	NZ	New Zealand	USA	United States of America	Pt	Point
Dom Rep	Dominican Republic	Nic	Nicaragua	U Volta	Upper Volta	Res	Reservoir
E Germ	East Germany	Nig	Nigeria	Urug	Uruguay	R	River
El Sal	El Salvador	Nor	Norway	Ven	Venezuela	S	Sea
Eng	England	Pak	Pakistan	Viet	Vietnam	Sd	Sound
Eq Guinea	Equatorial Guinea	PNG	Papua New Guinea	W Germ	West Germany	Str	Strait
Eth	Ethiopia	Par	Paraguay	Yugos	Yugoslavia	V	Valley
Fin	Finland	Phil	Philippines	Zim	Zimbabwe		

1

Alice Bacabal

Alice *USA* 24D4
Alice Springs *Aust* 30C3
Alicudi, I *Italy* 10C3
Alimniá, I *Greece* 11F3
Al Jaghbūb *Libya* 19B2
Al Jawf *Libya* 19B2
Aljezur *Port* 9A2
Al Khums *Libya* 19A1
Alkmaar *Neth* 6A2
Al Kufrah Oasis *Libya* 19B2
Al Lādhiqīyah *Syria* 14B2
Allahābād *India* 15G3
Allegheny Mts *USA* 25F3
Allen,Mt *NZ* 32A3
Aller, R *France* 8C2
Alma Ata *USSR* 15F1
Almada *Port* 9A2
Almagan, I *Pacific O* 17H5
Al Manāmah *Qatar* 14D3
Almansa *Spain* 9B2
Al Marj *Libya* 19B1
Almazán *Spain* 9B1
Almeria *Spain* 9B2
Älmhult *Sweden* 6C1
Almirós *Greece* 11E3
Almodôvar *Port* 9A2
Al Mukalla *S Yemen* 14C4
Alness *Scot* 4C3
Alnwick *Eng* 4E4
Alotau *PNG* 30E2
Aloysius,Mt *Aust* 30B3
Alpi Dolomitiche, Mts *Italy* 10C1
Alps, Mts *Europe* 10B1
Al Qaddāhiyah *Libya* 19A1
Al Qaryah Ash Sharqiyah *Libya* 19A1
Al Qatrūn *Libya* 19A2
Als, I *Den* 6B1
Alsace, Region *France* 8D2
Alsfeld *W Germ* 6B2
Alston *Eng* 4D4
Alta *Nor* 2J5
Alta Gracia *Arg* 27D4
Altai, Mts *Mongolia* 16B2
Altamira *Brazil* 29H4
Altamura *Italy* 10D2
Altanbulag *Mongolia* 16D1
Altata *Mexico* 26B2
Altay *China* 12K5
Altay *Mongolia* 13L5
Altay, Mts *USSR* 12K5
Alto Molócue *Mozam* 21D5
Altun Shan, Mts *China* 15G2
Alula *Somalia* 19E3
Älvdalen *Sweden* 2G6
Alvsbyn *Sweden* 2J5
Alytus *USSR* 2J8
Amadi *Sudan* 20D3
Amadjuak L *Can* 23L3
Åmål *Sweden* 2G7
Amalat, R *USSR* 13N4
Amaliás *Greece* 11E3
Amami, I *Japan* 16F4
Amami gunto, Arch *Japan* 16F4
Amapá *Brazil* 29H3
Amapá, State *Brazil* 29H3
Amarillo *USA* 24C3
Amazonas *Brazil* 29H4
Amazonas, State *Brazil* 28E4
Ambalavao *Madag* 21E6
Ambam *Cam* 20B3
Ambanja *Madag* 21E5
Ambarchik *USSR* 13S3
Ambato *Ecuador* 28C4
Ambato-Boeny *Madag* 21E5
Ambatolampy *Madag* 21E5
Ambatondrazaka *Madag* 21E5
Amberg *W Germ* 6C3
Ambergris Cay, I *Belize* 26D3
Ambilobe *Madag* 21E5
Amboasary *Madag* 21E6
Ambodifototra *Madag* 21E5
Ambohimahasoa *Madag* 21E6
Ambositra *Madag* 21E6
Ambovombe *Madag* 21E6
Ambriz *Angola* 21B4
Ambrym, I *Vanuatu* 31F2
Am Dam *Chad* 20C2
Amderma *USSR* 12H3
Ameca *Mexico* 26B2
Ameland, I *Neth* 6B2
American Samoa, Is *Pacific O* 31H2
Amersfoort *Neth* 6B2
Amfilokhía *Greece* 11E3
Amfissa *Greece* 11E3
Amga *USSR* 13P3
Amgal, R *USSR* 13P3
Amhara, Region *Eth* 20D2
Amherst *Can* 23M5
Amiens *France* 8C2
Amman *Jordan* 14B2
Ämmänsaari *Fin* 2K6
Amoda'ya, R *USSR* 14E1
Amos *Can* 23L5
Ampanihy *Madag* 21E6
Amposta *Spain* 9C1
Amsterdam *Neth* 6A2
Am Timan *Chad* 20C2
Amund Ringes I *Can* 23J2
Amundsen G *Can* 22F2
Amur, R *USSR* 13O4
Anabar, R *USSR* 13N2
Anaco *Ven* 28F2
Anaconda *USA* 24B2
Anadyr' *USSR* 13T3
Anadyr', R *USSR* 13T3
Anadyrskiy Zaliv, S *USSR* 13U3
Anadyrskoye Ploskogor'ye, Plat *USSR* 13T3
Anáfi, I *Greece* 11F3
Analalaya *Madag* 21E5
Anápolis *Brazil* 29J7
Anatahan, I *Pacific O* 17H5
Añatuya *Arg* 27D3
Anchorage *USA* 22D3
Ancohuma, Mt *Bol* 28E7
Ancón *Peru* 28C6
Ancona *Italy* 10C2
Ancud *Chile* 27B6
Andabuaylas *Peru* 28D6
Andalsnes *Nor* 2F6
Andalucia, Region *Spain* 9A2
Andaman Is *Burma* 15H4
Andaman S *Burma* 15H4
Andenes *Nor* 2H5
Andernach *W Germ* 6B2
Anderson, R *Can* 22F3
Andikíthira, I *Greece* 11E3
Andizhan *USSR* 12J5
Andkhui *Afghan* 12H6
Andorra, Principality *SW Europe* 9C1
Andorra-La-Vella *Andorra* 9C1
Andover *Eng* 5E6
Andreapol' *USSR* 7G1
Andria *Italy* 10D2
Andros, I *Bahamas* 25F4
Ándros, I *Greece* 11E3
Andújar *Spain* 9B2
Andulo *Angola* 21B5
Anéfis *Mali* 18C3
Aneityum, I *Vanuatu* 31F3
Angarsk *USSR* 13M4
Angel de la Guarda, I *Mexico* 26A2
Angelholm *Sweden* 2G7
Angemuk, Mt *Indon* 17G7
Angers *France* 8B2
Anglesey, I *Wales* 3C3
Angmagssalik *Greenland* 23P3
Angoche *Mozam* 21E5
Angol *Chile* 27B5
Angola, Republic *Africa* 21B5
Angoulême *France* 8C2
Angra do Heroismo *Açores* 18A1
Angumu *Zaïre* 20C4
Anholt, I *Den* 6C1
Anjak *USA* 22C3
Anjou, Region *France* 8B2
Anjouan, I *Comoros* 21E5
Anjozorobe *Madag* 21E5
Ankara *Turk* 14B2
Ankaratra, Mt *Madag* 21E5
Ankazoabo *Madag* 21E6
Ankazobe *Madag* 21E5
Anklam *E Germ* 6C2
Annaba *Alg* 18C1
An Nafūd *S Arabia* 14B3
Annan *Scot* 4D4
Annapolis *USA* 25F3
Annapurna, Mt *Nepal* 15G3
Annonay *France* 8C2
Ansbach *W Germ* 6C3
Anshan *China* 16F2
Anson B *Aust* 17F8
Ansongo *Mali* 18C3
Antalaha *Madag* 21F5
Antalya *Turk* 14B2
Antananarivo *Madag* 21E5
Antequera *Spain* 9B2
Anti-Atlas, Mts *Mor* 18B1
Anticosti I *Can* 23M5
Antipodes Is *NZ* 31G5
Antofagasta *Chile* 27B2
Antrim, County *N Ire* 4B4
Antrim *N Ire* 4B4
Antrim Hills *N Ire* 4B4
Antseranana *Madag* 21E5
Antsirabe *Madag* 21E5
Antsohiny *Madag* 21E5
Antwerpen *Belg* 6A2
An Uaimh *Irish Rep* 5B5
Anvik *USA* 22B3
Anxi *China* 13L5
Anyuysk *USSR* 13S3
Anzhero-Sudzhensk *USSR* 12K4
Anzio *Italy* 10C2
Aoba, I *Vanuatu* 31F2
Aosta *Italy* 10B1
Aouker, Desert Region *Maur* 18B3
Aoulef *Alg* 18C2
Aozou *Chad* 20B1
Apa, R *Brazil/Par* 27E2
Apalachee B *USA* 25E4
Apaporis, R *Colombia* 28D3
Apatin *Yugos* 11D1
Apatzingan *Mexico* 26B3
Apeldoorn *Neth* 6B2
Apia *Western Samoa* 31H2
Apoera *Suriname* 29G2
Aporé, R *Brazil* 29H7
Apostle Is *USA* 25D2
Appalachian Mts *USA* 25E3
Appennino Abruzzese, Mts *Italy* 10C2
Appennino Ligure, Mts *Italy* 10B2
Appennino Lucano, Mts *Italy* 10D2
Appennino Napoletano, Mts *Italy* 10D2
Appennino Tosco-Emilliano, Mts *Italy* 10C2
Appennino Umbro-Marchigiano, Mts *Italy* 10C2
Appleby *Eng* 5D4
Apucarana *Brazil* 27F2
Apure, R *Ven* 28E2
Apurimac, R *Peru* 28D6
Aqaba *Jordan* 14B2
Aqidauana *Brazil* 29G8
Arabian, S *Asia/Arabian Pen* 14E4
Aracajú *Brazil* 29L6
Aracati *Brazil* 29L4
Araçatuba *Brazil* 29H8
Aracena *Spain* 9A2
Araçuai *Brazil* 29K7
Arad *Rom* 11E1
Arada *Chad* 20C2
Arafura S *Indon/Aust* 30C1
Aragarças *Brazil* 29H7
Aragón, Region *Spain* 9B1
Aragon, R *Spain* 9B1
Araguaia, R *Brazil* 29H6
Araguaína *Brazil* 29J5
Araguari *Brazil* 29J7
Arak *Alg* 18C2
Aral'sk *USSR* 14E1
Aral'skoye More, S *USSR* 12G5
Aran, I *Irish Rep* 3B2
Aran, Is *Irish Rep* 3B3
Aranda de Duero *Spain* 9B1
Aranjuez *Spain* 9B1
Araouane *Mali* 18B3
Arapey, R *Urug* 27E4
Arapiraca *Brazil* 29L6
Ararangua *Brazil* 27G3
Araraquara *Brazil* 29J8
Ararat *Aust* 30D4
Arauca, R *Ven* 28E2
Arauea *Colombia* 28D2
Arawa *PNG* 31E1
Araxá *Brazil* 29J7
Arba Minch *Eth* 20D3
Arbatax *Sardegna* 10B3
Arbrå *Sweden* 2H6
Arbroath *Scot* 4D3
Arcachon *France* 8B3
Archipiélago de la Reina Adelaida, Arch *Chile* 27B8
Archipiélago de las Chones, Arch *Chile* 27B6
Archipiélago de las Perlas, Arch *Panama* 28C2
Arcos de la Frontera *Spain* 9A2
Arctic Red *Can* 22E3
Arctic Red R *Can* 22E3
Arctic Village *USA* 22D3
Arda, R *Bulg* 11F2
Ardar des Iforas, Upland *Alg/Mali* 18C2
Ardee *Irish Rep* 5B5
Ardennes, Region *Belg* 6B2
Ardila, R *Port* 9A2
Ardmore *USA* 24D3
Ardnamurchan, Pt *Scot* 4B3
Ardres *France* 5F6
Ardrishaig *Scot* 4C3
Ardrossan *Scot* 4C4
Areia Branca *Brazil* 29L4
Arendal *Nor* 2F7
Arequipa *Peru* 28D7
Arezzo *Italy* 10C2
Argenta *Italy* 10C2
Argentan *France* 8C2
Argentina, Republic *S America* 27C5
Argenton-sur-Creuse *France* 8C2
Argeşul, R *Rom* 11F2
Argolikós Kólpos, G *Greece* 11E3
Árgos *Greece* 11E3
Argostólion *Greece* 11E3
Argyle,L *Aust* 30B2
Argyll, Oilfield *N Sea* 4G3
Århus *Den* 2G7
Ariamsvlei *Namibia* 21C6
Aribinda *Upper Volta* 18B3
Arica *Chile* 27B1
Arinos, R *Brazil* 29G6
Aripuana *Brazil* 28F5
Aripuanã, R *Brazil* 28F5
Arisaig *Scot* 4C3
Arizona, State *USA* 24B3
Årjäng *Sweden* 2G7
Arka *USSR* 13Q3
Arkalya *USSR* 12H4
Arkansas, State *USA* 25D3
Arkansas, R *USA* 25D3
Arkhangel'sk *USSR* 12F3
Arkipelag Nordenshelda, Arch *USSR* 13K2
Arklow *Irish Rep* 3B3
Arlanzón, R *Spain* 9B1
Arles *France* 8C3
Arlon *Belg* 6B3
Armagh, County *N Ire* 5B4
Armagh *N Ire* 5B4
Armagós, I *Greece* 11F3
Armenia *Colombia* 28C3
Armidale *Aust* 30E4
Armyanskaya SSR, Republic *USSR* 12F5
Arnaud, R *Can* 23L3
Arnhem *Neth* 6B2
Arnhem,C *Aust* 30C2
Arnhem Land *Aust* 30C2
Arorae, I *Kiribati* 31G1
Arosa *Switz* 10B1
Arquipélago dos Bijagós, Arch *Guinea-Bissau* 18A3
Arran, I *Scot* 4C4
Arras *France* 8C1
Arrecife *Canary Is* 18A2
Arrochar *Scot* 4C3
Arrowtown *NZ* 32A2
Árta *Greece* 11E3
Artemovsk *USSR* 13L4
Artemovskiy *USSR* 13N4
Artesia *USA* 24C3
Arthurs P *NZ* 32B2
Artic Bay *Can* 23K2
Artigas *Urug* 27E4
Artillery L *Can* 22H3
Artois, Region *France* 8C1
Artsiz *USSR* 7F3
Aru *Zaïre* 20D3
Aruanã *Brazil* 29H6
Arusha *Tanz* 20D4
Aruwimi, R *Zaïre* 20C3
Arvayheer *Mongolia* 16D2
Arvida *Can* 23L5
Arvidsjaur *Sweden* 2H5
Arvika *Sweden* 2G7
Asawanwah, Well *Libya* 19A2
Aschaffenburg *W Germ* 6B3
Aschersleben *E Germ* 6C2
Ascoli Piceno *Italy* 10C2
Asedjirad, Upland *Alg* 18C2
Åsele *Sweden* 2H6
Aselle *Eth* 20D3
Asenovgrad *Bulg* 11E2
Ashburton *NZ* 31G5
Ashburton, R *Aust* 30A3
Asheville *USA* 25E3
Ashford *Eng* 5F6
Ashkhabad *USSR* 12G6
Ashland, Kentucky *USA* 25E3
Ashland, Oregon *USA* 24A2
Ashuanipi L *Can* 23M4
Asinara, I *Medit S* 10B2
Asino *USSR* 12K4
Askersund *Sweden* 2G7
Asmara *Eth* 20D2
Asosa *Eth* 20D2
Aspiring,Mt *NZ* 32A2
Assab *Eth* 20E2
Assen *Neth* 6B2
Assens *Den* 6C1
As Sidrah *Libya* 19A1
Assiniboia *Can* 22H5
Assiniboine,Mt *Can* 22G4
Assis *Brazil* 29H8
Assis *Brazil* 29H8
Assumption, I *Seychelles* 21E4
Asti *Italy* 10B2
Astipálaia, I *Greece* 11F3
Astorga *Spain* 9A1
Astoria *USA* 24A2
Astrakhan' *USSR* 12F5
Asturias, Region *Spain* 9A1
Asunción *Par* 27E3
Aswa, R *Uganda* 20D3
Aswân *Egypt* 19C2
Aswân High Dam *Egypt* 19C2
Asyût *Egypt* 19C2
Atafu, I *Tokelau Is* 31H1
Atakpamé *Togo* 18C4
Atangmik *Greenland* 23N3
Atar *Maur* 18A2
Atasu *USSR* 12J5
Atbara *Sudan* 20D2
Atbasar *USSR* 12H4
Atchafalaya B *USA* 25D4
Atchison *USA* 25D3
Atessa *Italy* 10C2
Athabasca, R *Can* 22G4
Athabasca L *Can* 22H4
Athens, Georgia *USA* 25E3
Athínai *Greece* 11E3
Athlone *Irish Rep* 3B3
Áthos, Mt *Greece* 11E2
Athy *Irish Rep* 5B5
Ati *Chad* 20B2
Atikoken *Can* 23J5
Atka *USSR* 13R3
Atlanta, Georgia *USA* 25E3
Atlantic City *USA* 25F3
Atlas Saharien, Mts *Alg* 18C1
Atlin *Can* 22E4
Atlin L *Can* 22E4
Atmore *USA* 25E3
Atofinandrahana *Madag* 21E6
Atrato, R *Colombia* 28C2
Attauapiskat *Can* 23K4
Attauapiskat, R *Can* 23K4
Atvidaberg *Sweden* 2H7
Aubagne *France* 8D3
Aubenas *France* 8C3
Auch *France* 8C3
Auckland *NZ* 31G4
Aude, R *France* 8C3
Auden *Can* 23K4
Augsburg *W Germ* 6C3
Augusta *Aust* 30A4
Augusta, Georgia *USA* 25E3
Augusta, Maine *USA* 25G2
Augustow *Pol* 7E2
Augustus,Mt *Aust* 30A3
Auk, Oilfield *N Sea* 4G3
Aurillac *France* 8C3
Aurora, Colorado *USA* 24C3
Ausert, Well *Mor* 18A2
Austin, Minnesota *USA* 25D2
Austin, Texas *USA* 24D3
Australian Alps, Mts *Aust* 30D4
Austria, Fed Republic *Europe* 6C3
Autlán *Mexico* 26B3
Autun *France* 8C2
Auvergne, Region *France* 8C2
Auxerre *France* 8C2
Aux Sources,Mt *Lesotho* 21C6
Avallon *France* 8C2
Avalon Pen *Can* 23N5
Aveíro *Brazil* 29G4
Aveiro *Port* 9A1
Avellaneda *Arg* 27E4
Avellino *Italy* 10C2
Avesta *Sweden* 2H6
Avezzano *Italy* 10C2
Aviemore *Scot* 4D3
Aviemore,L *NZ* 32B2
Avignon *France* 8C3
Avila *Spain* 9B1
Aviles *Spain* 9A1
Avon, County *Eng* 5D6
Avon, R, Dorset *Eng* 5E6
Avon, R, Warwick *Eng* 5E5
Avonmouth *Wales* 5D6
Avtovac *Yugos* 11D2
Awarem *Eth* 20E3
Awarua Pt *NZ* 32A2
Awash *Eth* 20E3
Awash, R *Eth* 20E3
Awatere, R *NZ* 32B2
Awbārī *Libya* 19A2
Aweil *Sudan* 20C3
Awjilan *Libya* 19B2
Axel Heiberg I *Can* 23J1
Axminster *Eng* 5D6
Ayacucho *Arg* 27E5
Ayacucho *Peru* 28D6
Ayaguz *USSR* 12K5
Ayakkum Hu, L *China* 15G2
Ayamonte *Spain* 9A2
Ayan *USSR* 13P4
Ayaviri *Peru* 28D6
Áyios Evstrátios, I *Greece* 11F3
Aykhal *USSR* 13N3
Aylesbury *Eng* 5E6
Ayn Zuwayyah, Well *Libya* 19B2
Ayod *Sudan* 20D3
Ayr *Aust* 30D2
Ayr *Scot* 4C4
Ayr, R *Scot* 4C4
Ayre,Pt of *Eng* 5C4
Ayvacik *Turk* 11F3
Ayvalik *Turk* 11F3
Azaouad, Desert Region *Mali* 18B3
Azeffal, Watercourse *Maur* 18A2
Azerbaydzhanskaya SSR, Republic *USSR* 12F5
Azogues *Ecuador* 28C4
Azoum, R *Chad* 20C2
Azuero,Pen de *Panama* 28B2
Azúl *Arg* 27E5

B

Baardheere *Somalia* 20E3
Babadag *Rom* 11F2
Babahoyo *Ecuador* 28C4
Babati *Tanz* 20D4
Babine L *Can* 22F4
Babo *Indon* 30C1
Bacabal *Brazil* 29J4

Bacău

Bindura

Bacău *Rom*	**11F1**
Bachu *China*	**15F2**
Back, R *Can*	**22J3**
Bacolod *Phil*	**17F5**
Badajoz *Spain*	**9A2**
Badalona *Spain*	**9C1**
Baden-Baden *W Germ*	**6B3**
Baden-Württemberg, State *W Germ*	**6B3**
Badgastein *Austria*	**6C3**
Bad-Godesberg *W Germ*	**6B2**
Bad Hersfeld *W Germ*	**6B2**
Bad Ischl *Austria*	**10C1**
Bad-Kreuznach *W Germ*	**6B3**
Bad Tolz *W Germ*	**6C3**
Baena *Spain*	**9B2**
Bafatá *Guinea-Bissau*	**18A3**
Baffin B *Greenland/Can*	**23L2**
Baffin I *Can*	**23L2**
Bafia *Cam*	**20B3**
Bafing, R *Mali*	**18A3**
Bafoulabé *Mali*	**18A3**
Bafoussam *Cam*	**20B3**
Bafwasende *Zaïre*	**20C3**
Bagamoyo *Tanz*	**21D4**
Bagé *Brazil*	**27F4**
Baghdad *Iraq*	**14C2**
Bagnoa *Ivory Coast*	**18B4**
Bagnols-sur-Cèze *France*	**8C3**
Bagoé, R *Mali*	**18B3**
Baguio *Phil*	**17F5**
Bahamas,The, Is *Caribbean*	**25F4**
Bahar Dar *Eth*	**20D2**
Bahia, State *Brazil*	**29K6**
Bahía Blanca *Arg*	**27D5**
Bahia Blanca, B *Arg*	**27D5**
Bahia de Banderas, B *Mexico*	**26B2**
Bahia de Campeche, B *Mexico*	**26C2**
Bahia de Corando, B *Costa Rica*	**28B2**
Bahia de la Ascension, B *Mexico*	**26D3**
Bahia de Petacalco, B *Mexico*	**26B3**
Bahia de Rio de Oro, B *Mor*	**18A2**
Bahía Grande, B *Arg*	**27C8**
Bahia Kino *Mexico*	**24B4**
Bahia Magdalena, B *Mexico*	**26A2**
Bahia Sebastia Vizcaino, B *Mexico*	**26A2**
Bahrain, Sheikdom *Arabian Pen*	**14D3**
Bahr Aouk, R *Chad/CAR*	**20C3**
Bahr el Arab, Watercourse *Sudan*	**20C3**
Bahr el Ghazal, R *Sudan*	**20D3**
Bahr el Ghazal, Watercourse *Chad*	**20B2**
Baia de Marajó, B *Brazil*	**29J4**
Baiá de Pemba, B *Mozam*	**21E5**
Baia de São Marcos, B *Brazil*	**29K4**
Baia de Setúbal, B *Port*	**9A2**
Baia de Todos os Santos B *Brazil*	**29L6**
Baia dos Tigres *Angola*	**21B5**
Baïbokoum *Chad*	**20B3**
Baie Antongila, B *Madag*	**21F5**
Baie-Comeau *Can*	**23M5**
Baie de Bombetoka, B *Madag*	**21E5**
Baie de Mahajamba, B *Madag*	**21E5**
Baie de St Augustin, B *Madag*	**21E6**
Baie des Chaleurs, B *Can*	**25G2**
Baie-du-Poste *Can*	**23L4**
Băilesti *Rom*	**11E2**
Baird Mts *USA*	**22B3**
Bairnsdale *Aust*	**30D4**
Baja *Hung*	**11D1**
Baja California, Pen *Mexico*	**26A1**
Bakala *CAR*	**20C3**
Bakel *Sen*	**18A3**
Baker, Montana *USA*	**24C2**
Baker, Oregon *USA*	**24B2**
Baker *USA*	**22G5**
Baker Foreland, Pt *Can*	**23J3**
Baker L *Can*	**22J3**
Baker Lake *Can*	**22J3**
Baker,Mt *USA*	**24A2**
Bakersfield *USA*	**24B3**
Bakkaflói, B *Iceland*	**2C1**
Bako *Eth*	**20D3**
Bakouma *CAR*	**20C3**
Baku *USSR*	**12F5**
Balaton, L *Hung*	**11D1**
Balbriggan *Irish Rep*	**5B5**
Balcarce *Arg*	**27E5**
Balchik *Bulg*	**11F2**
Balclutha *NZ*	**31F5**
Baldy Peak, Mt *USA*	**24C3**
Bali, I *Indon*	**30A1**
Balikesir *Turk*	**14A2**
Balikpapan *Indon*	**17E7**
Balkhash *USSR*	**12J5**
Ballachulish *Scot*	**4C3**
Ballantrae *Scot*	**4C4**
Ballantyne Str *Can*	**22G2**
Ballarat *Aust*	**30D4**
Ballater *Scot*	**4D3**
Ballina *Irish Rep*	**3B3**
Ballycastle *N Ire*	**4B4**
Ballymena *N Ire*	**4B4**
Ballymoney *N Ire*	**4B4**
Ballyshannon *Irish Rep*	**5A4**
Balombo *Angola*	**21B5**
Balranald *Aust*	**30D4**
Balsas *Brazil*	**29J5**
Balsas, R *Mexico*	**26B3**
Baltic S *N Europe*	**2H7**
Baltimore *USA*	**25F3**
Baltimore *USA*	**25F3**
Bama *Nig*	**20B2**
Bamako *Mali*	**18B3**
Bambari *CAR*	**20C3**
Bamberg *W Germ*	**6C3**
Bambili *Zaïre*	**20C3**
Bamenda *Cam*	**20B3**
Bamingui, R *CAR*	**20B3**
Bamingui Bangoran, National Park *CAR*	**20B3**
Banalia *Zaïre*	**20C3**
Banamba *Mali*	**18B3**
Banbridge *N Ire*	**5B4**
Banbury *Eng*	**5E5**
Banchory *Scot*	**4D3**
Banco Chinchorro, Is *Mexico*	**26D3**
Banda Aceh *Indon*	**17C6**
Bandama, R *Ivory Coast*	**18B4**
Bandar ' Abbās *Iran*	**14D3**
Bandar Seri Begawan *Brunei*	**17E6**
Banda S *Indon*	**17F7**
Bandiagara *Mali*	**18B3**
Bandundu *Zaïre*	**20B4**
Bandung *Indon*	**17D7**
Banes *Cuba*	**26E2**
Banff *Can*	**24B1**
Banff *Scot*	**4D3**
Banff, R *Can*	**22G4**
Bangalore *India*	**15F4**
Bangassou *CAR*	**20C3**
Bangkok *Thai*	**17D5**
Bangladesh, Republic *Asia*	**15G3**
Bangor, Maine *USA*	**25G2**
Bangor *N Ire*	**4B4**
Bangor *Wales*	**5C5**
Bangui *CAR*	**20B3**
Bangweulu, L *Zambia*	**21D5**
Bani, R *Mali*	**18B3**
Bani Bangou *Niger*	**18C3**
Banī Walīd *Libya*	**19A1**
Banja Luka *Yugos*	**10D2**
Banjarmasin *Indon*	**17E7**
Banjul *The Gambia*	**18A3**
Banks, Is *Vanuatu*	**31F2**
Banks I *Aust*	**17H8**
Banks I, British Columbia *Can*	**22E4**
Banks I, Northwest Territories *Can*	**22F2**
Banks Pen *NZ*	**32B2**
Bann, R *N Ire*	**4B4**
Banská Bystrica *Czech*	**7D3**
Bantry *Irish Rep*	**3B3**
Bantry, B *Irish Rep*	**3A3**
Baoshan *China*	**16C4**
Bar *Yugos*	**11D2**
Bara *Sudan*	**20D2**
Baraawe *Somalia*	**20E3**
Barabinsk *USSR*	**12J4**
Barabinskaya Step, Steppe *USSR*	**12J4**
Baracaldo *Spain*	**9B1**
Baranof I *USA*	**22E4**
Barbacena *Brazil*	**29K8**
Barbados, I *Caribbean*	**29G1**
Barbastro *Spain*	**9C1**
Barbezieux *France*	**8B2**
Barbôsa *Colombia*	**28D2**
Barcaldine *Aust*	**30D3**
Barcellona *Italy*	**10D3**
Barcelona *Spain*	**9C1**
Barcelona *Ven*	**28F1**
Barcoo, R *Aust*	**30D3**
Bardai *Chad*	**20B1**
Bardas Blancas *Arg*	**27C5**
Bardejov *Czech*	**7E3**
Bardsey, I *Wales*	**5C5**
Bareilly *India*	**15F3**
Barentsøya, I *Barents S*	**12D2**
Barents S *USSR*	**12D2**
Barentu *Eth*	**20D2**
Barguzin *USSR*	**13N4**
Barguzin, R *USSR*	**13N4**
Bari *Italy*	**10D2**
Barika *Alg*	**9D2**
Barinas *Ven*	**28D2**
Barjuj, Watercourse *Libya*	**19A2**
Barkly Tableland, Mts *Aust*	**30C2**
Barlee,L *Aust*	**30A3**
Barlee Range, Mts *Aust*	**30A3**
Barletta *Italy*	**10D2**
Barmouth *Wales*	**5C5**
Barnard Castle *Eng*	**5E4**
Barnaul *USSR*	**12K4**
Barnes Icecap *Can*	**23L2**
Barnsley *Eng*	**5E5**
Barnstaple *Eng*	**5C6**
Barquisimeto *Ven*	**28E1**
Barra *Brazil*	**29K6**
Barra, I *Scot*	**4B3**
Barragem do Castelo do Bode, Res *Port*	**9A2**
Barragem do Maranhão *Port*	**9A2**
Barra Head, Pt *Scot*	**4B3**
Barra Mansa *Brazil*	**29K8**
Barranca *Peru*	**28C6**
Barrancabermeja *Colombia*	**28D2**
Barrancas *Ven*	**28F2**
Barranquilla *Colombia*	**28D1**
Barra,Sound of, Chan *Scot*	**4B3**
Barreiras *Brazil*	**29K6**
Barreiro *Port*	**9A2**
Barreiros *Brazil*	**29L5**
Barren,C *Aust*	**30D5**
Barretos *Brazil*	**29J8**
Barrington,Mt *Aust*	**30E4**
Barrow *USA*	**22C2**
Barrow, R *Irish Rep*	**3B3**
Barrow, R *Irish Rep*	**5B5**
Barrow Creek *Aust*	**30C3**
Barrow I *Aust*	**30A3**
Barrow-in-Furness *Eng*	**5D4**
Barrow,Pt *USA*	**22C2**
Barrow Str *Can*	**23J2**
Barstow *USA*	**24B3**
Bar-sur-Aube *France*	**8C2**
Bartica *Guyana*	**29G2**
Bartle Frere,Mt *Aust*	**30D2**
Bartlesville *USA*	**24D3**
Bartolomeu Dias *Mozam*	**21D6**
Bartoszyce *Pol*	**7E2**
Basankusu *Zaïre*	**20B3**
Basel *Switz*	**10B1**
Basento, R *Italy*	**10D2**
Basilan *Phil*	**17F6**
Basildon *Eng*	**5F6**
Basingstoke *Eng*	**5E6**
Basin Region *USA*	**24B2**
Basra *Iraq*	**14C2**
Bassano *Italy*	**10C1**
Bassas da India, I *Mozam Chan*	**21D6**
Bass Str *Aust*	**30D5**
Båstad *Sweden*	**2G7**
Bastia *Corse*	**10B2**
Bastogne *Belg*	**6B3**
Bata *Eq Guinea*	**20A3**
Batang *China*	**16C3**
Batangafo *CAR*	**20B3**
Batangas *Phil*	**17F5**
Bath *Eng*	**5D6**
Batha, R *Chad*	**20B2**
Bathurst *Aust*	**30D4**
Bathurst *Can*	**23M5**
Bathurst,C *Can*	**22F2**
Bathurst I *Aust*	**30C2**
Bathurst I *Can*	**22H2**
Bathurst Inlet, B *Can*	**22H3**
Batna *Alg*	**18C1**
Baton Rouge *USA*	**25D3**
Battle Creek *USA*	**25E2**
Battle Harbour *Can*	**23N4**
Baubau *Indon*	**30B1**
Bauld,C *Can*	**23N4**
Baunt *USSR*	**13N4**
Bauru *Brazil*	**29J8**
Bautzen *E Germ*	**6C2**
Bawîti *Egypt*	**19B2**
Bayamo *Cuba*	**26E2**
Bayandzürh *Mongolia*	**16D2**
Bayan Har Shan, Mts *China*	**16C3**
Bay City, Michigan *USA*	**25E2**
Baydaratskaya Guba, B *USSR*	**12H3**
Baydhabo *Somalia*	**20E3**
Bayeaux *France*	**8B2**
Bayern, State *W Germ*	**6C3**
Baykalskiy Khrebet, Mts *USSR*	**16D1**
Baykit *USSR*	**13L3**
Baylik Shan, Mts *China/Mongolia*	**13L5**
Bayonne *France*	**8B3**
Bayreuth *W Germ*	**6C3**
Baza *Spain*	**9B2**
Bazaliya *USSR*	**7F3**
Bazas *France*	**8B3**
Beachy Head *Eng*	**5F6**
Bealanana *Madag*	**21E5**
Beatrice *USA*	**24D2**
Beatrice, Oilfield *N Sea*	**4D2**
Beatton River *Can*	**22F4**
Beatty *USA*	**24B3**
Beauchene Is *Falkland Is*	**27E8**
Beaufort S *Can*	**22D2**
Beauly *Scot*	**4C3**
Beaumont, Texas *USA*	**25D3**
Beaune *France*	**8C2**
Beauvais *France*	**8C2**
Beaver Creek *Can*	**22D3**
Beccles *Eng*	**5F5**
Bečej *Yugos*	**11E1**
Béchar *Alg*	**18B1**
Beckley *USA*	**25E3**
Bedford, County *Eng*	**5E5**
Bedford *Eng*	**5E5**
Beechey, Pt *USA*	**22D2**
Beeville *USA*	**24D4**
Befale *Zaïre*	**20C3**
Befandriana *Madag*	**21E5**
Beijing *China*	**16E2**
Beirut *Leb*	**14B2**
Bei Shan, Mts *China*	**16C2**
Beja *Port*	**9A2**
Bejaïa *Alg*	**18C1**
Béjar *Spain*	**9A1**
Békéscsaba *Hung*	**7E3**
Bekily *Madag*	**21E6**
Belau, Republic *Pacific O*	**17G6**
Belaya Tserkov *USSR*	**7G3**
Belcher Chan *Can*	**23J2**
Belcher Is *Can*	**23L4**
Belém *Brazil*	**29J4**
Belén *Colombia*	**28C3**
Belen *USA*	**24C3**
Belet Uen *Somalia*	**20E3**
Belfast *N Ire*	**4B4**
Belfast Lough, Estuary *N Ire*	**4B4**
Belfodio *Eth*	**20D2**
Belford *Eng*	**4E4**
Belfort *France*	**8D2**
Belgatanga *Ghana*	**18B3**
Belgium, Kingdom *N W Europe*	**6A2**
Bel Hedan *Libya*	**19A2**
Belize *Belize*	**26D3**
Belize, Republic *C America*	**26D3**
Bellac *France*	**8C2**
Bella Coola *Can*	**22F4**
Belle Fourche *USA*	**24C2**
Bellegarde *France*	**8D2**
Belle I *Can*	**23N4**
Belle-Ile, I *France*	**8B2**
Belle Isle,Str of *Can*	**23N4**
Belleville *Can*	**23L5**
Bellin *Can*	**23L3**
Bellingham *USA*	**24A2**
Bellinzona *Switz*	**10B1**
Bello *Colombia*	**28C2**
Bellona Reefs *Nouvelle Calédonie*	**31E3**
Bell Pen *Can*	**23K3**
Belluno *Italy*	**10C1**
Bell Ville *Arg*	**27D4**
Belmonte *Brazil*	**29L7**
Belmopan *Belize*	**26D3**
Beloha *Madag*	**21E6**
Belo Horizonte *Brazil*	**29K7**
Beloit, Wisconsin *USA*	**25E2**
Belomorsk *USSR*	**12E3**
Belorusskaya SSR, Republic *USSR*	**7F2**
Belo-Tsiribihina *Madag*	**21E5**
Beloye More, S *USSR*	**12E3**
Bel'tsy *USSR*	**7F3**
Belukha, Mt *USSR*	**12K5**
Bembe *Angola*	**21B4**
Bemidji *USA*	**25D2**
Bena Dibele *Zaïre*	**20C4**
Ben Attow, Mt *Scot*	**4C3**
Benavente *Spain*	**9A1**
Benbecula, I *Scot*	**4B3**
Bencubbin *Aust*	**30A4**
Bend *USA*	**24A2**
Ben Dearg, Mt *Scot*	**4C3**
Bender Beyla *Somalia*	**19E3**
Bendery *USSR*	**7F3**
Bendigo *Aust*	**30D4**
Benešov *Czech*	**6C3**
Benevento *Italy*	**10C2**
Bengal,B of *Asia*	**15G4**
Ben Gardane *Libya*	**19A1**
Benghāzī *Libya*	**19B1**
Benguela *Angola*	**21B5**
Ben Hope, Mt *Scot*	**4C2**
Beni *Zaïre*	**20C3**
Béni, R *Bol*	**28E6**
Beni Abbes *Alg*	**18B1**
Benicarló *Spain*	**9C1**
Benidji *USA*	**23J5**
Benidorm *Spain*	**9B2**
Beni Mansour *Alg*	**9C2**
Beni Mazar *Egypt*	**19C2**
Benin, Republic *Africa*	**18C4**
Benin City *Nig*	**18C4**
Beni Suef *Egypt*	**19C2**
Ben Kilbreck, Mt *Scot*	**4C2**
Ben Lawers, Mt *Scot*	**3C2**
Ben Macdui, Mt *Scot*	**4D3**
Ben More Assynt, Mt *Scot*	**4C2**
Benmore,L *NZ*	**32B2**
Ben Nevis, Mt *Scot*	**4C3**
Bénoué, R *Cam*	**20B3**
Benson, Arizona *USA*	**24B3**
Bentiu *Sudan*	**20C3**
Ben Wyvis, Mt *Scot*	**4C3**
Benxi *China*	**16F2**
Beograd *Yugos*	**11E2**
Berat *Alb*	**11D2**
Berber *Sudan*	**20D2**
Berbera *Somalia*	**20E2**
Berbérati *CAR*	**20B3**
Berdichev *USSR*	**7F3**
Berens, R *Can*	**22J4**
Berens River *Can*	**22J4**
Berettyoújfalu *Hung*	**7E3**
Bereza *USSR*	**7F2**
Berezhany *USSR*	**7E3**
Berezina, R *USSR*	**7F2**
Berezniki *USSR*	**12G4**
Berezovo *USSR*	**12H3**
Bergamo *Italy*	**10B1**
Bergen *Nor*	**2F6**
Bergerac *France*	**8C3**
Beringovskiy *USSR*	**13U3**
Bering S *USSR/USA*	**13T3**
Bering Str *USSR/USA*	**22B3**
Berja *Spain*	**9B2**
Berkeley *USA*	**24A3**
Berkovitsa *Bulg*	**11E2**
Berkshire, County *Eng*	**5E6**
Berlin *E Germ*	**6C2**
Bermejo *Bol*	**28F8**
Bermejo, R *Arg*	**27E3**
Bern *Switz*	**10B1**
Bernburg *E Germ*	**6C2**
Bernier B *Can*	**23K2**
Berounka, R *Czech*	**6C3**
Berry, Region *France*	**8C2**
Berry Is *Bahamas*	**25F4**
Bertoua *Cam*	**20B3**
Beru, I *Kiribati*	**31G1**
Berwick-upon-Tweed *Eng*	**4D4**
Berwyn, Mts *Wales*	**5D5**
Besalampy *Madag*	**21E5**
Besançon *France*	**8D2**
Beskidy Zachodnie, Mts *Pol*	**7E3**
Betafo *Madag*	**21E5**
Betanzos *Spain*	**9A1**
Bethel, Alaska *USA*	**22B3**
Bethune *France*	**8C1**
Betioky *Madag*	**21E6**
Betou *Congo*	**20B3**
Betpak Dala, Steppe *USSR*	**15E1**
Betroka *Madag*	**21E6**
Betsiamites *Can*	**23M5**
Beyla *Guinea*	**18B4**
Béziers *France*	**8C3**
Beznosova *USSR*	**16D1**
Bhutan, Kingdom *Asia*	**15G3**
Biak, I *Indon*	**17G7**
Biala Podlaska *Pol*	**7E2**
Bialograd *Pol*	**6D2**
Bialystok *Pol*	**7E2**
Biargtangar, C *Iceland*	**2A1**
Biarritz *France*	**8B3**
Bibala *Angola*	**21B5**
Biberach *W Germ*	**6B3**
Bibiani *Ghana*	**18B4**
Bicaz *Rom*	**11F1**
Bideford *Eng*	**5C6**
Bideford B *Eng*	**5C6**
Bidon 5 *Alg*	**18C2**
Bié *Angola*	**21B5**
Biebrza *Pol*	**7E2**
Biel *Switz*	**10B1**
Bielawa *Pol*	**6D2**
Bielefeld *W Germ*	**6B2**
Biella *Italy*	**10B1**
Bielsk Podlaski *Pol*	**7E2**
Biferno, R *Italy*	**10C2**
Bigadiç *Turk*	**11F3**
Big Delta *USA*	**22D3**
Biggar *Can*	**22H4**
Big Horn Mts *USA*	**24C2**
Bight of Benin, B *W Africa*	**18C4**
Bight of Biafra, B *Cam*	**18C4**
Big I *Can*	**23L3**
Bignona *Sen*	**18A3**
Big River *Can*	**22H4**
Big Spring *USA*	**24C3**
Big Trout L *Can*	**23J4**
Big Trout Lake *Can*	**23K4**
Bihać *Yugos*	**10D2**
Biharamulo *Tanz*	**20D4**
Bijeljina *Yugos*	**11D2**
Bikoro *Zaïre*	**20B4**
Bilbao *Spain*	**9B1**
Bilé, R *Czech*	**6D3**
Bileća *Yugos*	**11D2**
Bili, R *Zaïre*	**20C3**
Bilibino *USSR*	**13S3**
Billings *USA*	**24C2**
Bilma *Niger*	**20B2**
Biloxi *USA*	**25E3**
Biltine *Chad*	**20C2**
Bindura *Zim*	**21D5**

Cachoeira de Paulo Afonso **Chongoroi**

Cachoeira de Paulo Afonso, Waterfall *Brazil* **29L5**
Cachoeira do Sul *Brazil* **27F4**
Cachoeiro de Itapemirim *Brazil* **29K8**
Cacolo *Angola* **21B5**
Caconda *Angola* **21B5**
Caculuvar, R *Angola* **21B5**
Čadca *Czech* **7D3**
Cader Idris, Mts *Wales* **5D5**
Cadillac *USA* **25E2**
Cadiz *Spain* **9A2**
Caen *France* **8B2**
Caernarfon *Wales* **5C5**
Caernarfon B *Wales* **5C5**
Caetité *Brazil* **29K6**
Cafayate *Arg* **27C3**
Cagayan de Oro *Phil* **17F6**
Cagliari *Sardegna* **10B3**
Cahir *Irish Rep* **5B5**
Cahore Pt *Irish Rep* **5B5**
Cahors *France* **8C3**
Caia *Mozam* **21D5**
Caianda *Angola* **21C5**
Caicó *Brazil* **29L5**
Caicos Pass *Bahamas* **25F4**
Cairngorms, Mts *Scot* **4D3**
Cairns *Aust* **30D2**
Cairo *Egypt* **19C1**
Cairo *USA* **25E3**
Cajabamba *Peru* **28C5**
Cajamarca *Peru* **28C5**
Calabar *Nig* **18C4**
Calafat *Rom* **11E2**
Calafate *Arg* **27B8**
Calahorra *Spain* **9B1**
Calais *France* **8C1**
Calama *Chile* **27C2**
Calamar *Colombia* **28D3**
Calanscio Sand Sea *Libya* **19B2**
Calarasi *Rom* **11F2**
Calatayud *Spain* **9B1**
Calcutta *India* **15G3**
Caldas da Rainha *Port* **9A2**
Caldas Novas *Brazil* **29J7**
Caldera *Chile* **27B3**
Caldwell *USA* **24B2**
Caleta Olivia *Arg* **27C7**
Calexico *USA* **24B3**
Calgary *Can* **22G4**
Cali *Colombia* **28C3**
Caliente, Nevada *USA* **24B3**
California, State *USA* **24A3**
Callander *Scot* **4C3**
Callao *Peru* **28C6**
Caltanissetta *Italy* **10C3**
Caluango *Angola* **21B4**
Calulo *Angola* **21B5**
Caluquembe *Angola* **21B5**
Calvi *Corse* **10B2**
Camagüey *Cuba* **26E2**
Camagüey,Arch de, Is *Cuba* **26E2**
Camaná *Peru* **28D7**
Camargo *Bol* **28F8**
Camarones *Arg* **27C6**
Camaxilo *Angola* **21B4**
Cambatela *Angola* **21B4**
Cambodia, Republic *SE Asia* **17D5**
Camborne *Eng* **5C6**
Cambrai *France* **8C1**
Cambrian Mts *Wales* **5D5**
Cambridge, County *Eng* **5E5**
Cambridge *Eng* **5F5**
Cambridge *NZ* **32C1**
Cambridge Bay *Can* **22H3**
Cambridge G *Aust* **17F8**
Camden, Arkansas *USA* **25D3**
Cameron I *Can* **22H2**
Cameron Mts *NZ* **32A3**
Cameroon, Federal Republic *Africa* **20B3**
Cameroun, Mt *Cam* **20A3**
Cametá *Brazil* **29J4**
Camiri *Bol* **28F8**
Camocim *Brazil* **29K4**
Camooweal *Aust* **30C2**
Campana, I *Chile* **27A7**
Campbell,C *NZ* **32B2**
Campbell,Mt *Can* **22E3**
Campbell River *Can* **22F5**
Campbellton *Can* **23M5**
Campbeltown *Scot* **4C4**
Campeche *Mexico* **26C3**
Campina Grande *Brazil* **29L5**
Campinas *Brazil* **29J8**
Campo *Cam* **20A3**
Campobasso *Italy* **10C2**
Campo Gallo *Arg* **27D3**
Campo Grande *Brazil* **27F2**
Campo Maior *Brazil* **29K4**
Campo Mourão *Brazil* **27F2**
Campos *Brazil* **29K8**
Camrose *Can* **22G4**
Camucuio *Angola* **21B5**
Canacupa *Angola* **21B5**
Canada, Commonwealth Nation *N America* **22F3**
Cañada de Gomez *Arg* **27D4**
Canadian, R *USA* **24C3**
Cananea *Mexico* **26A1**
Canatlán *Mexico* **26B2**
Canaveral,C *USA* **25E4**
Canavieriras *Brazil* **29L7**
Canberra *Aust* **30D4**
Candala *Somalia* **19E3**
Çandarli Körfezi, B *Turk* **11F3**
Canelones *Urug* **27E4**
Cangamba *Angola* **21C5**
Cangombe *Angola* **21C5**
Caniapiscau, R *Can* **23M4**
Caniapiscau,L *Can* **23M4**
Canicatti *Italy* **10C3**
Canindé *Brazil* **29L4**
Canna, I *Scot* **4B3**
Cannes *France* **8D3**
Canõas *Brazil* **27F3**
Canora *Can* **22H4**
Cansore Pt *Irish Rep* **5B5**
Canterbury *Eng* **5F6**
Canterbury Bight, B *NZ* **32B2**
Canterbury Plains *NZ* **32B2**
Can Tho *Viet* **17D5**
Canton, Ohio *USA* **25E2**
Canton, I *Phoeniz Is* **31H1**
Canzar *Angola* **21C4**
Capanema *Brazil* **29J4**
Capbreton *France* **8B3**
Cap Corse, C *Corse* **10B2**
Cap d'Ambre, C *Madag* **21E5**
Cap de la Hague, C *France* **8B2**
Cap de Nouvelle-France, C *Can* **23L3**
Capdepera *Spain* **9C2**
Cape Breton I *Can* **23N5**
Cape Coast *Ghana* **18B4**
Cape Dorset *Can* **23L3**
Capelongo *Angola* **21B5**
Cape Mendocino *USA* **22F5**
Capenda Camulemba *Angola* **21B4**
Cape Perry *Can* **22F2**
Cape Province *S Africa* **21C7**
Cape Tatnam *Can* **23J4**
Cape Town *S Africa* **21B7**
Cape Verde, Is *Atlantic O* **19A4**
Cape York Pen *Aust* **30D2**
Capim, R *Brazil* **29J4**
Capo Isola de Correnti, C *Italy* **10D3**
Capo Rizzuto, C *Italy* **10D3**
Capo Santa Maria di Leuca, C *Italy* **11D3**
Capo San Vito *Italy* **10C3**
Capo Spartivento, C *Italy* **10D3**
Capri, I *Italy* **10C2**
Caprivi Strip, Region *Namibia* **21C5**
Cap Rosso, C *Corse* **10B2**
Cap Vert, C *Sen* **18A3**
Caquetá, R *Colombia* **28D4**
Caracal *Rom* **11E2**
Caracaraí *Brazil* **28F3**
Caracas *Ven* **28E1**
Carahue *Chile* **27B5**
Carangola *Brazil* **29K8**
Caransebeş *Rom* **11E1**
Caravaca *Spain* **9B2**
Carbonia *Sardegna* **10B3**
Carborear *Can* **23N5**
Carcaion *Can* **22G4**
Carcar Mts *Somalia* **19D3**
Carcassonne *France* **8C3**
Carcross *Can* **22E3**
Cardenas *Cuba* **26D2**
Cardiff *Wales* **5D6**
Cardigan *Wales* **5C5**
Cardigan B *Wales* **5C5**
Carei *Rom* **11E1**
Careiro *Brazil* **29G4**
Carhaix-Plouguer *France* **8B2**
Carhué *Arg* **27D5**
Cariacica *Brazil* **29K0**
Caribou *Can* **22J4**
Caribou Mts, Alberta *Can* **22G4**
Caribou Mts, British Columbia *Can* **22F4**
Caripito *Ven* **28F1**
Carlingford Lough, Inlet *N Ire* **5B4**
Carlisle *Eng* **4D4**
Carlow, County *Irish Rep* **5B5**
Carlow *Irish Rep* **5B5**
Carlsbad, New Mexico *USA* **24C3**
Carlyle *Can* **22H5**
Carmarthen *Wales* **5C6**
Carmarthen B *Wales* **5C6**
Carmen, I *Mexico* **24B4**
Carmen de Patagones *Arg* **27D6**
Carmona *Spain* **9A2**
Carnarvon *Aust* **30A3**
Carndonagh *Irish Rep* **4B4**
Carnegi,L *Aust* **30B3**
Carnot *CAR* **20B3**
Carolina *Brazil* **29J5**
Caroline, Is *Pacific O* **17G6**
Carpatii Orientali, Mts *Rom* **7F3**
Carpentaria,G of *Aust* **30C2**
Carpenter Ridge *Indian O* **15G5**
Carpentras *France* **8D3**
Carpi *Italy* **10C2**
Carrara *Italy* **10C2**
Carrauntoohill, Mt *Irish Rep* **3B3**
Carrickmacross *Irish Rep* **5B5**
Carrick-on-Suir *Irish Rep* **5B5**
Carrington *USA* **22J5**
Carrington *USA* **24D2**
Carrión, R *Spain* **9B1**
Carroll *USA* **25D2**
Carson City *USA* **24B3**
Cartagena *Spain* **9B2**
Cartago *Colombia* **28C3**
Cartago *Costa Rica* **26D4**
Cartegena *Colombia* **28D1**
Carterton *NZ* **32C2**
Cartier I *Timor S* **30B2**
Cartwright *Can* **23N4**
Caruaru *Brazil* **29L5**
Carúpano *Ven* **28F1**
Casablanca *Mor* **18B1**
Casa Grande *USA* **24B3**
Casale Monferrato *Italy* **10B1**
Cascade Pt *NZ* **32A2**
Cascade Range, Mts *USA* **24A2**
Cascavel *Brazil* **27F2**
Caserta *Italy* **10C2**
Cashel *Irish Rep* **5B5**
Casino *Aust* **31E3**
Casma *Peru* **28C5**
Caspe *Spain* **9C1**
Casper *USA* **24C2**
Caspian S *USSR* **12G5**
Cassamba *Angola* **21C5**
Cassiar Mts *Can* **22E3**
Cassino *Italy* **10C2**
Castellane *France* **8D3**
Castellon de la Plana *Spain* **9C1**
Castelo *Brazil* **29K5**
Castelo Branco *Port* **9A2**
Castelsarrasin *France* **8C3**
Castelvetrano *Italy* **10C3**
Castilla La Nueva, Region *Spain* **9B2**
Castilla La Vieja, Region *Spain* **9B1**
Castlebar *Irish Rep* **3B3**
Castlebay *Scot* **4B3**
Castle Douglas *Scot* **4D4**
Castres-sur-l'Agout *France* **8C3**
Castro *Arg* **27B6**
Castro *Brazil* **27F2**
Castro Alves *Brazil* **29L6**
Castrovillari *Italy* **10D3**
Caswell Sd *NZ* **32A2**
Cat, I *Bahamas* **26E2**
Catacaos *Peru* **28B5**
Cataluña, Region *Spain* **9C1**
Catamarca *Arg* **27C3**
Catamarca, State *Arg* **27C3**
Catandica *Mozam* **21D5**
Catanduva *Brazil* **27G2**
Catania *Italy* **10D3**
Catanzaro *Italy* **10D3**
Cateraggio *Corse* **10B2**
Catete *Angola* **21B4**
Catio *Guinea-Bissau* **18A3**
Cat Lake *Can* **23J4**
Cato, I *Aust* **31E3**
Catoche,C *Mexico* **26D2**
Cauca, R *Colombia* **28D2**
Caucaia *Brazil* **29L4**
Caucasia *Colombia* **28C2**
Caungula *Angola* **21B4**
Cauquenes *Chile* **27B5**
Cavaillon *France* **8D3**
Cavally, R *Lib* **18B4**
Cavan, County *Irish Rep* **5B5**
Cavan *Irish Rep* **5B5**
Caxias *Brazil* **28D4**
Caxias *Brazil* **29K4**
Caxias do Sul *Brazil* **27F3**
Caxito *Angola* **21B4**
Cayenne *French Guiana* **29H3**
Cayman Brac, I *Caribbean* **26E3**
Caynabo *Somalia* **20E3**
Cayo Romana, I *Cuba* **26E2**
Cayos Mistikos, Is *Nic* **26D3**
Cazombo *Angola* **21C5**
Ceara, State *Brazil* **29K5**
Cebu *Phil* **17F5**
Cecina *Italy* **10C2**
Cedar City *USA* **24B3**
Cedar L *Can* **22J4**
Cedar Rapids *USA* **25D2**
Cedros, I *Mexico* **26A2**
Ceduna *Aust* **30C4**
Ceelbuur *Somalia* **20E3**
Ceerigaabo *Somalia* **19D3**
Cefalù *Italy* **10C3**
Cegléd *Hung* **7D3**
Cela *Angola* **21B5**
Celaya *Mexico* **26B2**
Celebes S *S E Asia* **17F6**
Celje *Yugos* **10D1**
Celle *W Germ* **6C2**
Celtic S *UK* **5B6**
Cendrawasih, Pen *Indon* **17G7**
Central, Region *Scot* **4C3**
Central African Republic *Africa* **20B3**
Centralia, Washington *USA* **24A2**
Central Range, Mts *PNG* **17H7**
Ceram Sea *Indonesia* **17F7**
Ceres *Brazil* **29J7**
Cergy-Pontoise *France* **8C2**
Cerignola *Italy* **10D2**
Cerralvo, I *Mexico* **24C4**
Cerro de Pasco *Peru* **28C6**
Cesena *Italy* **10C2**
České Budějovice *Czech* **6C3**
České Zemé, Region *Czech* **6C3**
Českomoravská Vysočina *U Czech* **6D3**
Cesme *Turk* **11F3**
Cessnock *Aust* **30E4**
Cetina, R *Yugos* **10D2**
Chaa-Khol *USSR* **13L4**
Chachapoyas *Peru* **28C5**
Chaco, State *Arg* **27D3**
Chad, Republic *Africa* **20B2**
Chad, L *C Africa* **20B2**
Chadron *USA* **24C2**
Chagda *USSR* **13P4**
Chaine des Mitumba, Mts *Zaïre* **21C4**
Chala *Peru* **28D7**
Chalabesa *Zambia* **21D5**
Chalons-sur-Marne *France* **8C2**
Chalon sur Saône *France* **8C2**
Cham *W Germ* **6C3**
Chambéry *France* **8D2**
Champagne, Region *France* **8C2**
Chile, Republic *S America* **27B6**
Champaign *USA* **25E2**
Champlain,L *USA* **25F2**
Chañaral *Chile* **27B3**
Chandalar *USA* **22D3**
Chandalar, R *USA* **22D3**
Changara *Mozam* **21D5**
Changchun *China* **16F2**
Chang-hua *Taiwan* **16F4**
Channel Is *UK* **8B2**
Channel Is *USA* **24B3**
Channel Port-aux-Basques *Can* **23N5**
Chapada Diamantina, Mts *Brazil* **29K6**
Chapadinha *Brazil* **29K4**
Chapecó *Brazil* **27F3**
Chapleau *Can* **23K5**
Chardzhou *USSR* **14E2**
Charente, R *France* **8C2**
Chari, R *Chad* **20B2**
Chari Baguirmi, Region *Chad* **20B2**
Charity *Guyana* **29G2**
Charleroi *Belg* **6A2**
Charles,C *USA* **25F3**
Charleston, S Carolina *USA* **25F3**
Charleston, W Virginia *USA* **25E3**
Charlesville *Zaïre* **20C4**
Charleville *Aust* **30D3**
Charleville-Mézières *France* **8C2**
Charlotte, N Carolina *USA* **25E3**
Charlottesville *USA* **25F3**
Charlottetown *Can* **23M5**
Charlton I *Can* **25F1**
Charters Towers *Aust* **30D3**
Chartres *France* **8C2**
Chascomús *Arg* **27E5**
Châteaubriant *France* **8B2**
Châteaudun *France* **8C2**
Châteaulin *France* **8B2**
Châteauroux *France* **8C2**
Château-Thierry *France* **8C2**
Châtellerault *France* **8C2**
Chatham *Eng* **5F6**
Chatham, New Brunswick *Can* **23M5**
Chatham Is *NZ* **31H5**
Châtillon *France* **8C2**
Chattanooga *USA* **25E3**
Chaumont *France* **8D2**
Chaves *Port* **9A1**
Cheb *Czech* **6C2**
Cheboksary *USSR* **12F4**
Cheboygan *USA* **25E2**
Chechersk *USSR* **7G2**
Chegga *Maur* **18B2**
Chegutu *Zim* **21D5**
Cheju *S Korea* **16F3**
Chekunda *USSR* **13P4**
Chelkar *USSR* **14D1**
Chelm *Pol* **7E2**
Chelmno *Pol* **7D2**
Chelmsford *Eng* **5F6**
Cheltenham *Eng* **5D6**
Chelyabinsk *USSR* **12H4**
Chemba *Mozam* **21D5**
Chenachen *Alg* **18B2**
Chengdu *China* **16D3**
Chepén *Peru* **28C5**
Cher, R *France* **8C2**
Cherbourg *France* **8B2**
Cheremkhovo *USSR* **13M4**
Chernobyl *USSR* **7G2**
Cherry, I *Solomon Is* **31F2**
Cherskiy *USSR* **13S3**
Chervonograd *USSR* **7E2**
Chesapeake Bay *USA* **25F3**
Cheshire, County *Eng* **5D5**
Chester *Eng* **5D5**
Chesterfield *Eng* **5E5**
Chesterfield Inlet *Can* **23J3**
Chetumal *Mexico* **26D3**
Cheviot *NZ* **32B2**
Cheviots, Hills *Eng/Scot* **3C2**
Chiange *Angola* **21B5**
Chibia *Angola* **21B5**
Chibougamou *Can* **23L4**
Chicago *USA* **25E2**
Chichester *Eng* **5E6**
Chichi-jima, I *Japan* **16H4**
Chickamauga L *USA* **25E3**
Chickasha *USA* **24D3**
Chiclayo *Peru* **28B5**
Chico *USA* **24A3**
Chico, R *Arg* **27C6**
Chicoa *Mozam* **21D5**
Chicoutimi *Can* **23L5**
Chicualacuala *Mozam* **21D6**
Chidley,C *Can* **23M3**
Chiehn *Lib* **18B4**
Chiengi *Zambia* **21C4**
Chieti *Italy* **10C2**
Chigmit Mts *USA* **22C2**
Chihuahua *Mexico* **26B2**
Chikwawa *Malawi* **21D5**
Chililabombwe *Zambia* **21C5**
Chilko L *Can* **22F4**
Chillán *Chile* **27B5**
Chilmborazo, Mt *Ecuador* **28C4**
Chilongozi *Zambia* **21D5**
Chilpancingo *Mexico* **26C3**
Chiltern Hills, Upland *Eng* **5E6**
Chilumba *Malawi* **21D5**
Chi-lung *Taiwan* **16F4**
Chilwa, L *Malawi* **21D5**
Chimbay *USSR* **12G5**
Chimbote *Peru* **28C5**
Chimkent *USSR* **12H5**
Chimoio *Mozam* **21D5**
Chinandega *Nic* **26D3**
Chincha Alta *Peru* **28C6**
Chinde *Mozam* **21D5**
Chingola *Zambia* **21C5**
Chinguar *Angola* **21B5**
Chinguetti *Maur* **18A2**
Chinhoyi *Zim* **21D5**
Chinko, R *CAR* **20C3**
Chinsali *Zambia* **21D5**
Chioggia *Italy* **10C1**
Chipata *Zambia* **21D5**
Chipinge *Zim* **21D6**
Chippenham *Eng* **5D6**
Chippewa Falls *USA* **25D2**
Chipuriro *Zim* **21D5**
Chira, R *Peru* **28B4**
Chiredzi *Zim* **21D6**
Chirfa *Niger* **20B1**
Chiriqui, Mt *Panama* **28B2**
Chirpan *Bulg* **11F2**
Chirrípo Grande, Mt *Costa Rica* **28B2**
Chirstchurch *NZ* **31G5**
Chirundu *Zim* **21C5**
Chisamba *Zambia* **21C5**
Chita *USSR* **16E1**
Chitado *Angola* **21B5**
Chitembo *Angola* **21B5**
Chitré *Panama* **28B2**
Chittagong *Bang* **15H3**
Chiume *Angola* **21C5**
Chivilcoy *Arg* **27D4**
Chivu *Zim* **21D5**
Chocontá *Colombia* **28D2**
Choele Choel *Arg* **27C5**
Choiseul, I *Solomon Is* **31E1**
Choix *Mexico* **26B2**
Chojnice *Pol* **7D2**
Choke, Mts *Eth* **20D2**
Chokurdakh *USSR* **13Q2**
Cholet *France* **8B2**
Choluteca *Honduras* **28A1**
Choma *Zambia* **21C5**
Chomutov *Czech* **6C2**
Chona, R *USSR* **13M3**
Chone *Ecuador* **28C4**
Chongoroi *Angola* **21B5**

Chongqing Deer Lodge

Chongqing *China* 16D4
Chortkov *USSR* 7F3
Chorzow *Pol* 7D2
Choszczno *Pol* 6D2
Choybalsan *Mongolia* 13N5
Chranbrey Inlet, B *Can* 23J3
Christchurch *NZ* 32B2
Christian,C *Can* 23M2
Christianshab *Greenland* 23N3
Chu *USSR* 12J5
Chu, R *USSR* 12J5
Chubut, State *Arg* 27C6
Chubut, R *Arg* 27C6
Chudskoye Ozer, L *USSR* 12D4
Chugach Mts *USA* 22D3
Chukotskiy Khrebet, Mts *USSR* 13T3
Chukotskiy Poluostrov, Pen *USSR* 13U3
Chulman *USSR* 16F1
Chulucanas *Peru* 28B5
Chulumani *Bol* 28E7
Chulym *USSR* 12K4
Chulym, R *USSR* 13K4
Chuma, R *USSR* 13L4
Chumikan *USSR* 13P4
Chunya *Tanz* 21D4
Chunya, R *USSR* 13M3
Chuquicamata *Chile* 27C2
Chur *Switz* 10B1
Churapcha *USSR* 13P3
Churchill *Can* 23J4
Churchill, R, Labrador *Can* 23M4
Churchill, R, Manitoba *Can* 23J4
Churchill,C *Can* 23J4
Churchill Falls *Can* 23M4
Churchill L *Can* 22H4
Chuxiong *China* 16D4
Ciechanow *Pol* 7E2
Ciedad Ojeda *Ven* 28D1
Ciego de Avila *Cuba* 26E2
Ciénaga *Colombia* 28D1
Cienfuegos *Cuba* 26D2
Cieszyn *Pol* 7D3
Cieza *Spain* 9B2
Cîmpina *Rom* 11F1
Cinca, R *Spain* 9C1
Činčer, Mt *Yugos* 10D2
Cincinatti *USA* 25E3
Cindrelu, Mt *Rom* 11E1
Cine, R *Turk* 11F3
Circle, Alaska *USA* 22D3
Cirebon *Indon* 17D7
Cirencester *Eng* 5E6
Citlaltepetl, Mt *Mexico* 26C3
Citta del Vaticano *Italy* 10C2
Città di Castello *Italy* 10C2
Ciudad Acuña *Mexico* 26B2
Ciudad Bolivar *Ven* 28F2
Ciudad Camargo *Mexico* 26B2
Ciudad del Carmen *Mexico* 26C3
Ciudadela *Spain* 9C2
Ciudad Guayana *Ven* 28F2
Ciudad Guzman *Mexico* 26B3
Ciudad Juárez *Mexico* 26B1
Ciudad Lerdo *Mexico* 24C4
Ciudad Madero *Mexico* 26C2
Ciudad Obregon *Mexico* 26B2
Ciudad Piar *Ven* 28F2
Ciudad Real *Spain* 9B2
Ciudad Rodrigo *Spain* 9A1
Ciudad Valles *Mexico* 26C2
Ciudad Victoria *Mexico* 26C2
Civitavecchia *Italy* 10C2
Clacton-on-Sea *Eng* 5F6
Claire,L *Can* 22G4
Clara *Irish Rep* 5B5
Clarence, R *NZ* 32B2
Clarence Str *Aust* 30C2
Clarenville *Can* 23N5
Claresholm *Can* 22G4
Clarión, I *Mexico* 26A3
Clark Hill Res *USA* 25E3
Clarksdale *USA* 25D3
Claromecó *Arg* 27E5
Claymore, Oilfield *N Sea* 4E2
Clayton, New Mexico *USA* 24C3
Clear, C *Irish Rep* 3B3
Clearwater *USA* 25E4
Cleburne *USA* 24D3
Clermont *Aust* 30D3
Clermont-Ferrand *France* 8C2
Cleveland, County *Eng* 5E4
Cleveland, Ohio *USA* 25E2
Clew, B *Irish Rep* 3B3
Clinton *Can* 22F4
Clinton-Colden L *Can* 22H3
Clipperton I *Pacific O* 26B3
Cliza *Bol* 28E7
Cloncurry *Aust* 30D3
Clones *Irish Rep* 5B4
Clonmel *Irish Rep* 5B5
Cloquet *USA* 25D2
Clovis, New Mexico *USA* 24C3
Cluj-Napoca *Rom* 11E1
Clutha, R *NZ* 32A3
Clwyd, County *Wales* 5D5
Clyde *Can* 23M2
Clyde *NZ* 32A3
Clyde, R *Scot* 4C4
Coari, R *Brazil* 28F5
Coast Mts *Can* 22E4
Coast Range *USA* 24A3
Coast Ranges, Mts *USA* 24A2
Coatbridge *Scot* 4C4
Coats I *Can* 23K3
Coatzacoalcas *Mexico* 26C3
Cobalt *Can* 23L5
Cobán *Guatemala* 26C3
Cobar *Aust* 30D4
Cobija *Bol* 28E6
Cobourg *Can* 23L5
Cobourg Pen *Aust* 30C2
Coburg *W Germ* 6C2
Coca *Ecuador* 28C4
Cochabamba *Bol* 28E7
Cochrane, Ontario *Can* 23K5
Coco, R *Honduras/Nic* 26D3
Cocobeach *Gabon* 20A3
Cod, Oilfield *N Sea* 4G3
Cod,C *USA* 25F2
Codfish I *NZ* 32A3
Cod I *Can* 23M4
Codó *Brazil* 29K4
Cody *USA* 24C2
Coen *Aust* 17H8
Coesfeld *W Germ* 6B2
Coeur d'Alene *USA* 24B2
Coffeyville *USA* 24D3
Cognac *France* 8B2
Coihaique *Chile* 27B7
Coimbra *Port* 9A1
Cojimies *Ecuador* 28B3
Colac *Aust* 30D4
Colatina *Brazil* 29K7
Colchester *Eng* 5F6
Col du Grand St Bernard P *Switz/Italy* 10B1
Col du Mont Cenis, P *Italy/France* 10B1
Col du Mt Cenis, P *Italy* 8D2
Coleraine *N Ire* 4B4
Coleridge,L *NZ* 32B2
Colima *Mexico* 26B3
Coll, I *Scot* 4B3
Colle de Tende, P *Italy/France* 10B2
Collie *Aust* 30A4
Collier B *Aust* 30B2
Collingwood *NZ* 32B2
Collinson Pen *Can* 22H2
Collinsville *Aust* 30D3
Colmar *France* 8D2
Colombia, Republic *S America* 28D3
Colombo *Sri Lanka* 15F5
Colón *Arg* 27E4
Colon *Cuba* 26D2
Colón *Panama* 28C2
Colonia *Urug* 27E4
Colonia Las Heras *Arg* 27C7
Colonsay, I *Scot* 4B3
Colorado, State *USA* 24C3
Colorado, R, Arizona *USA* 24B3
Colorado, R, Buenos Aires *Arg* 27D5
Colorado, R, Texas *USA* 24D3
Colorado Plat *USA* 24B3
Colorado Springs *USA* 24C3
Columbia, Missouri *USA* 25D3
Columbia, S Carolina *USA* 25E3
Columbia, Tennessee *USA* 25E3
Columbia, R *USA* 24A2
Columbia,Mt *Can* 22G4
Columbus, Georgia *USA* 25E3
Columbus, Mississippi *USA* 25E3
Columbus, Nebraska *USA* 24D2
Columbus, Ohio *USA* 25E2
Colville, R *USA* 22C3
Colville,C *NZ* 32C1
Colville L *Can* 22F3
Colwyn Bay *Wales* 5D5
Comayagua *Honduras* 26D3
Comber *N Ire* 5C4
Comeragh, Mts *Irish Rep* 5B5
Comitán *Mexico* 26C3
Committees B *Can* 23K3
Como *Italy* 10B1
Comodoro Rivadavia *Arg* 27C7
Comoros, Is *Indian O* 21E5
Compiègne *France* 8C2
Conakry *Guinea* 18A4
Concarneau *France* 8B2
Conceição do Araguaia *Brazil* 29J5
Concepción *Chile* 27B5
Concepción *Par* 27E2
Concepción, R *Arg* 27E4
Concepcion del Oro *Mexico* 26B2
Conception,Pt *USA* 24A3
Conchos, R *Mexico* 24C4
Concord, New Hampshire *USA* 25F2
Concordia *Arg* 27E4
Concordia *USA* 24D3
Condobolin *Aust* 30D4
Condrina *Brazil* 29H8
Connecticut, State *USA* 25F2
Constanţa *Rom* 11F1
Constantine *Alg* 18C1
Constitución *Chile* 27B5
Contas, R *Brazil* 29K6
Contuoyto L *Can* 22H3
Conway, Arkansas *USA* 25D3
Conwy *Wales* 5D5
Coober Pedy *Aust* 30C3
Cook Inlet, B *USA* 22C3
Cook,Mt *NZ* 32B2
Cook Str *NZ* 31G5
Cooktown *Aust* 30D2
Coolgardie *Aust* 30B4
Cooper Creek *Aust* 30C3
Cootamundra *Aust* 30D4
Cootehill *Irish Rep* 5B4
Copiapó *Chile* 27B3
Copper Centre *USA* 22D3
Coppermine *Can* 22G3
Coppermine, R *Can* 22G3
Coquimbo *Chile* 27B3
Corabia *Rom* 11E2
Coral Harbour *Can* 23K3
Coral S *Aust/PNG* 30E2
Coral Sea Island Territories *Aust* 30E2
Corantijn, R *Suriname/Guyana* 29G3
Corcubíon *Spain* 9A1
Cordele *USA* 25E3
Cordillera Cantabrica, Mts *Spain* 9A1
Cordillera de los Andes, Mts *Peru* 28C5
Cordillera del Toro, Mt *Arg* 27C3
Cordillera de Mérida *Ven* 28D2
Cordillera Isabelia, Mts *Nicaragua* 26D3
Cordillera Occidental, Mts *Colombia* 28C2
Cordillera Oriental, Mts *Colombia* 28C3
Córdoba *Arg* 27D4
Córdoba *Mexico* 26C3
Córdoba *Spain* 9B2
Córdoba, State *Arg* 27D4
Cordova *USA* 22D3
Corigliano Calabro *Italy* 10D3
Coringa Is *Aust* 30E2
Corinth, Mississippi *USA* 25E3
Corinto *Brazil* 29K7
Cork *Irish Rep* 3B3
Cornel Fabriciano *Brazil* 29K7
Corner Brook *Can* 23N5
Cornwall *Can* 23L5
Cornwall, County *Eng* 5C6
Cornwall,C *Eng* 5C6
Cornwall I *Can* 22H2
Cornwallis I *Can* 23J2
Coro *Ven* 28E1
Coroatá *Brazil* 29K4
Coroico *Bol* 28E7
Coromandel Pen *NZ* 32C1
Coromandel Range, Mts *NZ* 32C1
Coronation G *Can* 22G3
Coronel *Chile* 27B5
Coronel Oviedo *Par* 27E3
Coronel Pringles *Arg* 27D5
Coropuna, Mt *Peru* 28D7
Corps *France* 8D3
Corpus Christi *USA* 24D4
Corrientes *Arg* 27E3
Corrientes, State *Arg* 27E3
Corrigin *Aust* 30A4
Corse, I *Medit S* 10B2
Corsewall, Pt *Scot* 4C4
Corsicana *USA* 24D3
Corte *Corse* 10B2
Cortez *USA* 24C3
Cortina d'Ampezzo *Italy* 10C1
Corumbá *Brazil* 29G7
Corvo, I *Açores* 18A1
Corwen *Wales* 5D5
Cosenza *Italy* 10D3
Cosmoledo, Is *Seychelles* 21E5
Costa Blanca, Region *Spain* 9B2
Costa Brava, Region *Spain* 9C1
Costa de la Luz, Region *Spain* 9B2
Costa del Sol, Region *Spain* 9B2
Costa Rica, Republic *C America* 26D3
Cotagaita *Bol* 28E8
Côte d'Azur, Region *France* 8D3
Cotonou *Benin* 18C4
Cotopaxi, Mt *Ecuador* 28C4
Cotswold Hills, Upland *Eng* 5D6
Cottbus *E Germ* 6C2
Council *USA* 22B3
Council Bluffs *USA* 24D2
Coutances *France* 8B2
Coventry *Eng* 5E5
Covilhã *Spain* 9A1
Coxim *Brazil* 29H7
Craig *USA* 24C2
Crailsheim *W Germ* 6C3
Craiova *Rom* 11E2
Cranbrook *Can* 22G5
Crateus *Brazil* 29K5
Crato *Brazil* 29L5
Crawley *Eng* 5E6
Cree L *Can* 22H4
Cremona *Italy* 10C1
Cres, I *Yugos* 10C2
Crescent City *USA* 24A2
Crete,S of *Greece* 11E3
Creuse, R *France* 8C2
Crewe *Eng* 5D5
Crianlarich *Scot* 4C3
Criciuma *Brazil* 27G3
Crieff *Scot* 4D3
Croatia, Region *Yugos* 10D1
Croker I *Aust* 30C2
Cromarty *Scot* 4C3
Cromer *Eng* 5F5
Cromwell *NZ* 32A3
Crooked, I *Bahamas* 25F4
Crookston *USA* 24D2
Crossett *USA* 25D3
Crotone *Italy* 10D3
Croydon *Aust* 30D2
Croydon *Eng* 5E6
Crozier Chan *Can* 22F2
Cruz Alta *Brazil* 27F3
Cruz,C *Cuba* 26E3
Cruz del Eje *Arg* 27D4
Cruzeiro do Sul *Brazil* 28D5
Cuamba *Mozam* 21D5
Cuando, R *Angola* 21C5
Cuangar *Angola* 21B5
Cuauhtémoc *Mexico* 26B2
Cuba, Republic *Caribbean* 26D2
Cubango, R *Angola* 21B5
Cuchi *Angola* 21B5
Cuchi, R *Angola* 21B5
Cucui *Brazil* 28E3
Cúcuta *Colombia* 28D2
Cue *Aust* 30A3
Cuenca *Ecuador* 28C4
Cuenca *Spain* 9B1
Cuernavaca *Mexico* 26C3
Cuiabá *Brazil* 29G7
Cuiabá *Brazil* 29G7
Cuillin Hills, Mts *Scot* 4B3
Cuilo, R *Angola* 21B4
Cuito, R *Angola* 21B5
Cuito Cunavale *Angola* 21B5
Culiacán *Mexico* 26B2
Culverden *NZ* 32B2
Cumaná *Ven* 28F1
Cumberland, Maryland *USA* 25F3
Cumberland, R *USA* 25E3
Cumberland Pen *Can* 23M3
Cumberland Sd *Can* 23M3
Cumbria *Eng* 5D4
Cumnock *Scot* 4C4
Cunene, R *Angola/Namibia* 21B5
Cuneo *Italy* 10B2
Cunnamulla *Aust* 30D3
Cupar *Scot* 4D3
Ćuprija *Yugos* 11E2
Curaçao, I *Neth* 28E1
Curicó *Chile* 27B4
Curitiba *Brazil* 27G3
Curoca, R *Angola* 21B5
Curvelo *Brazil* 29K7
Cuttack *India* 15G3
Cuvelai *Angola* 21B5
Cuxhaven *W Germ* 6B2
Cuzco *Peru* 28D6
Cyangugu *Zaïre* 20C4
Cyprus, Republic *Medit S* 14B2
Cyrus Field B *Can* 23M3
Czechoslovakia, Republic *Europe* 7D3
Częstochowa *Pol* 7D2

D

Dabaro *Somalia* 19D4
Dabat *Eth* 20D2
Dabola *Guinea* 18A3
Dabou *Ivory Coast* 18B4
Dabrowa Gorn *Pol* 7D2
Dachau *W Germ* 6C3
Dachstein, Mt *Austria* 10C1
Dadu He, R *China* 16D3
Dagabur *Eth* 20E3
Dagana *Sen* 18A3
Dagestanskaya ASSR, Republic *USSR* 12F5
Da Hinggan Line, Mts *China* 13O5
Dahra *Libya* 19A2
Dahra, Region *Alg* 9C2
Daitō, Is *Pacific Oc* 16G4
Dajarra *Aust* 30C3
Dakar *Sen* 18A3
Dakhla *Mor* 18A2
Dakhla Oasis *Egypt* 19B2
Dakoro *Niger* 18C3
Dakovica *Yugos* 11E2
Dakovo *Yugos* 11D1
Dala *Angola* 21C5
Dalaba *Guinea* 18A3
Dalandzadgad *Mongolia* 16D2
Dalanjargalan *Mongolia* 16D2
Dalby *Aust* 30E3
Dalen *Nor* 2F7
Dales,The, Upland *Eng* 5D4
Dalhart *USA* 24C3
Dalhousie,C *Can* 22E2
Dallas *USA* 24D3
Dallol, R *Niger* 18C3
Dalmatia, Region *Yugos* 10D2
Daloa *Ivory Coast* 18B4
Daly, R *Aust* 30C2
Daly Waters *Aust* 30C2
Damar, I *Indon* 30B1
Damara *CAR* 20B3
Damascus *Syria* 14B2
Damavand, Mt *Iran* 14D2
Damba *Angola* 21B4
Damot *Eth* 20E3
Dampier *Aust* 30A3
Danané *Lib* 18B4
Da Nang *Viet* 17D5
Dangila *Eth* 20D2
Daniels Harbour *Can* 23N4
Dannebrogs Øy, I *Greenland* 23P3
Dannevirke *NZ* 32C2
Danville, Illinois *USA* 25E2
Danville, Kentucky *USA* 25E3
Danville, Virginia *USA* 25F3
Da Qaidam *China* 16C3
Dar'ā *Syria* 14B2
Daraj *Libya* 19A1
Dar Es Salaam *Tanz* 21D4
Dargaville *NZ* 32B1
Darjeeling *India* 15G3
Darling, R *Aust* 30D4
Darling Pen *Can* 23L1
Darlington *Eng* 5E4
Darmstadt *W Germ* 6B3
Darnah *Libya* 19B1
Darnley B *Can* 22F3
Daroca *Spain* 9B1
Dar Rounga, Region *CAR* 20C3
Dart, R *Eng* 5D6
Dartmoor, Moorland *Eng* 3C3
Dartmoor Nat Pk *Eng* 5D6
Dartmouth *Can* 23M5
Dartmouth *Eng* 5D6
Daru *PNG* 30D1
Daruvar *Yugos* 10D1
Darwin *Aust* 30C2
Dasht e Lūt, Salt Desert *Iran* 14D2
Daugava, R *USSR* 2K7
Dauguard Jensen Land *Greenland* 23M1
Dauphin *Can* 22H4
Dauphiné, Region *France* 8D2
Daura *Nig* 18C3
Davao *Phil* 17F6
Davenport, Iowa *USA* 25D2
David *Panama* 28B2
Davidson Mts *USA* 22D3
Davis Inlet *Can* 23M4
Davis Str *Greenland/Can* 23N3
Dawa, R *Eth* 20E3
Dawson *Can* 22E3
Dawson, R *Aust* 30D3
Dawson Creek *Can* 22F4
Dax *France* 8B3
Dayr az Zawr *Syria* 14C2
Dayton, Ohio *USA* 25E3
Daytona Beach *USA* 25E4
Dease Arm, B *Can* 22F3
Dease Lake *Can* 22E4
Death V *USA* 24B3
Deauville *France* 8C2
Debica *Pol* 7E2
Deblin *Pol* 7E2
Débo,L *Mali* 18B3
Debra Birhan *Eth* 20D3
Debra Markos *Eth* 20D2
Debra Tabor *Eth* 20D2
Debrecen *Hung* 7E3
Decatur, Alabama *USA* 25E3
Decatur, Illinois *USA* 25E3
Decazeville *France* 8C3
Deccan *India* 15F4
Dedza *Malawi* 21D5
Dee, R, Dumfries and Galloway *Scot* 4C4
Dee, R *Eng/Wales* 5D5
Dee, R, Grampian *Scot* 4D3
Deer Lake *Can* 23N5
Deer Lodge *USA* 24B2

Deésaguadero **En Nahud**

Deésaguadero, R *Bol* **28E7**
Dêgê *China* **16C3**
De Grey, R *Aust* **30A3**
Dehibat *Tunisia* **18D1**
Deim Zubeir *Sudan* **20C3**
De Kastri *USSR* **13Q4**
Dekese *Zaïre* **20C4**
Dekoa *CAR* **20B3**
Delano *USA* **24B3**
Delaware, State *USA* **25F3**
Delaware B *USA* **25F3**
Delgado, C *Mozam* **21E5**
Delhi *India* **15F3**
Delicias *Mexico* **26B2**
Delmenhorst *W Germ* **2F8**
Deloraine *Can* **22H5**
Del Rio *USA* **24C4**
Delta *USA* **24B3**
Dembidollo *Eth* **20D3**
Demidov *USSR* **7G1**
Demirköy *Turk* **11F2**
Denain *France* **8C1**
Denau *USSR* **15E2**
Denbigh *Wales* **5D5**
Dendi, Mt *Eth* **20D3**
Den Helder *Neth* **6A2**
Denia *Spain* **9C2**
Deniliquin *Aust* **30D4**
Denison, Texas *USA* **24D3**
Denizli *Turk* **14A2**
Denmark, Kingdom *Europe* **2F7**
Denmark Str *Greenland/ Iceland* **23Q3**
Denpasar *Indon* **17E7**
Denton, Texas *USA* **24D3**
D'Entrecasteaux Is *PNG* **30E1**
Denver *USA* **24C3**
Déo, R *Cam* **20B3**
Dépression du Mourdi, Desert Region *Chad* **20C2**
Deputatskiy *USSR* **13Q3**
Derby *Aust* **30B2**
Derby, County *Eng* **5E5**
Derby *Eng* **5E5**
Derna *Libya* **19B1**
Derudeb *Sudan* **20D2**
Deseado *Arg* **27C7**
Deseado, R *Arg* **27C7**
Deserta Grande, I *Medeira* **18A1**
Desierto de Atacama, Desert *Chile* **27C2**
Des Moines, Iowa *USA* **25D2**
Desolación, I *Chile* **27B8**
Dessau *E Germ* **6C2**
Dessye *Eth* **20D2**
Deta *Rom* **11E1**
Dete *Zim* **21C5**
Detroit *USA* **25E2**
Deva *Rom* **11E1**
Deventer *Neth* **6B2**
Deveron, R *Scot* **4D3**
Devil's Hole, Region *N Sea* **4F3**
Devils Lake *USA* **24D2**
Devizes *Eng* **5E6**
Devoll, R *Alb* **11E2**
Devon, County *Eng* **5C6**
Devon I *Can* **23J2**
Devonport *Aust* **30D5**
Dewey Res *USA* **25E3**
Dhākā *Bang* **15H3**
Dhar Oualata, Desert Region *Maur* **18B3**
Dhíkti Óri, Mt *Greece* **11F3**
Dhomokós *Greece* **11E3**
Diamantina *Brazil* **29K7**
Diamantina, R *Aust* **00D0**
Dibaya *Zaïre* **21C4**
Dickinson *USA* **24C2**
Diéma *Mali* **18B3**
Diepholz *W Germ* **6B2**
Dieppe *France* **8C2**
Digby *Can* **23M5**
Digne *France* **8D3**
Digoin *France* **8C2**
Digul, R *Indon* **30C1**
Dijon *France* **8C2**
Dik *Chad* **20B3**
Dikhil *Djibouti* **20E2**
Dikson *USSR* **12K2**
Dili *Indon* **30B1**
Dilling *Sudan* **20C2**
Dillon *USA* **24B2**
Dilolo *Zaïre* **21C5**
Dimbelenge *Zaïre* **20C4**
Dimitrovgrad *Bulg* **11F2**
Dinan *France* **8B2**
Dinder, R *Sudan* **20D2**
Dingle *Irish Rep* **3A3**
Dingle, B *Irish Rep* **3A3**
Dinguiraye *Guinea* **18A3**
Dingwall *Scot* **4C3**
Diouloulou *Sen* **18A3**
Diredawa *Eth* **20E3**
Dirk Hartog, I *Aust* **30A3**
Dirkou *Niger* **20B2**
Dirri *Somalia* **20E3**
Disappointment,C *South Georgia* **27J8**
Disappointment,L *Aust* **30B3**
Disko *Greenland* **23N3**
Disko Bugt, B *Greenland* **23N3**
Diskorjord *Greenland* **23N3**
Disna, R *USSR* **7F1**
Divinópolis *Brazil* **29K8**
Dixon Entrance, Sd *Can/ USA* **22E4**
Diyarbakir *Turk* **14B2**
Dja, R *Cam* **20B3**
Djado,Plat du *Niger* **20B1**
Djambala *Congo* **20B4**
Djanet *Alg* **18C2**
Djebel Bouhalla, Mt *Mor* **9A2**
Djéma *CAR* **20C3**
Djenné *Mali* **18B3**
Djibo *Upper Volta* **18B3**
Djibouti *Djibouti* **20E2**
Djibouti, Republic *E Africa* **20E2**
Djolu *Zaïre* **20C3**
Djugu *Zaïre* **20D3**
Djúpivogur *Iceland* **2C2**
Djurdjura, Mts *Alg* **9C2**
Dnepropetrovosk *USSR* **12E5**
Doba *Chad* **20B3**
Dobele *USSR* **7E1**
Dobo *Indon* **30C1**
Doboj *Yugos* **11D2**
Doce, R *Brazil* **29K7**
Doctor R P Peña *Arg* **27D2**
Dodge City *USA* **24C3**
Dodoma *Tanz* **20D4**
Dogger Bank, Sand-bank *N Sea* **4G4**
Dogondoutchi *Niger* **18C3**
Doha *Qatar* **14D3**
Dolak, I *Indon* **30C1**
Dolbeau *Can* **23L5**
Dôle *France* **8D2**
Dolgellau *Wales* **5D5**
Dolo *Eth* **20E3**
Dolores *Arg* **27E5**
Dolphin and Union Str *Can* **22G3**
Dolphin,C *Falkland Is* **27E8**
Dom, Mt *Indon* **17G7**
Dombarovskiy *USSR* **12G4**
Dombas *Nor* **2F6**
Dombóvár *Hung* **11D1**
Domfront *France* **8B2**
Dominion,C *Can* **23L3**
Domino *Can* **23N4**
Domna *USSR* **16E1**
Domodossola *Italy* **10B1**
Domuyo, Mt *Arg* **27B5**
Dom-yanskoya *USSR* **12H4**
Don, R *Scot* **4D3**
Donaghadee *N Ire* **4B4**
Donau, R *Austria* **6C3**
Donau, R *W Germ* **6C3**
Donauwörth *W Germ* **6C3**
Don Benito *Spain* **9A2**
Doncaster *Eng* **5E5**
Dondo *Angola* **21B4**
Dondo *Mozam* **21D5**
Donegal, County *Irish Rep* **4B4**
Donegal *Irish Rep* **3B3**
Donegal, B *Irish Rep* **3B3**
Donegal, Mts *Irish Rep* **4A4**
Donetsk *USSR* **12E5**
Dongara *Aust* **30A3**
Donggala *Indon* **30A1**
Donggi Cona, L *China* **16C3**
Dongola *Sudan* **20D2**
Dongsha Qundao, I *China* **16E4**
Dunji Vukuf *Yugos* **10D2**
Dönna, I *Nor* **2G5**
Dorchester *Eng* **5D6**
Dorchester,C *Can* **23L3**
Dordogne, R *France* **8C2**
Dordrecht *Neth* **6A2**
Dori *Upper Volta* **18B3**
Dornbirn *Austria* **6B3**
Dornoch *Scot* **4C3**
Dornoch Firth, Estuary *Scot* **4C3**
Dorotea *Sweden* **2H6**
Dorset, County *Eng* **5D6**
Dortmund *W Germ* **6B2**
Doruma *Zaïre* **20C3**
Dosatuy *USSR* **13N4**
Dossor *USSR* **12G5**
Dothan *USA* **25E3**
Douai *France* **8C1**
Douala *Cam* **20A3**
Doubs, R *France* **8B2**
Doubtful Sd *NZ* **32A3**
Douentza *Mali* **18B3**
Douglas, Arizona *USA* **24C3**
Douglas *Eng* **5C4**
Douglas, Wyoming *USA* **24C2**
Dourados *Brazil* **29H8**
Douro, R *Port* **9A1**
Dove, R *Eng* **5E5**
Dover *Eng* **5F6**
Dover *USA* **25F3**
Dover,Str of *Eng/France* **5F6**
Dovsk *USSR* **7G2**
Down, County *N Ire* **5B4**
Downpatrick *N Ire* **5C4**
Dr'aa, R *Mor* **18A2**
Draguignan *France* **8D3**
Drakensberg, Mts *S Africa* **21D6**
Dráma *Greece* **11E2**
Drammen *Nor* **2G7**
Drangajökull *Iceland* **2A1**
Drava, R *Yugos* **10D1**
Dresden *E Germ* **6C2**
Dreux *France* **8C2**
Drin, R *Alb* **11E2**
Drina, R *Yugos* **11D2**
Drissa, R *USSR* **7F1**
Drogheda *Irish Rep* **5B5**
Drogobych *USSR* **7E3**
Drumheller *Can* **22G4**
Druskininkai *USSR* **7E2**
Druzhina *USSR* **13Q3**
Dryden *Can* **23J5**
Dubai *UAE* **14D3**
Dubawnt, R *Can* **22H3**
Dubawnt L *Can* **22H3**
Dubbo *Aust* **30D4**
Dublin, County *Irish Rep* **5B5**
Dublin *Irish Rep* **5B5**
Dubossary *USSR* **7F3**
Dubrovica *USSR* **7F2**
Dubrovnik *Yugos* **11D2**
Dubuque *USA* **25D2**
Dudinka *USSR* **12K3**
Dudley *Eng* **5D5**
Dudypta, R *USSR* **13L2**
Duekoué *Ivory Coast* **18B4**
Duero, R *Spain* **9B1**
Duff Is *Solomon Is* **31F1**
Dufftown *Scot* **4D3**
Dugi Otok, I *Yugos* **10C2**
Duisburg *W Germ* **6B2**
Duk Faiwil *Sudan* **20D3**
Dulan *China* **16C3**
Duluth *USA* **25D2**
Dumas *USA* **24C3**
Dumbarton *Scot* **4C4**
Dumfries *Scot* **4D4**
Dumfries and Galloway, Region *Scot* **4C4**
Dumyat *Egypt* **19C1**
Dunărea, R *Rom* **11F2**
Dunary Head, Pt *Irish Rep* **5B5**
Dunav, R *Bulg* **11E2**
Dunav, R *Yugos* **11D1**
Dunayevtsy *USSR* **7F3**
Duncansby Head, Pt *Scot* **4D2**
Dundalk *Irish Rep* **5B4**
Dundalk B *Irish Rep* **5B5**
Dundas *Greenland* **23M2**
Dundas Pen *Can* **22G2**
Dundas Str *Aust* **17G8**
Dundee *Scot* **4D3**
Dundrum, B *N Ire* **5C4**
Dunedin *NZ* **31G5**
Dunfermline *Scot* **4D3**
Dungarvan *Irish Rep* **5B5**
Dungeness *Eng* **5F6**
Dungu *Zaïre* **20C3**
Dungunab *Sudan* **20D1**
Dunhuang *China* **16C2**
Dunkerque *France* **6A2**
Dunkirk *USA* **25F2**
Dunkur *Eth* **20D2**
Dunkwa *Ghana* **18B4**
Dun Laoghaire *Irish Rep* **3B3**
Dunnet Head, Pt *Scot* **4D2**
Dune *Scot* **1D1**
Dunstan Mts *NZ* **32A2**
Duque de Braganca *Angola* **21B4**
Durance, R *France* **8D3**
Durango *Mexico* **26B2**
Durango *Spain* **9B1**
Durango *USA* **24C3**
Durant *USA* **24D3**
Durazno *Urug* **27E4**
Durban *S Africa* **21D6**
Durham, County *Eng* **4E4**
Durham *Eng* **4E4**
Durham, N Carolina *USA* **25F3**
Durmitor, Mt *Yugos* **11D2**
Durness *Scot* **4C2**
Durrës *Alb* **11D2**
Dursunbey *Turk* **11F3**
D'Urville I *NZ* **32B2**
Dushanbe *USSR* **15E2**
Dusky Sd *NZ* **32A3**
Düsseldorf *W Germ* **6B2**
Dyer,C *Can* **23M3**
Dyersburg *USA* **25E3**
Dyfed, County *Wales* **5C5**
Dzag *Mongolia* **16C2**
Dzaoudzi *Mayotte* **21E5**
Dzarnïn Üüd *Mongolia* **16D2**
Dzavhan Gol, R *Mongolia* **16C2**
Dzehezkazgan *USSR* **14E1**
Dzhalinda *USSR* **13O4**
Dzhambul *USSR* **12J5**
Dzhungarskiy Alatau, Mts *USSR* **12J5**
Dzierzoniow *Pol* **6D2**
Dzungaria, Basin *China* **15G1**

E

Eabamet L *Can* **23K4**
Eagle Pass *USA* **24C4**
Eagle Plain *Can* **22E3**
Eastbourne *Eng* **5F6**
East,C *NZ* **31G4**
East China Sea *China/ Japan* **16F3**
Eastern Ghats, Mts *India* **15F4**
East Falkland, I *Falkland Is* **27E8**
East Germany, Republic *Europe* **6C2**
East London *S Africa* **21C7**
Eastmain *Can* **23L4**
Eastmain, R *Can* **23L4**
East Retford *Eng* **5E5**
East St Louis *USA* **25D3**
East Siberian S *USSR* **13R2**
East Sussex, County *Eng* **5F6**
Eauripik, I *Pacific O* **17H6**
Ebebiyin *Eq Guinea* **20B3**
Eberswalde *E Germ* **6C2**
Ebinur, L *China* **12K5**
Eboli *Italy* **10D2**
Ebolowa *Cam* **20B3**
Ebro, R *Spain* **9B1**
Echo Bay *Can* **22G3**
Ecija *Spain* **9A2**
Eclipse Sd *Can* **23K2**
Ecuador, Republic *S America* **28C4**
Eday, I *Scot* **4D2**
Edd *Eth* **20E2**
Edda, Oilfield *N Sea* **4G3**
Ed Da'ein *Sudan* **20C2**
Ed Damer *Sudan* **20D2**
Ed Debba *Sudan* **20D2**
Eddrachillis, B *Scot* **4C2**
Ed Dueim *Sudan* **20D2**
Edea *Cam* **20A3**
Eden, R *Eng* **4D4**
Edendale *NZ* **32A3**
Edgell I *Can* **23M3**
Edgeøya, I *Barents S* **12D2**
Edhessa *Greece* **11E2**
Edinburgh *Scot* **4D3**
Edirne *Bulg* **11F2**
Edmonton *Can* **22G4**
Edmundston *Can* **23M5**
Edolo *Italy* **10C1**
Edremit Körfezi, B *Turk* **11F3**
Edrengiyn Nuruu, Mts *Mongolia* **16C2**
Edson *Can* **22G4**
Edward,L *Zaïre/Uganda* **20C4**
Edwards Plat *USA* **24C3**
Efate, I *Vanuatu* **31F2**
Effingham *USA* **25E3**
Egedesminde *Greenland* **23N3**
Eger *Hung* **7E3**
Egersund *Nor* **2F7**
Eglinton I *Can* **22G2**
Egmont,C *NZ* **32B1**
Egmont,Mt *NZ* **32B1**
Egvekinot *USSR* **13T3**
Egypt, Republic *Africa* **19B2**
Eibar *Spain* **9B1**
Eigg, I *Scot* **4B3**
Eight Degree Chan *Indian O* **15F5**
Eighty Mile Beach *Aust* **30B2**
Eindhoven *Neth* **6B2**
Eisenach *E Germ* **6C2**
Eisenerz *Austria* **6C3**
Eketahuna *NZ* **32C2**
Ekibastuz *USSR* **12J4**
Ekimchan *USSR* **13P4**
Eksjo *Sweden* **2H7**
Ekwen, R *Can* **25E1**
El Asnam *Alg* **18C1**
El' Atrun Oasis *Sudan* **20C2**
Elba, I *Italy* **10C2**
El Balyana *Egypt* **19C2**
El Banco *Colombia* **28D2**
Elbasan *Alb* **11E2**
Elbe, R *E Germ/W Germ* **6C2**
Elbert,Mt *USA* **24C3**
Elbeuf *France* **8C2**
Elblag *Pol* **7D2**
El Bolson *Arg* **27B6**
Elburz, Mts *Iran* **14D2**
Elche *Spain* **9B2**
Elda *Spain* **9B2**
El'dikan *USSR* **13P3**
El Diviso *Colombia* **28C3**
El Djouf, Desert Region *Maur* **18B2**
El Dorado, Arkansas *USA* **25D3**
El Dorado, Kansas *USA* **24D3**
El Dorado *Mexico* **26B2**
El Dorado *Ven* **28F2**
Eldoret *Kenya* **20D3**
El Eglab, Region *Alg* **18B2**
El Escorial *Spain* **9B1**
Eleuthera, I *Bahamas* **25F4**
El Farsia, Well *Mor* **18B2**
El Fasher *Sudan* **20C2**
El Ferrol del Caudillo *Spain* **9A1**
El Fula *Sudan* **20C2**
El Gassi *Alg* **18C1**
El Geteina *Sudan* **20D2**
El Gezīra, Region *Sudan* **20D2**
Elgin, Illinois *USA* **25E2**
Elgin *Scot* **4D3**
El Golea *Alg* **18C1**
Elgon,Mt *Uganda/Kenya* **20D3**
El Goran *Eth* **20E3**
El Guettara, Well *Mali* **18B2**
El Hamurre *Somalia* **19D4**
El Haricha, Desert Region *Mali* **18B2**
El Harrach *Alg* **9C2**
Elira,C *Can* **22H2**
Elisenvaara *Fin* **2K6**
Elizabeth *Aust* **30C4**
Elizabeth City *USA* **25F3**
El Jebelein *Sudan* **20D2**
Elk *Pol* **7E2**
El Kamlin *Sudan* **20D2**
El Khenachich, Desert Region *Mali* **18B2**
Elkhovo *Bulg* **11F2**
Elko *USA* **24B2**
El Lagowa *Sudan* **20C2**
Ellef Ringnes I *Can* **22H2**
Ellensburg *USA* **24A2**
Ellesmere I *Can* **23K2**
Ellesmere,L *NZ* **32B2**
Elliot Lake *Can* **23K5**
El Maghra, L *Egypt* **19B1**
El Merelé, Desert Region *Maur* **18B3**
El Minya *Egypt* **19C2**
Elmira, New York *USA* **25F2**
El Mreitl, Well *Maur* **18B2**
Elmsborn *W Germ* **6B2**
El Muglad *Sudan* **20C2**
El Mzereb, Well *Mali* **18B2**
El Obeid *Sudan* **20D2**
El Paso *USA* **24C3**
El Puerto del Sta Maria *Spain* **9A2**
El Reno *USA* **24D3**
Elsa *Can* **22E3**
El Salvador, Republic *C America* **26D3**
Elsterwerda *E Germ* **6C2**
El Teleno, Mt *Spain* **9A1**
Eltham *NZ* **32B1**
El Tigre *Ven* **28F2**
Elvas *Port* **9A2**
Elvira *Brazil* **28D5**
Ely *Eng* **5F5**
Ely, Minnesota *USA* **25D2**
Ely, Nevada *USA* **24B3**
Eman, R *Sweden* **6D1**
Embalse Cerros Colorados, L *Arg* **27C5**
Embalse de Alarcón, Res *Spain* **9B2**
Embalse de Alcántarà, Res *Spain* **9A2**
Embalse de Almendra, Res *Spain* **9A1**
Embalse de Garcia de Sola, Res *Spain* **9A2**
Embalse de Guri, L *Ven* **28F2**
Embalse de Mequinenza, Res *Spain* **9B1**
Embalse de Ricobayo, Res *Spain* **9A1**
Embalse de Rio Negro, Res *Urug* **27E4**
Embalse Ezequil Ramos Mexia, L *Arg* **27C5**
Embalse Florentine Ameghino, L *Arg* **27C6**
Embalse Gabriel y Galan, Res *Spain* **9A1**
Embarcación *Arg* **27D2**
Embarras Portage *Can* **22G4**
Embu *Kenya* **20D4**
Emden *W Germ* **6B2**
Emerald *Aust* **30D3**
Emeri *Can* **23M4**
Emerson *Can* **22J5**
Emi Koussi, Mt *Chad* **20B1**
Emmen *Neth* **6B2**
Emory Peak, Mt *USA* **24C4**
Empalme *Mexico* **26A2**
Empedrado *Arg* **27E3**
Ems, R *W Germ* **6B2**
Enard, B *Scot* **4C2**
Encarnación *Par* **27E3**
Ende *Indon* **30B1**
England, Country *UK* **3C3**
Englee *Can* **23N4**
English Channel *Eng/ France* **3C3**
Enji, Well *Maur* **18B3**
Enkoping *Sweden* **2H7**
Enna *Italy* **10C3**
En Nahud *Sudan* **20C2**

Ennedi Gedser

Ennedi, Desert Region *Chad* 20C2
Ennis *Irish Rep* 3B3
Enniscorthy *Irish Rep* 5B5
Enniskillen *N Ire* 5B4
Enns, R *Austria* 6C3
Enschede *Neth* 2F8
Enschede *Neth* 6B2
Ensenada *Mexico* 26A1
Entebbe *Uganda* 20D4
Enugu *Nig* 18C4
Epernay *France* 8C2
Epi, I *Vanuatu* 31F2
Épinal *France* 8D2
Equatorial Guinea, Republic *Africa* 20A3
Erdenet *Mongolia* 16D2
Erdi, Desert Region *Chad* 20C2
Erechim *Brazil* 27F3
Erenhot *China* 16E2
Eresma, R *Spain* 9B1
Erfurt *E Germ* 6C2
Erg Chech, Desert Region *Alg* 18B2
Erg du Djourab, Desert Region *Chad* 20B2
Erg Du Ténéré, Desert Region *Niger* 18D3
Erg Iguidi, Region *Alg* 18B2
Ergli *USSR* 7F1
Erguig, R *Chad* 20B2
Ergun', R *USSR* 13N4
Ergun, R *USSR* 16E1
Ergun Zuoqi *China* 13O4
Eriba *Sudan* 20D2
Erie *USA* 25F2
Erie,L *USA/Can* 25E2
Eriskay, I *Scot* 4B3
Erlangen *W Germ* 6C3
Er Rahad *Sudan* 20D2
Errego *Mozam* 21D5
Errigal, Mt *Irish Rep* 3B2
Erris Head, Pt *Irish Rep* 3A3
Erromanga, I *Vanuatu* 31F2
Er Roseires *Sudan* 20D2
Erzgebirge, Upland *E Germ* 6C2
Erzurum *Turk* 14C2
Esara, R *Spain* 8C3
Esbjerg *Den* 6B1
Escalón *Mexico* 24C4
Escanaba *USA* 25E2
Escárcega *Mexico* 26C3
Escuinapa *Mexico* 26B2
Escuintla *Guatemala* 26C3
Eséka *Cam* 20B3
Esera, R *Spain* 9C1
Eşfahān *Iran* 14D2
Eskdale *NZ* 32C1
Eskifjörður *Iceland* 2C1
Eskilstuna *Sweden* 2H7
Eskimo L *Can* 22E3
Eskimo Point *Can* 23J3
Esla, R *Spain* 9A1
Esmeraldas *Ecuador* 28C3
Esmerelda, I *Chile* 27A7
Espalion *France* 8C3
Esperance *Aust* 30B4
Espirito Santo, State *Brazil* 29K7
Espiritu Santo, I *Vanuatu* 31F2
Espungabera *Mozam* 21D6
Esquel *Arg* 27B6
Essen *W Germ* 6B2
Essequibo *Guyana* 29G3
Essex, County *Eng* 5F6
Esslingen *W Germ* 6B3
Estância *Brazil* 29L6
Esteli *Nic* 28A1
Esteros *Par* 27D2
Estevan *Can* 22H5
Estrecho de Magallanes, Str *Chile* 27B8
Estremoz *Port* 9A2
Esztergom *Hung* 7D3
Etah *Can* 23L2
Etampes *France* 8C2
Ethiopia, Republic *Africa* 20D3
Etna, Mt *Italy* 10C3
Etosha Nat Pk *Namibia* 21B5
Etosha Pan, Salt L *Namibia* 21B5
Eua, I *Tonga* 31H3
Eugene *USA* 24A2
Euphrates, R *Iraq* 14C2
Eure, R *France* 8C2
Eureka *Can* 23K1
Eureka, Nevada *USA* 24B3
Eureka, Sd *Can* 23K2
Europa, I *Mozam Chan* 21E6
Euskirchen *W Germ* 6B2
Evans,C *Can* 23K1
Evans,L *Can* 23L4
Evans Str *Can* 23K3
Evanston, Wyoming *USA* 24B2
Evansville, Indiana *USA* 25E3
Everard,L *Aust* 30C4
Everest,Mt *Nepal/China* 15G3
Everett, Washington *USA* 24A2
Everglades,The, Swamp *USA* 25E4
Evesham *Eng* 5E5
Evinayong *Eq Guinea* 20B3
Evje *Nor* 2F7
Évora *Port* 9A2
Evreux *France* 8C2
Évvoia, I *Greece* 11E3
Ewo *Congo* 20B4
Exeter *Eng* 5D6
Exmoor Nat Pk *Eng* 5D6
Exmouth *Eng* 5D6
Extremadura, Region *Spain* 9A2
Exuma Sd *Bahamas* 26E2
Eyasi, L *Tanz* 20D4
Eyemouth *Scot* 4D4
Eyl *Somalia* 19D4
Eyre *Aust* 30B4
Eyre Creek, R *Aust* 30C3
Eyre,L *Aust* 30C3
Eyre Pen *Aust* 30C4
Ezine *Turk* 11F3

F

Faber L *Can* 22G3
Fåborg *Den* 2F7
Fabriano *Italy* 10C2
Fachi *Niger* 20B2
Fada *Chad* 20C2
Faenza *Italy* 10C2
Faeringehavn *Greenland* 23N3
Faerøerne, Is 2D3
Fafa, R *CAR* 20B3
Fafan, R *Eth* 20E3
Făgăras *Rom* 11E1
Faguibine,L, L *Mali* 18B3
Faiol, I *Açores* 18A1
Fairbanks *USA* 22D3
Fairbault *USA* 23J5
Fairbury *USA* 24D2
Fair Head, Pt *N Ire* 4B4
Fair Isle, I *Scot* 3C2
Fairlie *NZ* 32B2
Fairweather,Mt *USA* 22E4
Fais, I *Pacific O* 17H6
Faisalabad *India* 15F2
Faither,The, Pen *Scot* 4E1
Fakaofo, I *Tokeau Is* 31H1
Fakenham *Eng* 5F5
Fakfak *Indon* 30C1
Falcon Res *USA/Mexico* 26C2
Falémé, R *Mali/Sen* 18A3
Falkenberg *Sweden* 2G7
Falkirk *Scot* 4D4
Falkland Is, Dependency *S Atlantic* 27D8
Falkland Sd *Falkland Is* 27E8
Falköping *Sweden* 2G7
Fallon *USA* 24B3
Falmouth *Eng* 5C6
Falso,C *Mexico* 26A2
Falster, I *Den* 6C2
Fălticeni *Rom* 11F1
Falun *Sweden* 2H6
Fangak *Sudan* 20D3
Fano *Italy* 10C2
Faradje *Zaïre* 20C3
Farafangana *Madag* 21E6
Farafra Oasis *Egypt* 19B2
Farallon de Medinilla, I *Pacific O* 17H5
Faranah *Guinea* 18A3
Faraulep, I *Pacific O* 17H6
Fareham *Eng* 5E6
Farewell,C *NZ* 31G5
Farewell Spit, Pt *NZ* 32B2
Fargo *USA* 24D2
Faribault *USA* 25D2
Farmington, New Mexico *USA* 24C3
Farne Deep *N Sea* 4E4
Faro *Port* 9A2
Fåro, I *Sweden* 2H7
Farrar, R *Scot* 4C3
Fársala *Greece* 11E3
Fatima du Sul *Brazil* 29H7
Fauske *Nor* 2H5
Fawn, R *Can* 23K4
Fax, R *Sweden* 2H6
Faxaflói, B *Iceland* 2A2
Faya *Chad* 20B2
Fayetteville, Arkansas *USA* 25D3
Fayetteville, N Carolina *USA* 25F3
Fdérik *Maur* 18A2
Fear,C *USA* 25F3
Federated States of Micronesia, Is *Pacific O* 17H6
Fehmarn, I *W Germ* 6C2
Feijó *Brazil* 28D5
Feilding *NZ* 32C2
Feira *Zambia* 21D5
Feira de Santan *Brazil* 29L6
Feldkirch *Austria* 6B3
Felixstowe *Eng* 3D3
Femund, L *Nor* 2G6
Fenoarivo Atsinanana *Madag* 21E5
Fergana *USSR* 15F1
Fermanagh, County *N Ire* 5B4
Ferrara *Italy* 10C2
Ferreñafe *Peru* 28C5
Fès *Mor* 18B1
Feteşti *Rom* 11F2
Fetlar, I *Scot* 4E1
Feyzabad *Afghan* 12J6
Fianarantsoa *Madag* 21E6
Fiche *Eth* 20D3
Fier *Alb* 11D2
Fife, Region *Scot* 4D3
Fife Ness, Pen *Scot* 4D3
Figeac *France* 8C3
Figueira da Foz *Port* 9A1
Figueras *Spain* 9C1
Fiji, Is *Pacific O* 31G2
Filadelpia *Par* 29G8
Filiaşi *Rom* 11E2
Filiatrá *Greece* 11E3
Filicudi, I *Italy* 10C3
Findhorn, R *Scot* 4C3
Findlay *USA* 25E2
Fingoè *Mozam* 21D5
Finke, R *Aust* 30C3
Finland,G of *N Europe* 2J7
Finlay, R *Can* 22F4
Finlay Forks *Can* 22F4
Finnsnes *Nor* 2H5
Finschhafen *PNG* 17H7
Finspång *Sweden* 2H7
Finsterwalde *E Germ* 6C2
Fintona *N Ire* 5B4
Fiordland Nat Pk *NZ* 32A3
Firenze *Italy* 10C2
Firth of Clyde, Estuary *Scot* 4C4
Firth of Forth, Estuary *Scot* 4D3
Firth of Lorn, Estuary *Scot* 4B3
Firth of Tay, Estuary *Scot* 3C2
Fisher Str *Can* 23K3
Fishguard *Wales* 5C6
Fiskenaesset *Greenland* 23N3
Fitful Head, Pt *Scot* 4E2
Fitzroy, R *Aust* 30B2
Fitzroy Crossing *Aust* 30B2
Fizi *Zaïre* 20C4
Flagstaff *USA* 24B3
Flamborough Head, C *Eng* 5E4
Flaming Gorge Res *USA* 24C2
Flannan Isles, Is *Scot* 4B2
Flathead L *USA* 24B2
Flattery,C *Aust* 17H8
Flattery,C *USA* 24A2
Fleetwood *Eng* 5D5
Flekkefjord, Inlet *Nor* 2F7
Fleming Deep *Pacific Oc* 16H4
Flensburg *W Germ* 6B2
Flinders, I *Aust* 30C4
Flinders, I *Aust* 30D5
Flinders, R *Aust* 30D2
Flinders Range, Mts *Aust* 30C4
Flin Flon *Can* 22H4
Flint *USA* 25E2
Flint *Wales* 5D5
Flint, R *USA* 25E3
Florence, Alabama *USA* 25E3
Florence, S Carolina *USA* 25F3
Florencia *Colombia* 28C3
Flores *Guatemala* 26D3
Flores, I *Açores* 18A1
Flores, I *Indon* 30B1
Flores S *Indon* 17E7
Floriano *Brazil* 29K5
Florianópolis *Brazil* 27G3
Florida, State *USA* 26D2
Florida *Urug* 27E4
Florida Is *Solomon Is* 31E1
Florida Keys, Is *USA* 25E4
Florida,Strs of *USA* 25E4
Flórina *Greece* 11E2
Florø *Nor* 2F6
Fly, R *PNG* 30D1
Focsani *Rom* 11F1
Foggia *Italy* 10D2
Fogo, I *Cape Verde* 18A4
Foix *France* 8C3
Foley I *Can* 23L3
Foligno *Italy* 10C2
Folkestone *Eng* 5F6
Follonica *Italy* 10C2
Fond-du-Lac *Can* 22H4
Fond du Lac *USA* 25E2
Fontainbleau *France* 8C2
Fontenay-le-Comte *France* 8B2
Fonyód *Hung* 11D1
Forde *Nor* 2F6
Forécarian *Guinea* 18A4
Forel,Mt *Greenland* 23P3
Forfar *Scot* 4D3
Forlì *Italy* 10C2
Formentera, I *Spain* 9C2
Formia *Italy* 10C2
Formigas, I *Açores* 18A1
Formosa *Arg* 27E3
Formosa *Brazil* 29J7
Formosa, State *Arg* 27D2
Forres *Scot* 4D3
Forrest *Aust* 30B4
Forrest City *USA* 25D3
Forsayth *Aust* 30D2
Forssa *Fin* 2J6
Fort Albany *Can* 23K4
Fortaleza *Brazil* 29L4
Fort Augustus *Scot* 4C3
Fort Chimo *Can* 23M4
Fort Collins *USA* 24C2
Fort-de-France *Martinique* 28F1
Fort Dodge *USA* 25D2
Fortescue, R *Aust* 30A3
Fort Frances *Can* 23J5
Fort Frances *Can* 25D2
Fort Franklin *Can* 22F3
Fort George *Can* 23L4
Fort Good Hope *Can* 22F3
Forth, R *Scot* 4C3
Fort Hope *Can* 23K4
Forties, Oilfield *N Sea* 4F3
Fort Laird *Can* 22F3
Fort Lallemand *Alg* 18C1
Fort Lauderdale *USA* 25E4
Fort Mackay *Can* 22G4
Fort Macleod *Can* 22G5
Fort McMurray *Can* 22G4
Fort McPherson *Can* 22E3
Fort Morgan *USA* 24C2
Fort Myers *USA* 25E4
Fort Nelson *Can* 22F4
Fort Norman *Can* 22F3
Fort Peck Res *USA* 24C2
Fort Pierce *USA* 25E4
Fort Providence *Can* 22G3
Fort Resolution *Can* 22G3
Fort Rousset *Congo* 20B4
Fort Rupert *Can* 23L4
Fort St James *Can* 22F4
Fort Selkirk *Can* 22E3
Fort Severn *Can* 23K4
Fort Simpson *Can* 22F3
Fort Smith *Can* 22G3
Fort Smith *USA* 25D3
Fort Stockton *USA* 24C3
Fort Vermillion *Can* 22G4
Fort Wayne *USA* 25E2
Fort William *Scot* 4C3
Fort Worth *USA* 24D3
Fougamou *Gabon* 20B4
Fougères *France* 8B2
Foula, I *Scot* 4D1
Foulness I *Eng* 5F6
Foulwind,C *NZ* 32B2
Foumban *Cam* 20B3
Fourmies *France* 8C1
Foúrnoi, I *Greece* 11F3
Fouta Djallon, Mts *Guinea* 18A3
Foveaux Str *NZ* 31F5
Fowey *Eng* 5C6
Foxe Basin, G *Can* 23K3
Foxe Chan *Can* 23K3
Foxe Pen *Can* 23L3
Foxton *NZ* 32C2
Foz do Cuene *Angola* 21B5
Foz do Iguaçu *Brazil* 27F3
Franca *Brazil* 29J8
France, Republic *Europe* 8C2
France Ville *Gabon* 20B4
Franche Comté, Region *France* 8D2
Frankfort, Kentucky *USA* 25E3
Frankfurt *W Germ* 6B2
Frankfurt-an-der-Oder *E Germ* 6C2
Fränkischer Alb, Upland *W Germ* 6C3
Franklin, Region *Can* 22G2
Franklin B *Can* 22F2
Franklin Mts *Can* 22F3
Franklin Str *Can* 22J2
Franz Josef Glacier *NZ* 32B2
Fraser, R *Can* 22F5
Fraserburgh *Scot* 4D3
Fredericia *Den* 6B1
Fredericton *Can* 23M5
Frederikshåb *Greenland* 23N3
Frederikshavn *Den* 2G7
Fredrikstad *Nor* 2G7
Freetown *Sierra Leone* 18A4
Freiburg *W Germ* 6B3
Freistadt *Austria* 6C3
Fremantle *Aust* 30A4
French Guiana, Dependency *S America* 29H3
Fresnillo *Mexico* 26B2
Fresno *USA* 24B3
Fria *Guinea* 18A3
Fribourg *Switz* 10B1
Friedrichshafen *W Germ* 6B3
Frobisher B *Can* 23M3
Frobisher Bay *Can* 23M3
Frobisher L *Can* 22H4
Frome *Eng* 5D6
Frome, R *Eng* 5D6
Frome,L *Aust* 30C4
Frontera *Mexico* 26C3
Frosinone *Italy* 10C2
Frunze *USSR* 15F1
Fuerte, R *Mexico* 26B2
Fuerte Olimpo *Par* 27E2
Fuerteventura, I *Canary Is.* 18A2
Fuhai *China* 16B2
Fukang *China* 12K5
Fukuoka *Japan* 16G3
Fulda *W Germ* 6B2
Fulda, R *W Germ* 6B2
Funafuti, I *Tuvalu* 31G1
Funchal *Medeira* 18A1
Fundy,B of *Can* 23M5
Funhalouro *Mozam* 21D6
Furancungo *Mozam* 21D5
Furneaux Group, Is *Aust* 30D5
Fürstenwalde *E Germ* 6C2
Fürth *W Germ* 6C3
Fury and Hecla St *Can* 23K3
Fushun *China* 16F2
Füssen *W Germ* 6C3
Fuyun *China* 16B2
Fuzhou *China* 16E4
Fyn, I *Den* 6C1

G

Gaalkacyo *Somalia* 20E3
Gabela *Angola* 21B5
Gabès *Tunisia* 18D1
Gabon, Republic *Africa* 20B4
Gaborone *Botswana* 21C6
Gabrovo *Bulg* 11F2
Gadsen *USA* 25E3
Gads L *Can* 25D1
Gaeta *Italy* 10C2
Gaferut, I *Pacific O* 17H6
Gafsa *Tunisia* 18C1
Gagnon *Can* 23M4
Gaimán *Arg* 27C6
Gainsborough *Eng* 5E5
Gairloch *Scot* 4C3
Galadi *Eth* 20E3
Galana, R *Kenya* 20D4
Galashiels *Scot* 4D4
Galaţi *Rom* 11F1
Galena, Alaska *USA* 22C3
Galicia, Region *Spain* 9A1
Gállego, R *Spain* 9B1
Gallipoli *Italy* 11D2
Galloway, District 4C4
Galloway,Mull of, C *Scot* 5C4
Galveston *USA* 26C2
Galveston B *USA* 25D4
Galway *Irish Rep* 3B3
Galway, B *Irish Rep* 3B3
Gambia, R *The Gambia/Sen* 18A3
Gambia,The, Republic *Africa* 18A3
Gamboma *Congo* 20B4
Gambos *Angola* 21B5
Ganale Dorya, R *Eth* 20E3
Ganda *Angola* 21B5
Gandajika *Zaïre* 21C4
Gander *Can* 23N5
Gandia *Spain* 9B2
Ganga, R *India* 15G3
Gangdise Shan, Mts *China* 15G2
Gantsevichi *USSR* 2K8
Gao *Mali* 18C3
Gaoual *Guinea* 18A3
Gap *France* 8D3
Garanhuns *Brazil* 29L5
Gardner, I *Phoenix Is* 31H1
Gardula *Eth* 20D3
Garissa *Kenya* 20D4
Garmisch-Partenkirchen *W Germ* 6C3
Garnett Peak, Mt *USA* 24B2
Garonne, R *France* 8C3
Garry, R *Scot* 4C3
Garyarsa *China* 15G2
Gary L *Can* 22H3
Gascogne, Region *France* 8B3
Gascoyne, R *Aust* 30A3
Gashaka *Nig* 20B3
Gaspé *Can* 25G2
Gaspé,C *Can* 25G2
Gaspé Pen *Can* 25G2
Gateshead *Eng* 4E4
Gaua, I *Vanuatu* 31F2
Gauja, R *USSR* 7E1
Gavdhos, I *Greece* 11E4
Gävle *Sweden* 2H6
Gaysin *USSR* 7F3
Gazaintep *Turk* 14B2
Gbaringa *Lib* 18B4
Gdańsk *Pol* 7D2
Gdańsk,G of *Pol* 7D2
Gdov *USSR* 2K7
Gdynia *Pol* 7D2
Gediz, R *Turk* 11F3
Gedser *Den* 6C2

Geelong Hasselt

Geelong *Aust*	30D4
Geita *Tanz*	20D4
Gela *Italy*	10C3
Gelibolu *Turk*	11F2
Gelting *W Germ*	2F8
Gemena *Zaïre*	20B3
Gemona *Italy*	10C1
Geneina *Sudan*	20C2
General Eugenio A Garay *Arg*	27D2
General Manuel Belgrano, Mt *Arg*	27C3
General Roca *Arg*	27C5
General Santos *Phil*	17F6
Genève *Switz*	10B1
Genil, R *Spain*	9B2
Genova *Italy*	10B2
Genthin *E Germ*	6C2
George, R *Can*	23M4
George Sd *NZ*	32A2
Georgetown *Guyana*	29G2
George Town *Malay*	17D6
Georgetown *The Gambia*	18A3
Georgia, State *USA*	25E3
Georgian Bay *Can*	25E2
Georgia,Str of *Can*	22F5
Georgina, R *Aust*	30C3
Gera *E Germ*	6C2
Geraldine *NZ*	32B2
Geraldton *Aust*	30A3
Geraldton *Can*	25E2
Gerdine,Mt *USA*	22C3
Gerona *Spain*	9C1
Gestro, R *Eth*	20E3
Getafe *Spain*	9B1
Gevgeliija *Yugos*	11E2
Ghadamis *Libya*	18C1
Ghana, Republic *Africa*	18B4
Gharyan *Libya*	19A1
Ghāt *Libya*	19A2
Ghazaouet *Alg*	9B2
Gheorgheni *Rom*	11F1
Gheorghiu G Dei *Rom*	11F1
Gialo *Libya*	19B2
Giamame *Somalia*	20E3
Giarre *Italy*	10D3
Gibraltar, Colony *SW Europe*	9A2
Gibraltar,Str of *Spain/ Africa*	9A2
Gibson Desert *Aust*	30B3
Giessen *W Germ*	6B2
Gigha, I *Scot*	4C4
Giglio, I *Italy*	10C2
Gijon *Spain*	9A1
Gilbert, R *Aust*	30D2
Gilbert Is *Pacific O*	31G1
Gilé *Mozam*	21D5
Gilf Kebir Plat *Egypt*	19B2
Gillam *Can*	23J4
Ginir *Eth*	20E3
Gióna, Mt *Greece*	11E3
Girardot *Colombia*	28D3
Girdle Ness, Pen *Scot*	4D3
Giri, R *Zaïre*	20B3
Gironde, R *France*	8B2
Girvan *Scot*	4C4
Gisborne *NZ*	32C2
Gitega *Burundi*	20C4
Giurgiu *Rom*	11F2
Gizhiga *USSR*	13S3
Gizycko *Pol*	7E2
Gjirokastër *Alb*	11E2
Gjoatlaven *Can*	22J3
Gjøvik *Nor*	2G6
Glace Bay *Can*	23M5
Glacier Str *Can*	23K2
Gladstone, Queensland *Aust*	30E3
Glama, Mt *Iceland*	2A1
Glåma, R *Nor*	2G6
Glasgow *Scot*	4C4
Glastonbury *Eng*	5D6
Gleisdorf *Austria*	6D3
Glen Afton *NZ*	32C1
Glendale *USA*	24B3
Glittertind, Mt *Nor*	2F6
Gliwice *Pol*	7D2
Głogów *Pol*	6D2
Glomfjord *Nor*	2G5
Gloucester *Eng*	5D6
Glubokoye *USSR*	7F1
Gmünd *Austria*	6D3
Gmunden *Austria*	6C3
Gniezno *Pol*	7D2
Goba *Eth*	20D3
Gobi,, Desert *China/ Mongolia*	16D2
Gobza, R *USSR*	7G1
Godhavn *Greenland*	23N3
Gods L *Can*	23J4
Godthab *Greenland*	23N3
Goiânia *Brazil*	29J7
Goiás, State *Brazil*	29J6
Gojab, R *Eth*	20D3
Gökçeada, I *Turk*	11F2
Gol'chikha *USSR*	12K2
Golden B *NZ*	32B2
Goleniów *Pol*	6C2
Golf de Paria, G *Ven*	28F1
Golfe d'Ajaccio, G *Corse*	10B2
Golfe de St Florent, G *Corse*	10B2
Golfe de St-Malo, B *France*	8B2
Golfe du Lion, G *France*	8C3
Golfo Corcovado, G *Chile*	27B6
Golfo de Almeira, G *Spain*	9B2
Golfo de Ancud, G *Chile*	27B6
Golfo de Batabano, G *Cuba*	26D2
Golfo de Cadiz, G *Spain*	9A2
Golfo de Cagliari, G *Sardegna*	10B3
Golfo de California, G *Mexico*	26A1
Golfo de Chiriqui, G *Panama*	26D4
Golfo de Fonseca *Honduras*	26D3
Golfo de Guayaquil, G *Ecuador*	28B4
Golfo de los Mosquitos, G *Panama*	28B2
Golfo del Papagaya, G *Nic*	28A1
Golfo de Mazarrón, G *Spain*	9B2
Golfo de Nicoya, G *Costa Rica*	28A2
Golfo de Oristano, G *Sardegna*	10B3
Golfo de Panamá, G *Panama*	26E4
Golfo de Papagayo, G *Costa Rica*	26D3
Golfo de Penas, G *Chile*	27B7
Golfo de San Jorge, G *Spain*	9C1
Golfo de Tehuantepec, G *Mexico*	26C3
Golfo de Torugas, G *Colombia*	28C3
Golfo de Uraba, G *Colombia*	28C2
Golfo de Valencia, G *Spain*	9C2
Golfo di Genova, G *Italy*	10B2
Golfo di Policastro, G *Italy*	10D3
Golfo di Squillace, G *Italy*	10D3
Golfo di Taranto, G *Italy*	10D2
Golfo di Venezia, G *Italy*	10C1
Golfo Dulce, G *Costa Rica*	26D4
Golfo San Jorge, G *Arg*	27C7
Golfo San Matías, G *Arg*	27D6
Golmud *China*	16C3
Golocha *Eth*	20E3
Goma *Zaïre*	20C4
Gomel *USSR*	7G2
Gomera, I *Canary Is*	18A2
Gómez Palacio *Mexico*	26B2
Gonam, R *USSR*	13O4
Gondar *Eth*	20D2
Gonen, R *Turk*	11F3
Good Hope,C of *S Africa*	21B7
Goole *Eng*	5E5
Goomalling *Aust*	30A4
Goose Bay *Can*	23N4
Gora Munku Sardyk, Mt *USSR*	13L4
Goražde *Yugos*	11D2
Goré *Chad*	20B3
Gore *Eth*	20D3
Gore *NZ*	32A3
Gore Topko, Mt *USSR*	13P4
Gorey *Irish Rep*	5B5
Gorizia *Italy*	10C1
Gorki, Belorusskaya S.S. R. *USSR*	7G2
Gor'kiy *USSR*	12F4
Gorlitz *E Germ*	6C2
Gorna Orjahovica *Bulg*	11F2
Gorno-Altaysk *USSR*	16B1
Gorodnya *USSR*	7G2
Gorodok, Belorusskaya S.S.R. *USSR*	7G1
Gorodok, Ukrainskaya S. S.R. *USSR*	7E3
Gorodok, Ukrainskaya S. S.R. *USSR*	7F3
Goroka *PNG*	30D1
Gorongosa *Mozam*	21D5
Gorontalo *Indon*	17F6
Goryachinsk *USSR*	13M4
Gory Byrranga, Mts *USSR*	13L2
Goryn', R *USSR*	7F3
Gory Putorana, Mts *USSR*	13L3
Góry Świetokrzyskie, Upland *Pol*	7E2
Gory Tel'pos-iz', Mt *USSR*	12G3
Gorzow Wielkopolski *Pol*	2H8
Gospić *Yugos*	10D2
Gostivar *Yugos*	11E2
Gostynin *Pol*	7D2
Göteborg *Sweden*	2G7
Gotel, Mts *Nig*	20B3
Gotland, I *Sweden*	2H7
Gotska Sandön, I *Sweden*	2H7
Gottwaldov *Czech*	7D3
Goudoumaria *Niger*	20B2
Goumbou *Mali*	18B3
Goundam *Mali*	18B3
Gouré *Niger*	20B2
Gourma Rharous *Mali*	18B3
Gouro *Chad*	20B2
Gove Pen *Aust*	17G8
Goz-Beída *Chad*	20C2
Gozo, I *Medit S*	10C3
Grafton *Aust*	31E3
Grajaú *Brazil*	29J5
Grajewo *Pol*	7E2
Grámmos, Mt *Greece/ Alb*	11E2
Grampian, Region *Scot*	4D3
Grampian, Mts *Scot*	4C3
Granada *Colombia*	28D3
Granada *Nic*	28A1
Granada *Spain*	9B2
Gran Canaria, I *Canary Is*	18A2
Gran Chaco, Region *Arg*	27D3
Grand Bahama, I *Bahamas*	25F4
Grand Bank *Can*	23N5
Grand Canyon *USA*	24B3
Grande, R, Bahia *Brazil*	29K6
Grande Comore, I *Comoros*	21E5
Grand Erg de Bilma, Desert Region *Niger*	20B2
Grand erg Occidental, Mts *Alg*	18C1
Grand erg Oriental, Mts *Alg*	18C2
Grande Rivière de la Baleine, R *Can*	23L4
Grand Falls, New Brunswick *Can*	23M5
Grand Falls, Newfoundland *Can*	23N5
Grândola *Port*	9A2
Grand Prairie *Can*	22G4
Grand Rapids *Can*	22J4
Grand Rapids *USA*	25E2
Grand Teton, Mt *USA*	24B2
Grangeburg *USA*	26D1
Granollérs *Spain*	9C1
Gran Paradiso, Mt *Italy*	10B1
Grantham *Eng*	5E5
Grantown-on-Spey *Scot*	4D3
Granville *France*	8B2
Granville L *Can*	22H4
Grasse *France*	8D3
Gravelbourg *Can*	22H5
Gravelotte *S Africa*	21D6
Graz *Austria*	6D3
Great Abaco, I *Bahamas*	25F4
Great Australian Bight, G *Aust*	30B4
Great Bahama Bank *Bahamas*	26E2
Great Barrier I *NZ*	32C1
Great Barrier Reef, Is *Aust*	30D2
Great Bear L *Can*	22F3
Great Dividing Range, Mts *Aust*	30D3
Great Driffield *Eng*	5E4
Greater London, Metropolitan County *Eng*	5E6
Greater Manchester, Metropolitan County *Eng*	5D5
Great Exuma, I *Bahamas*	26E2
Great Falls *USA*	24B2
Great Glen, V *Scot*	4C3
Great Inagua, I *Bahamas*	25F4
Great Karroo, Plat *S Africa*	21C7
Great Namaland, Region *Namibia*	21B6
Great Ormes Head, C *Wales*	5D5
Great Ragged, I *Bahamas*	25F4
Great Ruaha, R *Tanz*	21D4
Great Sand Sea *Libya/ Egypt*	19B2
Great Sandy Desert *Aust*	30B3
Great Sandy Desert *USA*	24A2
Great Slave L *Can*	22G3
Great Victoria Desert *Aust*	30B3
Great Yarmouth *Eng*	5F5
Greece, Republic *Europe*	11E3
Greely Fjord *Can*	23K1
Greenland, Dependency *N Atlantic*	23O2
Greenock *Scot*	4C4
Greensboro *USA*	25F3
Greenstone, Pt *Scot*	4C3
Greenville *Lib*	18B4
Greenwich *Eng*	5F6
Gregory Range, Mts *Aust*	30D2
Greifswald *E Germ*	6C2
Grenå *Den*	6C1
Grenada, I *Caribbean*	28F1
Grenoble *France*	8D2
Grenville,C *Aust*	30D2
Grey, R *NZ*	32B2
Grey Is *Can*	23N4
Greymouth *NZ*	32B2
Grey Range, Mts *Aust*	30D3
Greystones *Irish Rep*	5B5
Grim,C *Aust*	30D5
Grimsby *Eng*	5E5
Grimsey, I *Iceland*	2B1
Grimstad *Nor*	2F7
Grinnell Pen *Can*	23J2
Grise Fjord *Can*	23K2
Grobina *USSR*	2J7
Grodno *USSR*	7E2
Groningen *Neth*	6B2
Groote Eylandt, I *Aust*	30C2
Grootfontein *Namibia*	21B5
Grosseto *Italy*	10C2
Grossglockner, Mt *Austria*	6C3
Grudziadz *Pol*	7D2
Grutness *Scot*	4E2
Gruzinskaya SSR, Republic *USSR*	12F5
Grytviken *South Georgia*	27J8
Guadalajara *Mexico*	26B2
Guadalajara *Spain*	9B1
Guadalcanal, I *Solomon Is*	31E1
Guadalimar, R *Spain*	9B2
Guadalope, R *Spain*	9B1
Guadalquivir, R *Spain*	9B2
Guadalupe *Mexico*	26B2
Guadian, R *Spain*	9B2
Guadiana, R *Port*	9A2
Guadiana, R *Spain*	9B2
Guadix *Spain*	9B2
Guajará Mirim *Brazil*	28E6
Guajira,Pen de *Colombia*	28D1
Gualaceo *Ecuador*	28C4
Guam, I *Pacific O*	17H5
Guanare *Ven*	28E2
Guane *Cuba*	26D2
Guangzhou *China*	16E4
Guania, R *Colombia*	28E3
Guapa *Colombia*	28C2
Guaporé, R *Brazil/Bol*	28F6
Guaquí *Bol*	28E7
Guaranda *Ecuador*	28C4
Guarda *Port*	9A1
Guardafui,C *Somalia*	19E3
Guasave *Mexico*	24C4
Guatemala *Guatemala*	26C3
Guatemala, Republic *C America*	26C3
Guavrare, R *Colombia*	28D3
Guayaquil *Ecuador*	28B4
Guaymas *Mexico*	26A2
Guba *Eth*	20D3
Guba *Zaïre*	21C5
Guba Buorkhaya, B *USSR*	13P2
Guban, Region *Somalia*	20E3
Gubin *Pol*	6C2
Guelta Zemmur *Mor*	18A2
Guéréda *Chad*	20C2
Guéret *France*	8C2
Guernsey, I *UK*	8B2
Gughe, Mt *Eth*	20D3
Gugigu *China*	13O4
Guguan, I *Pacific O*	17H5
Guiglo *Ivory Coast*	10D4
Guildford *Eng*	5E6
Guinea, Republic *Africa*	18A3
Guinea-Bissau, Republic *Africa*	18A3
Guinea,G of *W Africa*	18C4
Guir, Well *Mali*	18B3
Güiria *Ven*	28F1
Guiyang *China*	16D4
Gulbene *USSR*	7F1
Gulf,The *S W Asia*	14D3
Gulu *Uganda*	20D3
Guna, Mt *Eth*	20D2
Gungu *Zaïre*	20B4
Gunza *Angola*	21B5
Gurupi, R *Brazil*	29J4
Gur'yev *USSR*	12G5
Gusev *USSR*	7E2
Guston *USA*	25E3
Gütersloh *W Germ*	6B2
Guyana, Republic *S America*	29G3
Guyenne, Region *France*	8B3
Gwane *Zaïre*	20C3
Gwent, County *Wales*	5D6
Gweru *Zim*	21C5
Gwynedd *Wales*	5D4
Gyaring Hu, L *China*	16C3
Gydanskiy Poluostrov, Pen *USSR*	12J2
Gyldenløues *Greenland*	23O3
Gyöngyös *Hung*	7D3
Györ *Hung*	7D3

H

Ha'apai Group, Is *Tonga*	31H2
Haapajärvi *Fin*	2K6
Haarlem *Neth*	6A2
Habana *Cuba*	26D2
Haddington *Scot*	4D4
Haderslev *Den*	6B1
Hadley B *Can*	22H2
Hadsund *Den*	6C1
Haffners Bjerg, Mt *Greenland*	23M2
Hafnarfjörður *Iceland*	2A2
Hagen *W Germ*	6B2
Hagunia, Well *Mor*	18A2
Haha-jima, I *Japan*	16H4
Hah Xil Hu, L *China*	16C3
Haifa *Israel*	14B2
Hailar *China*	13N5
Hailuoto, I *Fin*	2J5
Hainan, I *China*	17E5
Hainfeld *Austria*	6D3
Haiphong *Viet*	16D4
Haiya *Sudan*	20D2
Hajdúböszörmény *Hung*	7E3
Ḩalab *Syria*	14B2
Halaib *Sudan*	20D1
Halberstadt *E Germ*	6C2
Halden *Nor*	2G7
Halifax *Can*	23M5
Halifax *Eng*	5E5
Hall Basin, Sd *Can*	23M1
Hall Beach *Can*	23K3
Halle *E Germ*	6C2
Hallingdal, R *Nor*	2F6
Hall Pen *Can*	23M3
Hall's Creek *Aust*	30B2
Halmahera, I *Indon*	17F6
Halmstad *Sweden*	2G7
Haltern *W Germ*	6B2
Haltia, Mt *Nor*	2J5
Haltwhistle *Eng*	4D4
Hamada de Tinrhert, Desert Region *Alg*	18C2
Hamada du Dra, Upland *Alg*	18B2
Hamada Tounassine, Region *Alg*	18B2
Ḩamāh *Syria*	14B2
Hamar *Nor*	2G6
Hamburg *W Germ*	6B2
Hämeenlinna *Fin*	2J6
Hamersley Range, Mts *Aust*	30A3
Hamhŭng *N Korea*	16F2
Hami *China*	16C2
Hamilton *Can*	23L5
Hamilton *NZ*	32C1
Hamilton *Scot*	4C4
Hamilton Inlet, B *Can*	23N4
Hamina *Fin*	2K6
Hamm *W Germ*	6B2
Hammādāh al Hamra, Upland *Libya*	19A2
Hammerdal *Sweden*	2H6
Hammerfest *Nor*	2J4
Hampden *NZ*	32B3
Hampshire, County *Eng*	5E6
Handan *China*	16E3
Handeni *Tanz*	20D4
Hangö *Fin*	2J7
Hangzhou *China*	16F3
Hanmer Springs *NZ*	32B2
Hannover *W Germ*	6B2
Hanöbukten, B *Sweden*	2G7
Hanoi *Viet*	16D4
Hanover, I *Chile*	27B8
Hantay *Mongolia*	16D2
Hāora *India*	15G3
Haparanda *Sweden*	2J5
Hara Fanna *Eth*	20E3
Harar *Eth*	20E3
Harare *Zim*	21D5
Harazé *Chad*	20C2
Harbin *China*	16F2
Hardangerfjord, Inlet *Nor*	2F6
Hargeysa *Somalia*	20E3
Harhu, L *China*	16C3
Harlingen *Neth*	6B2
Harlow *Eng*	5F6
Härnösand *Sweden*	2H6
Harper *Lib*	18B4
Harricanaw, R *Can*	23L4
Harrington Harbour *Can*	23N4
Harris, District *Scot*	4B3
Harrisburg *USA*	25F2
Harrison,C *Can*	23N4
Harris,Sound of, Chan *Scot*	4B3
Harrogate *Eng*	5E4
Harstad *Nor*	2H5
Hårteigen, Mt *Nor*	2F6
Hartford *USA*	25F2
Hartkjølen, Mt *Nor*	2G6
Hartland Pt *Eng*	5C6
Hartlepool *Eng*	4E4
Har Us Nuur, L *Mongolia*	16C2
Harwich *Eng*	5F6
Haslemere *Eng*	5E6
Hasselt *Belg*	6B2

Hassi Inifel

Iznik Golü

Hassi Inifel *Alg* 18C2
Hassi Mdakane, Well *Alg* 18B2
Hassi Messaoud *Alg* 18C1
Hassleholm *Sweden* 2G7
Hastings *Eng* 5F6
Hastings, Nebraska *USA* 24D2
Hastings *NZ* 32C1
Hatteras,C *USA* 25F3
Hatvan *Hung* 7D3
Hau Atlas, Mts *Mor* 18B1
Haud, Region *Eth* 20E3
Haugesund *Nor* 2F7
Hauhungaroa Range, Mts *NZ* 32C1
Hauraki G *NZ* 32B1
Hauroko,L *NZ* 32A3
Haute Kotto, Region *CAR* 20C3
Havelock North *NZ* 32C1
Haverfordwest *West* 5C6
Havlíčkův Brod *Czech* 6D3
Havre-St-Pierre *Can* 23M4
Havre-St-Pierre *Can* 23M4
Havsa *Turk* 11F2
Hawea,L *NZ* 32A2
Hawera *NZ* 32B1
Hawick *Scot* 4D4
Hawkdun Range, Mts *NZ* 32A2
Hawke B *NZ* 32C1
Hay, R *Can* 22G3
Haycock *USA* 22B3
Hayes, R *Can* 23J4
Hayes Halvø, Region *Greenland* 23M2
Hay River *Can* 22G3
Hazel Str *Can* 22G2
Hazelton *Can* 22F4
Hazen L *Can* 23L1
Hearst *Can* 25E2
Hebron *Can* 23M4
Hecla and Griper B *Can* 22G2
Hector,Mt *NZ* 32C2
Hede *Sweden* 2G6
Hedemora *Sweden* 2H6
Heerenveen *Neth* 6B2
Heide *W Germ* 6B2
Heidelberg *W Germ* 6B3
Heidenheim *W Germ* 6C3
Heihe *China* 13O4
Heilbronn *W Germ* 6B3
Heiligenstadt *E Germ* 6C2
Heinola *Fin* 2K6
Hekla, Mt *Iceland* 23R3
Helena *USA* 24B2
Helensburgh *Scot* 4C3
Hellin *Spain* 9B2
Helmsdale *Scot* 4D2
Helsingborg *Sweden* 2G7
Helsingør *Den* 6C1
Helsinki *Fin* 2J6
Helston *Eng* 5C6
Hemse *Sweden* 2H7
Hen and Chicken Is *NZ* 32B1
Hengduan Shan, Mts *China* 16C4
Hengelo *Neth* 6B2
Henley-on-Thames *Eng* 5E6
Henrietta Maria,C *Can* 23K4
Henry Kater Pen *Can* 23M3
Hentiyn Nuruu, Mts *Mongolia* 16D2
Herbert *Can* 22H4
Herbertville *NZ* 32C2
Hereford *Eng* 5D5
Hereford & Worcester, County *Eng* 5D5
Heriot *NZ* 32A3
Herma Ness, Pen *Scot* 4E1
Hermitage *NZ* 32B2
Hermit Is *PNG* 30D1
Hermosillo *Mexico* 26A2
Herning *Den* 6B1
Herrera del Duque *Spain* 9B2
Hertford, County *Eng* 5E6
Hessen, State *W Germ* 6B2
Heuts Plateaux *Alg* 18B1
Hewett Hewett, Gasfield *N Sea* 5F5
Hexham *Eng* 4D4
Hicks Bay *NZ* 32C1
Hidalgo del Parral *Mexico* 26B2
Hierro, I *Canary Is* 18A2
Highland, Region *Scot* 4C3
High River *Can* 22G4
High Wycombe *Eng* 5E6
Hiiumaa, I *USSR* 2J7
Hikurangi *NZ* 32B1
Hildesheim *W Germ* 6B2
Hillerød *Den* 6C1
Hillswick *Scot* 4E1
Hilversum *Neth* 6B2
Himalaya, Mts *Asia* 15F2
Hims *Syria* 14B2
Hinnøya, I *Nor* 2H5
Hiroshima *Japan* 16G3
Hirşova *Rom* 11F2
Hirtshals *Den* 6B1
Hitchin *Eng* 5E6
Hitra, I *Nor* 2F6
Hjørring *Den* 6B1
Hobart *Aust* 30D5
Hobro *Den* 6B1
Hobyo *Somalia* 19D4
Hochkonig, Mt *Austria* 6C3
Hódmezö'hely *Hung* 11E1
Hodonin *Czech* 6D3
Hof *W Germ* 6C2
Hofsjökull, Mts *Iceland* 2B2
Hoggar, Upland *Alg* 18C2
Hohhot *China* 16E2
Höhn *Iceland* 23R3
Hoh Sai Hu, L *China* 16C3
Hoh Xil Shan, Mts *China* 15G2
Hoima *Uganda* 20D3
Hokianga Harbour, B *NZ* 32B1
Hokitika *NZ* 32B2
Hokkaidō, I *Japan* 16H2
Holitika *NZ* 32B2
Hollabrunn *Austria* 6D3
Holman Island *Can* 22G2
Holmsund *Sweden* 2J6
Holstebro *Den* 6B1
Holsteinborg *Greenland* 23N3
Holyhead *Wales* 5C5
Holy I *Eng* 4E4
Holy I *Wales* 5C5
Home B *Can* 23M3
Homer Tunnel *NZ* 32A2
Homoine *Mozam* 21D6
Hondo, R *Mexico* 26D3
Honduras, Republic *C America* 26D3
Honduras,G of *Honduras* 26D3
Hønefoss *Nor* 2G6
Hong Kong, Colony *SE Asia* 16E4
Hongor *Mongolia* 16E2
Honiara *Solomon Is* 31E1
Honningsvåg *Nor* 2K4
Honshu,, I *Japan* 16G3
Hook Head, C *Irish Rep* 5B5
Hoorn *Neth* 6A2
Hoover Dam *USA* 24B3
Hopedale *Can* 23M4
Hopen, I *Barents S* 12D2
Hopes Advance,C *Can* 23M3
Hordiyo *Somalia* 19E3
Hormuz,Str of *Oman/Iran* 14D3
Horn *Austria* 6D3
Horn, C *Iceland* 23Q3
Hornavan, L *Sweden* 2H5
Hornby *NZ* 32B2
Hornepayne *Can* 23K5
Horn Mts *Can* 22F3
Hornsea *Eng* 5E5
Horqueta *Par* 27E2
Horsens *Den* 6C1
Horsham *Eng* 5E6
Horten *Nor* 2G7
Hoste, I *Chile* 27C9
Hotan *China* 15F2
Hottah *Can* 22G3
Houston *USA* 25D4
Houtman, Is *Aust* 30A3
Hovd *Mongolia* 16C2
Hövsgol Nuur, L *Mongolia* 16D1
Hoy, I *Scot* 4D2
Høyanger *Nor* 2F6
Hradeç-Královė *Czech* 6D2
Hranice *Czech* 7D3
Hron, R *Czech* 7D3
Huacho *Peru* 28C6
Hua-lien *Taiwan* 16F4
Huallaga, R *Peru* 28C5
Huallanca *Peru* 28C5
Huamachuco *Peru* 28C5
Huambo *Angola* 21B5
Huanay *Bol* 28E7
Huancabamba *Peru* 28C5
Huancavelica *Peru* 28C6
Huancayo *Peru* 28C6
Huānuco *Peru* 28C5
Huanuni *Bol* 27C1
Huaráz *Peru* 28C5
Huarmey *Peru* 28C6
Huascarán, Mt *Peru* 28C5
Huayapan, R *Mexico* 26B2
Huddersfield *Eng* 5E5
Hudiksvall *Sweden* 2H6
Hudson B *Can* 23K4
Hudson Bay *Can* 22H4
Hudson Str *Can* 23L3
Hue *Viet* 17D5
Huelva *Spain* 9A2
Húercal Overa *Spain* 9B2
Huesca *Spain* 9B1
Hughenden *Aust* 30D3
Huiarau Range, Mts *NZ* 32C1
Huixtla *Mexico* 26C3
Hull *Eng* 5E5
Hull, I *Phoenix Is* 31H1
Hulla, Mt *Colombia* 28C3
Hultsfred *Sweden* 6D1
Hulun Nur, L *China* 13N5
Humaita *Brazil* 28F5
Humber, R *Eng* 5E5
Humberside, County *Eng* 5E5
Humboldt *Can* 22H4
Humboldt Gletscher, Gl *Greenland* 23M2
Humpata *Angola* 21B5
Húnaflói, B *Iceland* 2A1
Hunedoara *Rom* 11E1
Hungary, Republic *Europe* 7D3
Huntingdon *Eng* 5E5
Huntly *NZ* 32C1
Huntly *Scot* 4D3
Huntsville *USA* 25E3
Huon Peninsula, Pen *PNG* 17H7
Huron,L *USA/Can* 25E2
Hurunui, R *NZ* 32B2
Husavik *Iceland* 2B1
Huşi *Rom* 11F1
Huskvarna *Sweden* 2G7
Husum *W Germ* 6B2
Hvar, I *Yugos* 10D2
Hwange *Zim* 21C5
Hwange Nat Pk *Zim* 21C5
Hyargas Nuur, L *Mongolia* 16C2
Hyderābad *India* 15F4
Hyderabad *Pak* 15E3
Hyndman Peak, Mt *USA* 24B2
Hyvinkää *Fin* 2J6

I

Iaçu *Brazil* 29K6
Ialomiţa, R *Rom* 11F2
Iärpen *Sweden* 2G6
Iaşi *Rom* 11F1
Ibadan *Nig* 18C4
Ibagué *Colombia* 28C3
Ibar, R *Yugos* 11E2
Ibarra *Ecuador* 28C3
Ibiza *Spain* 9C2
Ibiza, I *Spain* 9C2
Ibo *Mozam* 21E5
Ibotirama *Brazil* 29K6
Ica *Peru* 28C6
Icá, R *Brazil* 28E4
Icana *Brazil* 28E3
Iceland, Republic *N Atlantic O* 2A1
Icha *USSR* 13R4
Idaho, State *USA* 24B2
Idehan Marzūg, Desert *Libya* 19A2
Idehan Ubari, Desert *Libya* 19A2
Idelés *Alg* 18C2
Iderlym Gol, R *Mongolia* 16C2
Ídhi Óros, Mt *Greece* 11E3
Ídhra, I *Greece* 11E3
Idiofa *Zaïre* 20B4
Idritsa *USSR* 2K7
Ierápetra *Greece* 11F3
Ifakara *Tanz* 21D4
Ifalik, I *Pacific* 17H6
Ifanadiana *Madag* 21E6
Iférouane *Niger* 18C3
Igarka *USSR* 12K3
Iggesund *Sweden* 2H6
Iglesias *Sardegna* 10B3
Igloolik *Can* 23K3
Ignace *Can* 25D2
Igoumenítsa *Greece* 11E3
Iguape *Brazil* 27G2
Iguatu *Brazil* 29L5
Iguéla *Gabon* 20A4
Ihosy *Madag* 21E6
Iisalmi *Fin* 2K6
Ijsselmeer, S *Neth* 6B2
Ikaría, I *Greece* 11F3
Ikela *Zaïre* 20C4
Ikhtiman *Bulg* 11E2
Ikopa, R *Madag* 21E5
Ilagan *Phil* 17F5
Ilanskiy *USSR* 16C1
Ile de Noirmoutier, I *France* 8B2
Ile de Ré, I *France* 8B2
Île des Pins, I *Nouvelle Calédonie* 31F3
Ile d'Ouessant, I *France* 8A2
Ile d'Yeu, I *France* 8B2
Îles Bélèp *Nouvelle Calédonie* 31F2
Îles Chesterfield *Nouvelle Calédonie* 31E2
Îles de Horn, Is *Pacific O* 31H2
Iles d'Hyères, Is *France* 8D3
Ilfracombe *Eng* 5C6
Ilha Bazaruto, I *Mozam* 21D6
Ilha De Maracá, I *Brazil* 29H3
Ilha de Marajó, I *Brazil* 29H4
Ilha do Bananal, Region *Brazil* 29H6
Ilhas Selvegens, I *Atlantic O* 18A2
Ilhéus *Brazil* 29L6
Ilin, R *USSR* 16D1
Iliodhrómia, I *Greece* 11E3
Illéla *Niger* 18C3
Îlles Wallis, Is *Pacific O* 31H2
Illiamna L *USA* 22C4
Illinois, State *USA* 25E2
Illizi *Alg* 18C2
Ilo *Peru* 28D7
Iloilo *Phil* 17F5
Ilomantsi *Fin* 2L6
Ilorin *Nig* 18C4
Il'yino *USSR* 7G1
Imbituba *Brazil* 27G3
Imi *Eth* 20E3
Imola *Italy* 10C2
Imperatriz *Brazil* 29J5
Imperia *Italy* 10B2
Impfondo *Congo* 20B3
In Afahleleh, Well *Alg* 18C2
In Amenas *Alg* 18C2
Inari *Fin* 2K5
Inarijärvi, L *Fin* 2K5
In Belbel *Alg* 18C2
Inch' ŏn *S Korea* 16F3
In Dagouber, Well *Mali* 18B2
Indals, R *Sweden* 2H6
Indefatigable, Gasfield *N Sea* 5G5
India, Federal Republic *Asia* 15F3
Indiana, State *USA* 25E2
Indianapolis *USA* 25E3
Indian Harbour *Can* 23N4
Indigirka, R *USSR* 13Q3
Indonesia, Republic *S E Asia* 17E7
Indore *India* 15F3
Indre, R *France* 8C2
Indus, R *Pak* 15E3
In Ebeggi, Well *Alg* 18C2
In Ecker *Alg* 18C2
In Ezzane *Alg* 18D2
Ingal *Niger* 18C3
Ingham *Aust* 30D2
Inglefield Land, Region *Can* 23M2
Inglewood *NZ* 32B1
Ingólfshöfði, I *Iceland* 2B2
Ingolstadt *W Germ* 6C3
In-Guezzam, Well *Alg* 18C3
Inhambane *Mozam* 21D6
Inharrime *Mozam* 21D6
Inirida, R *Colombia* 28E3
Inishowen, District *Irish Rep* 4B4
Inner Mongolia, Autonomous Region *China* 16D2
Innisfail *Aust* 30D2
Innsbruck *Austria* 6C3
Inongo *Zaïre* 20B4
Inoucdjouac *Can* 23L4
Inowrocław *Pol* 7D2
In Salah *Alg* 18C2
Interlaken *France* 8D2
International Date Line 31H3
Inuvik *Can* 22E3
Inveraray *Scot* 4C3
Invercargill *NZ* 32A3
Inverness *Scot* 4C3
Inverurie *Scot* 4D3
Inya *USSR* 16B1
Inya, R *USSR* 13Q3
Inyanga *Zim* 21D5
Inzia, R *Zaïre* 20B4
Ioánnina *Greece* 11E3
Iona, I *Scot* 4B3
Iôna Nat Pk *Angola* 21B5
Ionian S *Italy/Greece* 11D3
Ioníoi Nísoi, Is *Greece* 11E3
Íos, I *Greece* 11F3
Iowa, State *USA* 25D2
Ipiales *Colombia* 28C3
Ipoh *Malay* 17D6
Iporá *Brazil* 29H7
Ipsala *Turk* 11F2
Ipswich *Eng* 5F5
Iput, R *USSR* 7G2
Iquique *Chile* 27B2
Iquitos *Peru* 28D4
Iráklion *Greece* 11F3
Iran, Republic *S W Asia* 14D2
Irapuato *Mexico* 26B2
Iraq, Republic *S W Asia* 14C2
Irā Wan, Watercourse *Libya* 19A2
Irbit *USSR* 12H4
Ireng, R *Guyana* 29G3
Irian Jaya, Province *Indon* 17G7
Iriba *Chad* 20C2
Iringa *Tanz* 21D4
Iriomote, I *Japan* 16F4
Iriri, R *Brazil* 29H5
Irish S *Eng/Irish Rep* 5C5
Irkutsk *USSR* 13M4
Irlysh *USSR* 12J4
Iron Range *Aust* 30D2
Iroquois Falls *Can* 25E2
Irrawaddy, R *Burma* 15H3
Irtysh, R *USSR* 12H4
Irun *Spain* 9B1
Irvine *Scot* 4C4
Isachsen *Can* 22H2
Isachsen,C *Can* 22H2
Ísafjörður *Iceland* 23Q3
Isangi *Zaïre* 20C3
Isbister *Scot* 4E1
Ischia, I *Italy* 10C2
Isernia *Italy* 10C2
Ishigaki, I *Japan* 16F4
Ishim *USSR* 12H4
Ishim, R *USSR* 12H4
Isil'kul *USSR* 12J4
Isiolo *Kenya* 20D3
Isiro *Zaïre* 20C3
Iskitim *USSR* 12K4
Iskur, R *Bulg* 11E2
Isla Coiba, I *Panama* 28B2
Isla de Chiloé, I *Chile* 27B6
Isla de Cozumel, I *Mexico* 26D2
Isla del Maiz, I *Caribbean* 26D3
Isla de los Estados, I *Arg* 27D8
Isla de Santa Catarina, I *Brazil* 27G3
Isla du Diable, I *French Guiana* 29H2
Isla Fernando de Noronha, I *Brazil* 29M4
Isla Grande de Tierra del Fuego, I *Arg/Chile* 27C8
Islamabad *India* 15F2
Isla Magdalena, I *Mexico* 26A2
Island L *Can* 25D1
Islands,B of *NZ* 32B1
Isla Providencia, I *Colombia* 28B1
Isla Puná, I *Ecuador* 28B4
Isla Santa Margarita, I *Mexico* 26A2
Islas Baleares, Is *Spain* 9C2
Islas Canarias, Is *Atlantic O* 18A2
Islas Columbretes, Is *Spain* 9C2
Islas de la Bahia, Is *Honduras* 26D3
Islas de Margarita, Is *Ven* 28F1
Islas Diego Ramírez, Is *Chile* 27C9
Islas Galapagos, Is *Pacific O* 28N
Islas Juan Fernandez, Is *Pacific O* 28Q
Islas los Roques, Is *Ven* 28E1
Islas Wollaston, Is *Chile* 27C9
Isla Tidra, I *Maur* 18A3
Isla Wellington, I *Chile* 27B7
Islay, I *Scot* 4B4
Isle, R *France* 8C2
Isle of Wight, I *Eng* 5E6
Isles Glorieuses, Is *Madag* 21E5
Îsles Loyauté, Is *Nouvelle Calédonie* 31F3
Ismâ' ilîya *Egypt* 19C1
Isoanala *Madag* 21E6
Isoka *Zambia* 21D5
Isola Egadi, I *Italy* 10C3
Isola Ponziane, I *Italy* 10C2
Isole Lipari, Is *Italy* 10C3
Isoles Tremiti, Is *Italy* 10D2
Israel, Republic *S W Asia* 14B2
Isser, R *Alg* 9C2
Issoire *France* 8C2
Issoudun *France* 8C2
Istanbul *Turk* 14A1
Istiáia *Greece* 11E3
Istra, Pen *Yugos* 10C1
Istranca Dağlari, Upland *Turk* 11F2
Itacoatiara *Brazil* 29G4
Itagui *Colombia* 28C2
Itaituba *Brazil* 29G4
Itajaí *Brazil* 27G3
Italy, Repubic *Europe* 10C2
Itapetinga *Brazil* 29K7
Itapipoca *Brazil* 29L4
Iténez, R *Brazil/Bol* 28F6
Itimbiri, R *Zaïre* 20C3
Itivdleg *Greenland* 23N3
Itonomas, R *Bol* 28F6
Iturbe *Arg* 27C2
Itzehoe *W Germ* 6B2
Iul'tin *USSR* 13T3
Iurga *USSR* 12K4
Ivacevichi *USSR* 7F2
Ivalo *Fin* 2K5
Ivangrad *Yugos* 11D2
Ivano-Frankovsk *USSR* 12D5
Ivindo, R *Gabon* 20B3
Ivohibe *Madag* 21E6
Ivongo Soanierana *Madag* 21E5
Ivory Coast, Republic *Africa* 18B4
Ivrea *Italy* 10B1
Ivujivik *Can* 23L3
Iwo *Nig* 18C4
Iwo Jima, I *Japan* 16H4
Izhevsk *USSR* 12G4
Izmail *USSR* 7F3
Izmır *Turk* 14A2
Izmir Körfezi, B *Turk* 11F3
Iznik Golü, L *Turk* 11F2

Jabal al Akhdar Khatyrka

J

Jabal al Akhdar, Mts *Libya* 19B1
Jabal as Sawdā, Mts *Libya* 19A2
Jabalpur *India* 15F3
Jablonec nad Nisou *Czech* 6D2
Jaboatão *Brazil* 29L5
Jaca *Spain* 9B1
Jacareacanga *Brazil* 29G5
Jacarezinho *Brazil* 29H8
Jáchal *Arg* 27C4
Jackson *USA* 25D3
Jackson,C *NZ* 32B2
Jackson Head, Pt *NZ* 32A2
Jacksonville *USA* 25E3
Jacobina *Brazil* 29K6
Jaén *Peru* 28C5
Jaén *Spain* 9B2
Jaipur *India* 15F3
Jajce *Yugos* 10D2
Jakarta *Indon* 17D7
Jakobshavn *Greenland* 23N3
Jakobstad *Fin* 2J6
Jalapa *Mexico* 26C3
Jalón, R *Spain* 9B1
Jalo Oasis *Libya* 19B2
Jama *Ecuador* 28B4
Jamaica, I *Caribbean* 26E3
Jambi *Indon* 17D7
James B *Can* 23K4
Jameston *USA* 22J5
Jamshedpur *India* 15G3
Japan, Empire *SE Asia* 16G3
Japan,S of *Japan* 16G2
Japurá, R *Brazil* 28E4
Jarama, R *Spain* 9B1
Jardin, R *Spain* 9B2
Jari, R *Brazil* 29H3
Jarocin *Pol* 6D2
Jaroslaw *Pol* 7E2
Jaslo *Pol* 7E3
Jason Is *Falkland Is* 27D8
Jasper *Can* 22G4
Jastrowie *Pol* 6D2
Játiva *Spain* 9B2
Jatobá *Brazil* 29J4
Jauja *Peru* 28C6
Java S *Indon* 17D7
Java Tronch *Indon* 30A2
Jawa, I *Indon* 17D7
Jayapura *Indon* 17H7
Jbel Ouarkziz, Mts *Mor* 18B2
Jbel Sarhro, Mt *Mor* 18B1
Jebel Abyad, Desert Region *Sudan* 20C2
Jebel Asoteriba, Mt *Sudan* 20D1
Jebel Marra, Mt *Sudan* 20C2
Jebel Uweinat, Mt *Sudan* 20C1
Jedburgh *Scot* 4D4
Jedrzejów *Pol* 7E2
Jefferson City *USA* 25D3
Jefferson,Mt *USA* 24B3
Jelena Gora *Pol* 6D2
Jember *Indon* 17E7
Jena *E Germ* 6C2
Jensen Nunatakker, Mt *Greenland* 23O3
Jens Munk, I *Can* 23K3
Jequié *Brazil* 29L6
Jequitinhonha, R *Brazil* 29K7
Jerez de la Frontera *Spain* 9A2
Jerez de los Caballeros *Spain* 9A2
Jersey, I *UK* 8B2
Jersey City *USA* 25F2
Jerusalem *Jordan* 14B2
Jesenice *Yugos* 10C1
Jeseniky, Upland *Czech* 6D2
Jesup *USA* 25E3
Jezerce, Mt *Alb* 11D2
Jezioro Mamry, L *Pol* 7E2
Jezioro Śniardwy, L *Pol* 7E2
J H Kerr L *USA* 25F3
Jiayuguan *China* 16C3
Jiddah *S Arabia* 14B3
Jihlava *Czech* 6D3
Jilib *Somalia* 20E3
Jilin *China* 16F2
Jiloca, R *Spain* 9B1
Jimma *Eth* 20D3
Jinan *China* 16E3
Jinja *Uganda* 20D3
Jinzhou *China* 16F2
Jiparaná, R *Brazil* 28F5
Jipijapa *Ecuador* 28B4
Jiu, R *Rom* 11E2
Joal *Sen* 18A3
João Pessoa *Brazil* 29M5
João Pinheiro *Brazil* 29J7
Joensuu *Fin* 2K6
Johannesburg *S Africa* 21C6
Johan Pen *Can* 23L2
John O'Groats *Scot* 4D2
Joigny *France* 8C2
Joinville *Brazil* 27G3
Jokkmokk *Sweden* 2H5
Joliet *USA* 25E2
Joliette *Can* 23L5
Joma, Mt *China* 15H2
Jonava *USSR* 7E1
Jonesboro, Arkansas *USA* 25D3
Jones Sd *Can* 23K2
Joniškis *USSR* 7E1
Jönköping *Sweden* 2G7
Joplin *USA* 25D3
Jordan, Kingdom *S W Asia* 14B2
Jørpeland *Nor* 2F7
Jos *Nig* 18C4
Joseph Bonaparte G *Aust* 30B2
Josephine, Oilfield *N Sea* 4G3
Jotunheimen, Mt *Nor* 12B3
Jowhar *Somalia* 20E3
Juàjeiro *Brazil* 29K5
Juan de Fuca,Str of *USA/Can* 22F5
Juan de Nova, I *Mozam Chan* 21E5
Juazeiro *Brazil* 29K5
Juazeiro do Norte *Brazil* 29L5
Juba *Sudan* 20D3
Juba, R *Somalia* 20E3
Jucar, R *Spain* 9B2
Judenburg *Austria* 6C3
Juiz de Fora *Brazil* 29K8
Jujuy, State *Arg* 27C2
Juli *Peru* 28E7
Juliaca *Peru* 28D7
Julianatop, Mt *Suriname* 29G3
Julianehab *Greenland* 23O3
Junction City *USA* 24D3
Jundiaí *Brazil* 27G2
Juneau *USA* 22E4
Junee *Aust* 30D4
Jungfrau, Mt *Switz* 10B1
Junín *Arg* 27D4
Juquiá *Brazil* 27G2
Jur, R *Sudan* 20C3
Jura, I *Scot* 4C4
Jura, Mts *France* 8D2
Jura,Sound of, Chan *Scot* 4C3
Juruá, R *Brazil* 28E4
Juruena, R *Brazil* 29G6
Jutai, R *Brazil* 28E4
Juticalpa *Honduras* 26D3
Jylland, Pen *Den* 6B1
Jyväskyla *Fin* 2K6

K

K2, Mt *China/India* 15F2
Kabaena, I *Indon* 30B1
Kabala *Sierra Leone* 18A4
Kabale *Rwanda* 20D4
Kabalo *Zaïre* 20C4
Kabambare *Zaïre* 20C4
Kabarole *Uganda* 20D3
Kabia, I *Indon* 30B1
Kabinda *Zaïre* 20C4
Kabompo *Zambia* 21C5
Kabompo, R *Zambia* 21C5
Kabongo *Zaïre* 21C4
Kabul *Afghan* 15E2
Kachug *USSR* 13M4
Kadavu, I *Fiji* 25G2
Kadoma *Zim* 21C5
Kadugli *Sudan* 20C2
Kaduna *Nig* 18C3
Kaédi *Maur* 18A3
Kaffrine *Sen* 18A3
Kafue *Zambia* 21C5
Kafue, R *Zambia* 21C5
Kafue Nat Pk *Zambia* 21C5
Kagan *USSR* 12H6
Kagul *USSR* 7F3
Kahama *Tanz* 20D4
Kahemba *Zaïre* 21B4
Kaiapoi *NZ* 32B2
Kaieteur Fall *Guyana* 29G2
Kaikohe *NZ* 32B1
Kaikoura *NZ* 31G5
Kaikoura Pen *NZ* 32B2
Kaikoura Range, Mts *NZ* 32B2
Kaimana *Indon* 17G7
Kaipara Harbour, B *NZ* 32B1
Kaiserslautern *W Germ* 6B3
Kaisiadorys *USSR* 7E2
Kaitaia *NZ* 32B1
Kaitangata *NZ* 32A3
Kajaani *Fin* 2K6
Kajiado *Kenya* 20D4
Kaka *Sudan* 20D2
Kakamega *Kenya* 20D3
Kakhovskoye Vodokhranilishche, Res *USSR* 12E5
Kalabáka *Greece* 11E3
Kalabo *Zambia* 21C5
Kalahari Desert *Botswana* 21C6
Kalakan *USSR* 13N4
Kalámai *Greece* 11E3
Kalamazoo *USA* 25E2
Kalarsh *USSR* 7F3
Kalémié *Zaïre* 20C4
Kalgoorlie *Aust* 30B4
Kalima *Zaïre* 20C4
Kalimantan, Province *Indon* 17E7
Kálimnos, I *Greece* 11F3
Kaliningrad *USSR* 2J8
Kaliningrad *USSR* 7E2
Kalinovka *USSR* 7F3
Kalispell *USA* 24B2
Kalisz *Pol* 7D2
Kaliua *Tanz* 20D4
Kalix, R *Sweden* 2J5
Kalkfeld *Namibia* 21B6
Kallávesi, L *Fin* 2K6
Kallonis Kólpos, B *Greece* 11F3
Kalluk *USA* 22C4
Kalmar *Sweden* 2H7
Kalomo *Zambia* 21C5
Kalundborg *Den* 2G7
Kalush *USSR* 7E3
Kamanawa Mts *NZ* 32C1
Kamanjab *Namibia* 21B5
Kamara *China* 13O4
Kambia *Sierra Leone* 18A4
Kamchatka, Pen *USSR* 13S4
Kamenets Podolskiy *USSR* 7F3
Kamen-na-Obi *USSR* 12K4
Kamenskoya *USSR* 13S3
Kamilukuak L *Can* 22H3
Kamina *Zaïre* 21C4
Kaminak L *Can* 23J3
Kamloops *Can* 22F4
Kampala *Uganda* 20D3
Kampen *Neth* 6B2
Kanaaupscow, R *Can* 23L4
Kananga *Zaïre* 20C4
Kanbisha *USA* 22C3
Kandahar *Afghan* 14E3
Kandalaksha *USSR* 12E3
Kandalakshskaya Guba, B *USSR* 2L5
Kandy *Sri Lanka* 15G5
Kane Basin, B *Can* 23L1
Kanem, Desert Region *Chad* 20B2
Kangaba *Mali* 18B3
Kangâmiut *Greenland* 23N3
Kangaroo I *Aust* 30C4
Kanga'tsiaq *Greenland* 23N3
Kangchenjunga, Mt *Nepal* 15G3
Kangerdlugssuaq, B *Greenland* 23P3
Kangerdlugssvatsaiq, B *Greenland* 23P3
Kangetet *Kenya* 20D3
Kango *Gabon* 20B3
Kangto, Mt *China* 16C4
Kaniama *Zaïre* 21C4
Kanin Nos, Pt *USSR* 12F3
Kankaanpää *Fin* 2J6
Kankan *Guinea* 18B3
Kano *Nig* 18C3
Kānpur *India* 15G3
Kansas, State *USA* 24D3
Kansas City *USA* 25D3
Kansk *USSR* 16C1
Kao-hsiung *Taiwan* 16F4
Kaoka Veld, Plain *Namibia* 21B5
Kaolack *Sen* 18A3
Kaoma *Zambia* 21C5
Kapanga *Zaïre* 21C4
Kap Cort Adelaer, C *Greenland* 23O3
Kap Dalton, C *Greenland* 23Q3
Kapellskär *Sweden* 2H7
Kap Farvel, C *Greenland* 23O3
Kap Gustav Holm, C *Greenland* 23P3
Kapiri *Zambia* 21C5
Kaplice *Czech* 6C3
Kapona *Zaïre* 21C4
Kaposvár *Hung* 11D1
Kap Parry, C *Can* 23L2
Kap Ravn, C *Greenland* 23Q3
Kapuskasing *Can* 23K5
Kap York, C *Greenland* 23M2
Karacabey *Turk* 11F2
Karachi *Pak* 14E3
Karaftit *USSR* 16E1
Karaganda *USSR* 12J5
Karagayly *USSR* 12J5
Kara Kalpakskaya, Republic *USSR* 12G5
Karakoram, Mts *India* 15F2
Karakoro, R *Maur/Sen* 18A3
Karakumy, Desert *USSR* 12G6
Karamay *China* 12K5
Karamea *NZ* 32B2
Karamea Bight, B *NZ* 32B2
Kara S *USSR* 12J2
Karasjok *Nor* 2K5
Karasuk *USSR* 12J4
Kara Tau, Mts *USSR* 12H5
Karaul *USSR* 12K3
Karcag *Hung* 7E3
Kardhítsa *Greece* 11E3
Karesuando *Sweden* 2J5
Karet, Desert Region *Maur* 18B2
Kargasok *USSR* 12K4
Kariba *Zim* 21C5
Kariba, L *Zim/Zambia* 21C5
Kariba Dam *Zim/Zambia* 21C5
Karima *Sudan* 20D2
Karin *Somalia* 20E2
Karis *Fin* 2J6
Karishimbe, Mt *Zaïre* 20C4
Káristos *Greece* 11E3
Karkar, I *PNG* 17H7
Karlik Shan, Mt *China* 13L5
Karlino *Pol* 6D2
Karl Marx Stadt *E Germ* 6C2
Karlobag *Yugos* 10D2
Karlovac *Yugos* 10D1
Karlovo *Bulg* 11E2
Karlovy Vary *Czech* 6C2
Karlshamn *Sweden* 2G7
Karlskoga *Sweden* 2G7
Karlskrona *Sweden* 2H7
Karlsruhe *W Germ* 6B3
Karlstad *Sweden* 2G7
Karnobat *Bulg* 11F2
Karoi *Zim* 21C5
Karonga *Malawi* 21D4
Karora *Sudan* 20D2
Kárpathos, I *Greece* 11F3
Karrats Fjord *Greenland* 23N2
Karsakpay *USSR* 12H4
Karsakpay *USSR* 12H5
Kärsava *USSR* 7F1
Karshi *USSR* 14E2
Karstula *Fin* 2J6
Kartal *Turk* 11F2
Karymskoye *USSR* 16E1
Kasai, R *Zaïre* 20B4
Kasaji *Zaïre* 21C5
Kasama *Zambia* 21D5
Kasanga *Tanz* 21D4
Kasba L *Can* 22H3
Kasempa *Zambia* 21C5
Kasenga *Zaïre* 21C5
Kasese *Uganda* 20D3
Kashi *China* 15F2
Kashmir, State *India* 15F2
Kasko *Fin* 2J6
Kaslo *Can* 22G5
Kasonga *Zaïre* 20C4
Kasongo-Lunda *Zaïre* 21B4
Kásos, I *Greece* 11F3
Kassala *Sudan* 20D2
Kassel *W Germ* 6B2
Kasserine *Tunisia* 18C1
Kassinga *Angola* 21B5
Kastélli *Greece* 11E3
Kastoría *Greece* 11E2
Kástron *Greece* 11F3
Kasungu *Malawi* 21D5
Kataba *Zambia* 21C5
Katako-kombe *Zaïre* 20C4
Katalla *USA* 22D3
Katangli *USSR* 13Q4
Katanning *Aust* 30A4
Kateríni *Greece* 11E2
Kates Needle, Mt *Can/USA* 22E4
Katherine *Aust* 30C2
Kathmandu *Nepal* 15G3
Katima Mulilo *Namibia* 21C5
Katmai,Mt *USA* 22C4
Katowice *Pol* 7D2
Katrineholm *Sweden* 2H7
Katsina *Nig* 18C3
Kattakurgan *USSR* 12H6
Kattegat, Str *Denmark/Sweden* 2G7
Kaunas *USSR* 7E2
Kautokeino *Nor* 2J5
Kavadarci *Yugos* 11E2
Kavajë *Alb* 11D2
Kavála *Greece* 11E2
Kavieng *PNG* 30E1
Kawakawa *NZ* 32B1
Kawambwa *Zambia* 21C4
Kawerau *NZ* 32C1
Kawhia *NZ* 32B1
Kayes *Mali* 18A3
Kazach'ye *USSR* 13P2
Kazakhskaya SSR, Republic *USSR* 12G5
Kazakhskaya SSR, Republic *USSR* 12G5
Kazan' *USSR* 12F4
Kazanlŭk *Bulg* 11F2
Kazan Retto, Is *Japan* 16H4
Kazatin *USSR* 7F3
Kazincbarcika *Hung* 7E3
Kéa, I *Greece* 11E3
Kearney *USA* 24D2
Kébémer *Sen* 18A3
Kebnekaise, Mt *Sweden* 2H5
Kecskemet *Hung* 7D3
Kedainiai *USSR* 7E1
Kediri *Indon* 17E7
Kédougou *Sen* 18A3
Keetmanshoop *Namibia* 21B6
Keewatin, Region *Can* 23J3
Kefallinía, I *Greece* 11E3
Keflavik *Iceland* 2A2
Keg River *Can* 22G4
Keita *Niger* 18C3
Keith *Scot* 4D3
Keith Arm, B *Can* 22F3
Kekertuk *Can* 23M3
Kelang *Malay* 17D6
Kellé *Congo* 20B4
Kellet,C *Can* 22F2
Kelloselka *Fin* 12D3
Kells *Irish Rep* 5B5
Kells Range, Hills *Scot* 4C4
Kelme *USSR* 7E1
Kelowna *Can* 22G5
Kelsey Bay *Can* 22F4
Kelso *Scot* 4D4
Kem' *USSR* 12E3
Ke Macina *Mali* 18B3
Kemerovo *USSR* 12K4
Kemi *Fin* 2J5
Kemi, R *Fin* 2K5
Kemijärvi *Fin* 2K5
Kempten *W Germ* 6C3
Kenamuke Swamp *Sudan* 20D3
Kendal *Eng* 5D4
Kendari *Indon* 30B1
Kenema *Sierra Leone* 18A4
Kenge *Zaïre* 20B4
Kéniéba *Mali* 18A3
Kenitra *Mor* 18B1
Kenny Dam *Can* 22F4
Kenora *Can* 23J5
Kenosha *USA* 25E2
Kent, County *Eng* 5F6
Kent Pen *Can* 22H3
Kentucky, State *USA* 25E3
Kentucky L *USA* 25E3
Kenya, Republic *Africa* 20D3
Kenya,Mt *Kenya* 20D4
Kepaluan Tanimbar, Arch *Indon* 17G7
Kepno *Pol* 7D2
Kepulauan Aru, Arch *Indon* 17G7
Kepulauan Babar, I *Indon* 30B1
Kepulauan Banda, Arch *Indon* 17G7
Kepulauan Banggai, I *Indon* 30B1
Kepulauan Barat Daya, Is *Indon* 30B1
Kepulauan Kai, Arch *Indon* 17G7
Kepulauan Leti, I *Indon* 30B1
Kepulauan Mentawai, Arch *Indon* 17C7
Kepulauan Sermata, I *Indon* 30B1
Kepulauan Sula, I *Indon* 30B1
Kepulauan Togian, I *Indon* 30B1
Kepulauan Tukangbesi, Is *Indon* 30B1
Kerava *Fin* 2J6
Kerema *PNG* 30D1
Keren *Eth* 20D2
Kericho *Kenya* 20D4
Kerio, R *Kenya* 20D3
Kerki *USSR* 14E2
Kérkira *Greece* 11D3
Kérkira, I *Greece* 11D3
Kermadec Is *NZ* 31H3
Kermadec Trench *Pacific O* 31H4
Kermān *Iran* 14D2
Kerme Körfezi, B *Turk* 11F3
Kerulen, R *Mongolia* 13N5
Kerzaz *Alg* 18B2
Keşan *Turk* 11F2
Kestenga *USSR* 2L5
Keswick *Eng* 5D4
Ketchikan *USA* 22E4
Ketrzyn *Pol* 7E2
Kettering *Eng* 5E5
Kettlestone B *Can* 23L3
Key West *USA* 25E4
Kezhma *USSR* 13M4
K'félgyháza *Hung* 11D1
Khabarovsk *USSR* 13P5
Khāli *Yemen* 14C4
Khálki, I *Greece* 11F3
Khalkidhíki, Pen *Greece* 11E2
Khalkís *Greece* 11E3
Khambhat,G of *India* 15F3
Khaniá *Greece* 11E3
Khanty-Mansiysk *USSR* 12H3
Khapcheranga *USSR* 16E2
Khārga Oasis *Egypt* 19C2
Khar' kov *USSR* 12E4
Kharmanli *Bulg* 11F2
Khartoum *Sudan* 20D2
Khartoum North *Sudan* 20D2
Khashm el Girba *Sudan* 20D2
Khaskovo *Bulg* 11F2
Khatanga *USSR* 13M2
Khatangskiy Zaliv, Estuary *USSR* 13N2
Khatyrka *USSR* 13T3

Khemis **Lamego**

Khemis *Alg* 9C2
Kherrata *Alg* 9D2
Khilok *USSR* 13N4
Khíos *Greece* 11F3
Khíos, I *Greece* 11F3
Khodorov *USSR* 7E3
Kholm *USSR* 7G1
Khrebet Cherskogo, Mts *USSR* 13Q3
Khrebet Dzhugdzhur, Mts *USSR* 13P4
Khrebet Orulgan, Mts *USSR* 13O3
Khrebet Tarbagatay, Mts *USSR* 15G1
Khrebet Tukuringra, Mts *USSR* 13O4
Khust *USSR* 7E3
Khuwei *Sudan* 20C2
Kiambi *Zaïre* 21C4
Kibangou *Congo* 20B4
Kibaya *Tanz* 20D4
Kibombo *Zaïre* 20C4
Kibondo *Tanz* 20D4
Kibungu *Rwanda* 20D4
Kičevo *Yugos* 11E2
Kicking Horse P *Can* 22G4
Kidal *Mali* 18C3
Kidderminster *Eng* 5D5
Kidira *Sen* 18A3
Kidnappers,C *NZ* 32C1
Kiel *W Germ* 6C2
Kielce *Pol* 7E2
Kieler Bucht, B *W Germ* 6C2
Kiffa *Maur* 18A3
Kigoma *Tanz* 20C4
Kikhchik *USSR* 13R4
Kikinda *Yugos* 11E1
Kikládhes, Is *Greece* 11E3
Kikori *PNG* 17H7
Kikwit *Zaïre* 20B4
Kilbuck Mts *USA* 22C3
Kildare, County *Irish Rep* 5B5
Kildare *Irish Rep* 5B5
Kilifi *Kenya* 20E4
Kilimanjaro, Mt *Tanz* 20D4
Kilindoni *Tanz* 21D4
Kiliya *USSR* 7F3
Kilkenny, County *Irish Rep* 5B5
Kilkenny *Irish Rep* 5B5
Kilkís *Greece* 11E2
Killarney *Irish Rep* 3B3
Killin *Scot* 4C3
Killíni, Mt *Greece* 11E3
Kilmarnock *Scot* 4C4
Kilosa *Tanz* 21D4
Kilrush *Irish Rep* 3B3
Kilwa *Zaïre* 21C4
Kilwa Kisiwani *Tanz* 21D4
Kilwa Kivinje *Tanz* 21D4
Kimberley *S Africa* 21C6
Kimberley Plat *Aust* 30B2
Kími *Greece* 11E3
Kindia *Guinea* 18A3
Kindu *Zaïre* 20C4
Kingcome Inlet *Can* 22F4
King George Is *Can* 23L4
King I *Aust* 30D5
King Leopold Range, Mts *Aust* 30B2
Kingman *USA* 24B3
Kingombe *Zaïre* 20C4
King Sd *Aust* 30B2
King's Lynn *Eng* 5F5
Kingsmill Group, Is *Kiribati* 31G1
Kings Peak, Mt *USA* 24B2
Kingston *Aust* 30C4
Kingston *Can* 23L5
Kingston *Jamaica* 26E3
Kingston *NZ* 32A3
Kingstown *St Vincent* 28F1
Kingsville *USA* 24D4
Kingussie *Scot* 4C3
King William I *Can* 22J3
Kinkala *Congo* 20B4
Kinna *Sweden* 2G7
Kinnairds Head, Pt *Scot* 4D3
Kinross *Scot* 4D3
Kinshasa *Zaïre* 20B4
Kintyre, Pen *Scot* 4C4
Kinyeti, Mt *Sudan* 20D3
Kiparissía *Greece* 11E3
Kiparissiakós Kólpos, G *Greece* 11E3
Kipili *Tanz* 21D4
Kippure, Mt *Irish Rep* 5B5
Kipushi *Zaïre* 21C5
Kirensk *USSR* 13M4
Kirgizskaya SSR, Republic *USSR* 12J5
Kirgizskiy Khrebet, Mts *USSR* 15F1
Kiri *Zaïre* 20B4
Kiribati, Is *Pacific O* 31G1
Kirkağaç *Turk* 11F3
Kirkby Lonsdale *Eng* 5D4
Kirkcaldy *Scot* 4D3
Kirkcudbright *Scot* 4C4
Kirkenes *Nor* 2K5
Kirkland Lake *Can* 23K5
Kirksville *USA* 25D2
Kirkūk *Iraq* 14C2
Kirkwall *Scot* 4D2
Kirov *USSR* 12F4
Kirovskiy, Kamchatka *USSR* 13R4
Kiruna *Sweden* 2J5
Kisangani *Zaïre* 20C3
Kisii *Kenya* 20D4
Kisiju *Tanz* 21D4
Kiskunhalas *Hung* 7D3
Kislovodsk *USSR* 12F5
Kismaayo *Somalia* 20E4
Kissidougou *Guinea* 18B4
Kisumu *Kenya* 20D4
Kisvárda *Hung* 7E3
Kita *Mali* 18B3
Kitab *USSR* 12H6
Kita-Kyūshū *Japan* 16G3
Kitale *Kenya* 20D3
Kitalo, I *Japan* 16H4
Kitchener *Can* 23K5
Kitgum *Uganda* 20D3
Kíthira, I *Greece* 11E3
Kíthnos, I *Greece* 11E3
Kitimat *Can* 22F4
Kitinen, R *Fin* 2K5
Kittilä *Fin* 2J5
Kitunda *Tanz* 21D4
Kitwe *Zambia* 21C5
Kitzbühel *Austria* 6C3
Kitzingen *W Germ* 6C3
Kiumbi *Zaïre* 20C4
Kivercy *USSR* 7F2
Kivu,L *Zaïre/Rwanda* 20C4
Kiwalik *USA* 22B3
Kiyev *USSR* 12E4
Kiyevskoye Vodokhranilishche, Res *USSR* 7G2
Kizyl-Arvat *USSR* 14D2
Kladno *Czech* 6C2
Klagenfurt *Austria* 6C3
Klaipēda *USSR* 7E1
Klamath, R *USA* 24A2
Klamath Falls *USA* 24A2
Klatovy *Czech* 6C3
Kletnya *USSR* 7G2
Klimovichi *USSR* 7G2
Klintehamn *Sweden* 7D1
Ključ *Yugos* 10D2
Kłodzko *Pol* 6D2
Klondike Plat *USA/Can* 22D3
Klosterneuburg *Austria* 6D3
Kluczbork *Pol* 7D2
Knighton *Wales* 5D5
Knin *Yugos* 10D2
Knob,C *Aust* 30A4
Knoxville, Tennessee *USA* 25E3
Knud Ramsussens Land, Region *Greenland* 23Q3
Kobbermirebugt *Greenland* 23O3
Kōbe *Japan* 16G3
København *Den* 6C1
Koblenz *W Germ* 6B2
Kobroör, I *Indon* 17G7
Kočani *Yugos* 11E2
Koch I *Can* 23L3
Kodiak I *USA* 22C4
Kodok *Sudan* 20D3
Kodyma *USSR* 7F3
Koforidua *Ghana* 18B4
Køge *Den* 2G7
Kokchetav *USSR* 12H4
Kokemaki, L *Fin* 2J6
Kokkola *Fin* 2J6
Kokoda *PNG* 30D1
Kokonau *Indon* 17G7
Kokpekty *USSR* 12K5
Koksoak, R *Can* 23M4
Kolda *Sen* 18A3
Kolding *Den* 2F7
Kolín *Czech* 6D2
Köln *W Germ* 6B2
Kolo *Pol* 7D2
Kolobrzeg *Pol* 6D2
Kolokani *Mali* 18B3
Kolpakovskiy *USSR* 13R4
Kolpashevo *USSR* 12K4
Kólpos Merabéllou, B *Greece* 11F3
Kólpos Singitikós, G *Greece* 11E2
Kólpos Strimonikós, G *Greece* 11E2
Kólpos Toronaíos, G *Greece* 11E2
Kolvereid *Nor* 2G6
Kolwezi *Zaïre* 21C5
Kolyma, R *USSR* 13R3
Kolymskaya Nizmennost, Lowland *USSR* 13R3
Kolymstoye Nagor'ye, Mts *USSR* 13S3
Kom, Mt *Bulg/Yugos* 11E2
Koma *Eth* 20D3
Komandorskiye Ostrova, I *USSR* 13S4
Komárno *Czech* 7D3
Komi ASSR, Republic *USSR* 12G3
Kommunar *USSR* 16B1
Komoran, I *Indon* 17G7
Komotiní *Greece* 11F2
Komrat *USSR* 7F3
Komsomol'sk na Amure *USSR* 13P4
Konda, R *USSR* 12H4
Kondoa *Tanz* 20D4
Kong Christian IX Land, Region *Greenland* 23P3
Kong Frederik VI Kyst, Mts *Greenland* 23O3
Kong Karls Land, Is *Barents S* 12D2
Kongolo *Zaïre* 20C4
Kongsberg *Den* 2F7
Kongsvinger *Nor* 2G6
Konin *Pol* 7D2
Konjic *Yugos* 11D2
Końskie *Pol* 7E2
Konstanz *France* 8D2
Konya *Turk* 14B2
Kópasker *Iceland* 23R3
Kópavogur *Iceland* 2A2
Koper *Yugos* 10C1
Kopet Dag, Mts *Iran/USSR* 14D2
Köping *Sweden* 2H7
Koprivnica *Yugos* 10D1
Korakskoye Nagor'ye, Mts *USSR* 13S3
Korbach *W Germ* 6B2
Korbuk, R *USA* 22B3
Korçë *Alb* 11E2
Korčula, I *Yugos* 10D2
Korec *USSR* 7F2
Korf *USSR* 13S3
Korhogo *Ivory Coast* 18B4
Korinthiakós Kólpos, G *Greece* 11E3
Kórinthos *Greece* 11E3
Korkodon *USSR* 13R3
Korkodon, R *USSR* 13R3
Korla *China* 15G1
Kornat, I *Yugos* 10D2
Korogwe *Tanz* 20D4
Koror, Palau Is *Pacific O* 17G6
Körös, R *Hung* 7E3
Korostyshev *USSR* 7F2
Koro Toro *Chad* 20B2
Korsør *Den* 2G7
Kortrijk *Belg* 6A2
Kós, I *Greece* 11F3
Koscierzyna *Pol* 7D2
Kosciusko, Mt *Aust* 30D4
Košice *Czech* 7E3
Kosovska Mitrovica *Yugos* 11E2
Kossou, L *Ivory Coast* 18B4
Kosti *Sudan* 20D2
Kostopol' *USSR* 7F2
Kostrzyn *Pol* 6C2
Koszalin *Pol* 2H8
Kota Kinabalu *Malay* 17E6
Kotka *Fin* 2K6
Kotor *Yugos* 11D2
Kotto, R *CAR* 20C3
Kotuy, R *USSR* 13L3
Kotzebue Sd *USA* 22B3
Kouango *CAR* 20C3
Koulamoutou *Gabon* 20B4
Koulikoro *Mali* 18B3
Kourou *French Guiana* 29H2
Kouroussa *Guinea* 18B3
Kousséri *Cam* 20B2
Kouvola *Fin* 2K6
Kovdor *USSR* 2L5
Kozańi *Greece* 11E2
Kragerø *Nor* 2F7
Kragujevac *Yugos* 11E2
Kraków *Pol* 7D2
Kraljevo *Yugos* 11E2
Kramfors *Sweden* 2H6
Kranj *Yugos* 10C1
Krasino *USSR* 12G2
Kraśnik *Pol* 7E2
Krasnodar *USSR* 12E5
Krasnoyarsk *USSR* 13L4
Krasnystaw *Pol* 7E2
Kraulshavn *Greenland* 23N2
Krefeld *W Germ* 6B2
Kremenets *USSR* 7F2
Kribi *Cam* 20A3
Krinstinestad *Fin* 2J6
Kristiansand *Nor* 2F7
Kristianstad *Sweden* 2G7
Kristiansund *Nor* 12B3
Kristinehamn *Sweden* 2G7
Kríti, I *Greece* 11E3
Krivoy Rog *USSR* 12E5
Krk, I *Yugos* 10C1
Kronotskaya Sopka, Mt *USSR* 13S4
Kronpris Frederik Bjerge, Mts *Greenland* 23P3
Kronshtadt *USSR* 2K7
Kropotkin *USSR* 12F5
Kruger Nat Pk *S Africa* 21D6
Kruje *Alb* 11D2
Krupki *USSR* 7F2
Kruševac *Yugos* 11E2
Krustpils *USSR* 2K7
Krym, Pen *USSR* 12E5
Krzyz *Pol* 6D2
Kuala Lumpur *Malay* 17D6
Kuantan *Malay* 17D6
Kubor, Mt *PNG* 17H7
Kuching *Malay* 17E6
Kufstein *Austria* 6C3
Kūhha-ye Zāgros, Mts *Iran* 14D2
Kuhmo *Fin* 2K6
Kuigillingok *USA* 22B4
Kukës *Alb* 11E2
Kula *Turk* 11F3
Kulal,Mt *Kenya* 20D3
Kulata *Bulg* 11E2
Kulunda *USSR* 12J4
Kumanovo *Yugos* 11E2
Kumasi *Ghana* 18B4
Kumba *Cam* 20A3
Kumla *Sweden* 2H7
Kümüx *China* 15G1
Kunda *USSR* 2K7
Kungsbacka *Sweden* 2G7
Kunlun Shan, Mts *China* 15G2
Kunming *China* 16D4
Kuopio *Fin* 2K6
Kupa, R *Yugos* 10D1
Kupang *Indon* 30B2
Kupiano *PNG* 30D2
Kuqa *China* 15G1
Kürdzhali *Bulg* 11F2
Kureyka, R *USSR* 13L3
Kurgan *USSR* 12H4
Kurikka *Fin* 2J6
Kuril'skiye Ostrova, Is *USSR* 13Q5
Kurow *NZ* 32B2
Kurskiy Zaliv, Lg *USSR* 7E1
Kuruktag, R *China* 16B2
Kurunktag, R *China* 12K5
Kuşadasi Körfezi, B *Turk* 11F3
Kus Golü, L *Turk* 11F2
Kushva *USSR* 12H4
Kuskokwim Mts *USA* 22C3
Kustanay *USSR* 12H4
Kutná Hora *Czech* 6D3
Kutno *Pol* 7D2
Kutu *Zaïre* 20B4
Kutum *Sudan* 20C2
Kuusamo *Fin* 2K5
Kuwait *Kuwait* 14C3
Kuwait, Sheikdom *S W Asia* 14C3
Kuybyshev *USSR* 12G4
Kuybyshev *USSR* 12J4
Kuytun *USSR* 13M4
Kvigtind, Mt *Nor* 2G5
Kwale *Kenya* 20D4
Kwangju *S Korea* 16F3
Kwango, R *Zaïre* 20B4
Kwekwe *Zim* 21C5
Kwidzyn *Pol* 7D2
Kwoka, Mt *Indon* 17G7
Kyakhta *USSR* 16D1
Kyle of Lochalsh *Scot* 3B2
Kyoga, L *Uganda* 20D3
Kyōto *Japan* 16G3
Kyshtym *USSR* 12H4
Kyūshū *Japan* 16G3
Kyustendil *Bulg* 11E2
Kyusyur *USSR* 13O2
Kyzyl *USSR* 16C1
Kyzylkum, Desert *USSR* 12H5
Kzyl Orda *USSR* 12H5

L

Laas Caanood *Somalia* 20E3
Laas Qoray *Somalia* 19D3
La Asunción *Ven* 28F1
Labasa *Fiji* 25G2
Labé *Guinea* 18A3
Labe, R *Czech* 6D2
Labrador, Region *Can* 23M4
Labrador City *Can* 23M4
Labrador S *Greenland/Can* 23N4
Lábrea *Brazil* 28F5
Lac Bienville, L *Can* 23L4
Laccadive Is *India* 15F4
Lac de Gras, L *Can* 22G3
Lac des Bois, L *Can* 22F3
La Ceiba *Honduras* 26D3
La Châtre *France* 8C2
Lachlan, R *Aust* 30D4
La Chorrera *Panama* 28C2
Lac Joseph, L *Can* 23M4
Lac la Biche *Can* 22G4
Lac la Martre, L *Can* 22G3
Lac la Ronge, L *Can* 22H4
Lac L'eau Claire *Can* 23L4
Lac Léman, L *Switz/France* 10B1
Lac Manouane *Can* 23L4
Lac Manouane, L *Can* 25F1
Lac Mistassini, L *Can* 23L4
La Coruña *Spain* 9A1
La Crosse *USA* 25D2
La Cruces *USA* 24C3
Lac Seul, L *Can* 23J4
Lady Ann Str *Can* 23K2
Lae *PNG* 30D1
Laesø, I *Den* 6C1
Lafayette, Indiana *USA* 25E2
Lafayette, Louisiana *USA* 25D3
La Flèche *France* 8B2
Lagan, R *Sweden* 6C1
Lagarto *Brazil* 29L6
Lagoa dos Patos, Lg *Brazil* 27F4
Lago Agrio *Ecuador* 28C4
Lagoa mar Chiquita, L *Arg* 27D4
Lagoa Mirim, L *Urug/Brazil* 27F4
Lago Argentino, L *Arg* 27B8
Lago Buenos Aries, L *Arg* 27B7
Lago Cochrane, L *Chile/Arg* 27B7
Lago Colhué Huapi, L *Arg* 27C7
Lago de Chapala, L *Mexico* 26B2
Lago de Chiriqui, L *Panama* 28B2
Lago de la Laja, L *Chile* 27B5
Lago del Coghinas, L *Sardegna* 10B2
Lago de Maracaibo, L *Ven* 28D2
Lago de Perlas, L *Nic* 28B1
Lago di Bolsena, L *Italy* 10C2
Lago di Bracciano, L *Italy* 10C2
Lago di Como, L *Italy* 10B1
Lago di Garda, L *Italy* 10C1
Lago General Carrera, L *Chile* 27B7
Lago Maggiore, L *Italy* 10B1
Lago Musters, L *Arg* 27C7
Lago Nahuel Haupi, L *Arg* 27B6
Lago O'Higgins, L *Chile* 27B7
Lago Omodeo, L *Sardegna* 10B2
Lago Poopó, L *Bol* 28E7
Lago Ranco, L *Chile* 27B6
Lago Rogaguado, L *Bol* 28E6
Lagos *Nig* 18C4
Lagos *Port* 9A2
Lago San Martin, L *Chile/Arg* 27B7
Lagos de Moreno *Mexico* 26B2
Lago Titicaca *Bol/Peru* 28E7
Lago Viedma, L *Arg* 27B7
La Grande *USA* 24B2
La Grande Rivière, R *Can* 23L4
Lagrange *Aust* 30B2
La Grange, Georgia *USA* 25E3
La Gran Sabana, Mts *Ven* 28F2
Laguna de Caratasca, Lg *Honduras* 26D3
Laguna de Managua, L *Nicaragua* 26D3
Laguna de Nicaragua, L *Nicaragua* 26D3
Laguna de Tamiahua, Lg *Mexico* 26C2
Laguna de Términos, Lg *Mexico* 26C3
Laguna Madre, Lg *Mexico* 26C2
Laguna Seca *Mexico* 24C4
Lahore *India* 15F2
Lahti *Fin* 2K6
Lai *Chad* 20B3
Laihia *Fin* 2J6
Lairg *Scot* 4C2
Lajes *Brazil* 27F3
La Junta *USA* 24C3
Lake Charles *USA* 25D3
Lake District, Region *Eng* 5D4
Lake Eyre Basin *Aust* 30C3
Lake Harbour *Can* 23M3
Lake of the Woods *Can* 23J5
Lake Pukaki *NZ* 32B2
Lakeview *USA* 24A2
Lakonikós Kólpos, G *Greece* 11E3
Lakota *Ivory Coast* 18B4
Laksefjord, Inlet *Nor* 2K4
Lakselv *Nor* 2K4
La Libertad *Ecuador* 28B4
La Linea *Spain* 9A2
La Loche *Can* 22H4
La Malbaie *Can* 23L5
La Mancha, Region *Spain* 9B2
Lamar, Colorado *USA* 24C3
Lambaréné *Gabon* 20B4
Lambayeque *Peru* 28B5
Lamblon,C *Can* 22F2
Lamego *Port* 9A1

La Merced Luckenwalde

La Merced *Peru* 28C6
Lamía *Greece* 11E3
Lammermuir Hills *Scot* 4D4
Lammhult *Sweden* 2G7
Lamotrek, I *Pacific O* 17H6
Lampeter *Wales* 5C5
Lamu *Kenya* 20E4
Lanark *Scot* 4D4
Lancashire, County *Eng* 5D5
Lancaster *Eng* 5D4
Lancaster, Pennsylvania *USA* 25F3
Lancaster Sd *Can* 23K2
Landeck *Austria* 6C3
Lander *USA* 24C2
Landsberg *W Germ* 6C3
Lands End, C *Can* 22F2
Land's End, Pt *Eng* 5C6
Landshut *W Germ* 6C3
Làndskrona *Sweden* 2G7
Langenhagen *W Germ* 6B2
Langholm *Scot* 4D4
Langjökull, Mts *Iceland* 2A2
Langon *France* 8B3
Langres *France* 8D2
Lang Shan, Mts *China* 16D2
Languedoc, Region *France* 8C3
Lanin, Mt *Arg* 27B5
Lansdowne House *Can* 23K4
Lansing *USA* 25E2
Lanzarote, I *Canary Is* 18A2
Lanzhou *China* 16D3
Laoag *Phil* 17F5
Laois, County *Irish Rep* 5B5
La Oroya *Peru* 28C6
Laos, Republic *SE Asia* 17D5
Lapalisse *France* 8C2
La Palma, I *Canary Is* 18A2
La Palmas *Panama* 28C2
La Paragua *Ven* 28F2
La Paz *Arg* 27E4
La Paz *Bol* 28E7
La Paz *Mexico* 26A2
La Perouse,, Str *USSR/Japan* 16H2
La Plata *Arg* 27E4
Lappeenranta *Fin* 2K6
Lappland, Region *Sweden/Fin* 2H5
Laptev S *USSR* 13O2
Lapua *Fin* 2J6
La Purisma *Mexico* 24B4
Laqiya Arba'in, Well *Sudan* 20C1
La Quiaca *Arg* 27C2
L'Aquila *Italy* 10C2
Laramie *USA* 24C2
Laramie Range, Mts *USA* 24C2
Laredo *USA* 24D4
Largs *Scot* 4C4
La Rioja *Arg* 27C3
La Rioja, State *Arg* 27C3
Lárisa *Greece* 11E3
Larne *N Ire* 4B4
La Robla *Spain* 9A1
La Rochelle *France* 8B2
La Roche-sur-Yon *France* 8B2
La Roda *Spain* 9B2
La Ronge *Can* 22H4
Larvik *Nor* 2F7
Lar'yak *USSR* 12J3
La Sagra, Mt *Spain* 9B2
La Sarre *Can* 23L5
Lascombe *Can* 22G4
La Serena *Chile* 27B3
Las Flores *Arg* 27E5
La Sila, Mts *Italy* 10D3
Las Marismas, Marshland *Spain* 9A2
Las Palmas de Gran Canaria *Canary Is* 18A2
La Spezia *Italy* 10B2
Las Plumas *Arg* 27C6
Lastoursville *Gabon* 20B4
Lastovo, I *Yugos* 10D2
Las Tres Marias, Is *Mexico* 26B2
Las Vegas *USA* 24B3
Las Vegas *USA* 24C3
Latina *Italy* 10C2
La Tortuga, I *Ven* 28E1
La Tuque *Can* 23L5
Latviyskaya SSR, Fed Republic *USSR* 7E1
Lau Group, Is *Fiji* 31H2
Launceston *Aust* 30D5
Launceston *Eng* 5C6
La Unión *Chile* 27B6
La Union *El Salvador* 26D3
La Unión *Peru* 28C5
Laura *Aust* 30D2
Laurel, Mississippi *USA* 25E3
Lausanne *Switz* 10B1
Lautaro *Chile* 27B7
Lautoka, I *Fiji* 25G2
Laval *France* 8B2
Lavras *Brazil* 29K8
Lawrence *NZ* 32A3
Lawton *USA* 24D3
Laylo *Sudan* 20D3
La'youn *Mor* 18A2
Laz Daua *Somalia* 19D3
Lead *USA* 24C2
Leba *Pol* 7D2
Lebanon, Republic *S W Asia* 14B2
Lebombo, Mts *Mozam/S Africa/Swaziland* 21D6
Lebork *Pol* 7D2
Lebu *Chile* 27B5
Lecce *Italy* 11D2
Lecco *Italy* 10B1
Le Creusot *France* 8C2
Ledbury *Eng* 5D5
Leeds *Eng* 3C3
Leek *Eng* 5D5
Leer *W Germ* 6B2
Leeuwarden *Neth* 6B2
Leeuwin,C *Aust* 30A4
Legnica *Pol* 6D2
Leguan Inlet *Guyana* 29G2
Legulzamo *Colombia* 28D4
Le Harve *France* 8C2
Leibnitz *Austria* 6D3
Leicester, County *Eng* 5E5
Leicester *Eng* 5E5
Leichhardt, R *Aust* 30C2
Leiden *Neth* 6A2
Leigh Creek *Aust* 30C4
Leighton Buzzard *Eng* 5E6
Leine, R *W Germ* 6B2
Leinster, Region *Irish Rep* 5B5
Leipzig *E Germ* 6C2
Leiria *Port* 9A2
Leirvik *Nor* 2F7
Lek, R *Neth* 6A2
Lekemti *Eth* 20D3
Lelija, Mt *Yugos* 11D2
Leman Bank, Gasfield *N Sea* 5G5
Le Mans *France* 8C2
Lemicux Is *Can* 23M3
Lemmon *USA* 24C2
Lempdes *France* 8C2
Le Murge, Region *Italy* 10D2
Lena *USSR* 16D1
Lena, R *USSR* 13O3
Leninabad *USSR* 15E1
Leninakan *USSR* 12F5
Leningrad *USSR* 12E4
Leninogorsk *USSR* 16B1
Leninsk-Kuznetskiy *USSR* 12K4
Lensk *USSR* 13N3
Lentini *Italy* 10C3
Leoben *Austria* 10C1
Leominster *Eng* 5D5
Leon *Mexico* 26B2
León *Nic* 28A1
Leon, Region *Spain* 9A1
León *Spain* 9A1
Leonora *Aust* 30B3
Le Puy *France* 8C2
Léré *Chad* 20B3
Lérida *Spain* 9C1
Léros, I *Greece* 11F3
Lerwick *Scot* 3C1
Leskovac *Yugos* 11E2
Les Landes, Region *France* 8B3
Lesosibirsk *USSR* 13L4
Lesotho, Kingdom *Africa* 21C6
Les Sables-d'Olonne *France* 8B2
Lésvos, I *Greece* 11F3
Leszno *Pol* 6D2
Lethbridge *Can* 22G5
Lethem *Guyana* 29G3
Letichev *USSR* 7F3
Let Oktyobr'ya *USSR* 13N4
le Touquet-Paris-Plage *France* 5F6
Le Tréport *France* 8C1
Leuven *Belg* 6A2
Levádhia *Greece* 11E3
Levanger *Nor* 2G6
Levice *Czech* 7D3
Levin *NZ* 32C2
Lévis *Can* 23L5
Lévka Óri, Mt *Greece* 11E3
Levkás *Greece* 11E3
Levkás, I *Greece* 11E3
Lévque,C *Aust* 30B2
Levski *Bulg* 11F2
Lewes *Eng* 5F6
Lewis, I *Scot* 3B2
Lewis P *NZ* 32B2
Lewis Range, Mts *USA* 24B2
Lewiston, Idaho *USA* 24B2
Lewiston, Maine *USA* 25F2
Lewistown, Montana *USA* 24C2
Lexington, Kentucky *USA* 25E3
Lezhe *Alb* 11D2
Lhasa *China* 15H2
Lhunze *China* 16C4
Liard, R *Can* 22F3
Liard River *Can* 22F4
Libenge *Zaïre* 20B3
Liberal *USA* 24C3
Liberec *Czech* 6C2
Liberia, Republic *Africa* 18A4
Libourne *France* 8B3
Libreville *Gabon* 20A3
Libya, Republic *Africa* 19A2
Libyan Desert *Libya* 19B2
Libyan Plat *Egypt* 19B1
Licata *Italy* 10C3
Lichfield *Eng* 5E5
Lichinga *Mozam* 21D5
Lidköping *Sweden* 2G7
Lido di Ostia *Italy* 10C2
Liechtenstein, Principality *Europe* 10B1
Liège *Belg* 6B2
Lielupe, R *USSR* 7E1
Lienart *Zaïre* 20C3
Lienz *Austria* 6C3
Liepäja *USSR* 2J7
Liezen *Austria* 6C3
Liffey, R *Irish Rep* 5B5
Lifford *Irish Rep* 4B4
Lifu, I *Nouville Calédonie* 31F3
Ligonha, R *Mozam* 21D5
Ligurian, S *Italy* 10B2
Lihir Group, Is *PNG* 31E1
Likasi *Zaïre* 21C5
Lille *France* 8C1
Lillehammer *Nor* 2G6
Lillestrøm *Nor* 2G7
Lilongwe *Malawi* 21D5
Lim, R *Yugos* 11D2
Lima *Peru* 28C6
Lima *Spain* 9A1
Lima *USA* 25E2
Limavady *N Ire* 4B4
Limbe *Malawi* 21D5
Limburg *W Gem* 6B2
Limeira *Brazil* 29J8
Limerick *Irish Rep* 3B3
Limfjorden, L *Den* 6B1
Limmen Bight, B *Aust* 30C2
Límnos, I *Greece* 11F3
Limoeiro *Brazil* 29L5
Limoges *France* 8C2
Limón *Costa Rica* 26D4
Limon *USA* 24C3
Limousin, Region *France* 8C2
Linares *Chile* 27B5
Linares *Mexico* 24D4
Linares *Spain* 9B2
Lincang *China* 16C4
Lincoln *Arg* 27D4
Lincoln, County *Eng* 5E5
Lincoln *Eng* 5E5
Lincoln, Nebraska *USA* 24D2
Lincoln *NZ* 32B2
L'Incudina, Mt *Corse* 10B2
Lindau *W Germ* 6B3
Linden *Guyana* 29G2
Lindesnes, C *Nor* 2F7
Lindi *Tanz* 21D4
Lindi, R *Zaïre* 20C3
Lindos *Greece* 11F3
Lingen *W Germ* 6B2
Linguère *Sen* 18A3
Linhares *Brazil* 29L7
Linköping *Sweden* 2H7
Linxi *China* 16E2
Linz *Austria* 6C3
Lipari, I *Italy* 10C3
Lipova *Rom* 11E1
Lippe, R *W Germ* 6B2
Lira *Uganda* 20D3
Liranga *Congo* 20B4
Lisala *Zaïre* 20C3
Lisboa *Port* 9A2
Lisburn *N Ire* 5B4
Lisieux *France* 8C2
Lismore *Aust* 31E3
Litani, R *Suriname* 29H3
Lithgow *Aust* 30E4
Litovskaya SSR, Republic *USSR* 7E1
Little Abaco, I *Bahamas* 25F4
Little Barrier I *NZ* 32C1
Little Cayman, I *Caribbean* 26D3
Little Halibut Bank, Sand-bank *Scot* 4E2
Little Rock *USA* 25D3
Livanátais *Greece* 11E3
Livāni *USSR* 7F1
Liverpool *Can* 23M5
Liverpool *Eng* 5D5
Liverpool B *Can* 22E2
Liverpool B *Eng* 5D5
Liverpool,C *Can* 23L2
Livingston, Montana *USA* 24B2
Livno *Yugos* 10D2
Livorno *Italy* 10C2
Liwale *Tanz* 21D4
Lizard Pt *Eng* 5C7
Ljubljana *Yugos* 10C1
Ljungan, R *Sweden* 2G6
Ljungby *Sweden* 2G7
Ljusdal *Sweden* 2H6
Llandeilo *Wales* 5D6
Llandovery *Wales* 5D6
Llandrindod Wells *Wales* 5D5
Llandudno *Wales* 5D5
Llanelli *Wales* 5C6
Llangollen *Wales* 5D5
Llano Estacado, Plat *USA* 24C3
Llanos de Chiquitos, Region *Bol* 28F7
Llerena *Spain* 9A2
Lleyn, Pen *Wales* 5C5
Llimsk *USSR* 13M4
Lloydminster *Can* 22H4
Llullaillaco, Mt *Chile/Arg* 27C2
Loa, R *Chile* 27C2
Loan *France* 8C2
Loange, R *Zaïre* 20B4
Lobaye, R *CAR* 20B3
Lobito *Angola* 21B5
Loch Awe, L *Scot* 4C3
Lochboisdale *Scot* 4B3
Loch Bracadale, Inlet *Scot* 4B3
Loch Broom, Estuary *Scot* 4C3
Loch Doon, L *Scot* 4C4
Loch Earn, L *Scot* 4C3
Loch Eriboll, Inlet *Scot* 4C2
Loch Ericht, L *Scot* 4C3
Loches *France* 8C2
Loch Etive, Inlet *Scot* 4C3
Loch Ewe, Inlet *Scot* 4C3
Loch Fyne, Inlet *Scot* 4C3
Loch Hourn, Inlet *Scot* 4C3
Loch Indaal, Inlet *Scot* 4B4
Lochinver *Scot* 4C2
Loch Katrine, L *Scot* 4C3
Loch Leven, L *Scot* 4D3
Loch Linnhe, Inlet *Scot* 4C3
Loch Lochy, L *Scot* 4C3
Loch Lomond, L *Scot* 4C3
Loch Long, Inlet *Scot* 4C3
Lochmaddy *Scot* 4B3
Loch Maree, L *Scot* 4C3
Loch Morar, L *Scot* 4C3
Lochnagar, Mt *Scot* 4D3
Loch Ness, L *Scot* 4C3
Loch Rannoch, L *Scot* 4C3
Loch Roag, Inlet *Scot* 4B2
Loch Sheil, L *Scot* 4C3
Loch Shin, L *Scot* 4C2
Loch Snizort, Inlet *Scot* 4B3
Loch Sunart, Inlet *Scot* 4C3
Loch Tay, L *Scot* 4C3
Loch Torridon, Inlet *Scot* 4C3
Lockerbie *Scot* 4D4
Locri *Italy* 10D3
Lodi *Italy* 10B1
Lodja *Zaïre* 20C4
Lodwar *Kenya* 20D3
Łódź *Pol* 7D2
Lofoten, Is *Nor* 2G5
Logan, Utah *USA* 24B2
Logan,Mt *Can* 22D3
Logroño *Spain* 9B1
Lohja *Fin* 2J6
Loimaa *Fin* 2J6
Loir, R *France* 8C2
Loire, R *France* 8C2
Loja *Ecuador* 28C4
Loja *Spain* 9B2
Lokan Tekojärvi, Res *Fin* 2K5
Lokitaung *Kenya* 20D3
Loknya *USSR* 7F1
Lokolo, R *Zaïre* 20C4
Lokoro, R *Zaïre* 20C4
Loks Land, I *Can* 23M3
Lolland, I *Den* 6C2
Lom *Bulg* 11E2
Lomami, R *Zaïre* 21C4
Loma Mts *Sierra Leone/Guinea* 18A4
Lombok, I *Indon* 17E7
Lomé *Togo* 18C4
Lomela *Zaïre* 20C4
Lomela, R *Zaïre* 20C4
Lomond, Oilfield *N Sea* 4G3
Łomza *Pol* 7E2
Loncoche *Chile* 27B5
London *Can* 23K5
London *Eng* 5E6
Londonderry, County *N Ire* 4B4
Londonderry *N Ire* 4B4
Londonderry, I *Chile* 27B9
Londonderry,C *Aust* 30B2
Londres *Arg* 27C3
Londrina *Brazil* 27F2
Long, I *Bahamas* 25F4
Long, I *PNG* 17H7
Long Beach, California *USA* 24B3
Longford, County *Irish Rep* 5B5
Longford *Irish Rep* 5B5
Long Forties, Region *N Sea* 4E3
Long I *Can* 23L4
Long I *PNG* 30D1
Long I *USA* 25F2
Longlac *Can* 23K4
Longmont *USA* 24C2
Longquimay *Chile* 27B5
Longreach *Aust* 30D3
Longtown *Eng* 4D4
Longview, Texas *USA* 25D3
Longview, Washington *USA* 24A2
Longwy *France* 8D2
Lons-le-Saunier *France* 8D2
Lookout,C *USA* 25F3
Loolmalasin, Mt *Tanz* 20D4
Lopez, C *Gabon* 20A4
Lop Nur, L *China* 16C2
Lora del Rio *Spain* 9A2
Lorain *USA* 25E2
Lorca *Spain* 9B2
Lord Howe, I *Aust* 31E4
Lord Mayor B *Can* 23J3
Lordsburg *USA* 24C3
Lorient *France* 8B2
Lörrach *W Germ* 6B3
Lorraine, Region *France* 8D2
Los Alamos *USA* 24C3
Los Angeles *Chile* 27B5
Los Angeles *USA* 24B3
Lošinj, I *Yugos* 10C2
Los Mochis *Mexico* 26B2
Lossiemouth *Scot* 4D3
Los Vilos *Chile* 27B4
Lot, R *France* 8C3
Lothian, Region *Scot* 4D4
Lotikipi Plain *Sudan/Kenya* 20D3
Loto *Zaïre* 20C4
Lotta, R *Fin USSR* 2K5
Loudéac *France* 8B2
Louga *Sen* 18A3
Lough Allen, L *Irish Rep* 5B4
Lough Boderg, L *Irish Rep* 5B5
Loughborough *Eng* 5E5
Lough Bowna, L *Irish Rep* 5B5
Lough Conn, L *Irish Rep* 3B3
Lough Corrib, L *Irish Rep* 3B3
Lough Derg, L *Irish Rep* 3B3
Lough Derravaragh, L *Irish Rep* 5B5
Loughead I *Can* 22H2
Lough Ennell, L *Irish Rep* 5B5
Lough Erne, L *N Ire* 3B3
Lough Erne, L *N Ire* 5B4
Lough Foyle, Estuary *N Ire/Irish Rep* 3B2
Lough Neagh, L *N Ire* 3B3
Lough Oughter, L *Irish Rep* 5B4
Lough Ree, L *Irish Rep* 5B5
Lough Sheelin, L *Irish Rep* 5B5
Lough Swilly, Estuary *Irish Rep* 4B4
Louisiade Arch *Solomon Is* 31E2
Louisiana, State *USA* 25D3
Louisville, Kentucky *USA* 25E3
Lourdes *France* 8B3
Louth, County *Irish Rep* 5B5
Louth *Eng* 5E5
Louviers *France* 8C2
Lovech *Bulg* 11E2
Lóvere *Italy* 10C1
Low,C *Can* 23K3
Lowell, Massachusetts *USA* 25F2
Lower Hutt *NZ* 32B2
Lower Seal,L *Can* 23L4
Lowestoft *Eng* 5F5
Łowicz *Pol* 7D2
Loyd George Mt *Can* 22F4
Loznica *Yugos* 11D2
Lozva, R *USSR* 12H3
Lucacano *Angola* 21C5
Luachimo *Angola* 21C4
Lualaba, R *Zaïre* 20C4
Luampa *Zambia* 21C5
Luân *Angola* 21C5
Luanda *Angola* 21B4
Luando, R *Angola* 21B5
Luanginga, R *Angola* 21C5
Luangue, R *Angola* 21B4
Luangwa, R *Zambia* 21D5
Luanshya *Zambia* 21C5
Luapula, R *Zaïre* 21C5
Luarca *Spain* 9A1
Lubalo *Angola* 21B4
L'uban *USSR* 7F2
Lubango *Angola* 21B5
Lubbock *USA* 24C3
Lübeck *W Germ* 6C2
Lubefu *Zaïre* 20C4
Lubefu, R *Zaïre* 20C4
Lubero *Zaïre* 20C3
Lubilash, R *Zaïre* 21C4
Lublin *Pol* 7E2
Lubudi *Zaïre* 21C4
Lubudi, R *Zaïre* 21C4
Lubumbashi *Zaïre* 21C5
Lubutu *Zaïre* 20C4
Lucca *Italy* 10C2
Luce, B *Scot* 4C4
Lucenec *Czech* 7D3
Luckenwalde *E Germ* 6C2

Lucknow Mbarara

Lucknow *India* 15G3
Lucusse *Angola* 21C5
Lüda *China* 16F3
Lüderitz *Namibia* 21B6
Ludlow *Eng* 5D5
Ludogorie, Upland *Bulg* 11F2
Luduş *Rom* 11E1
Ludvika *Sweden* 2H6
Ludwigsburg *W Germ* 6B3
Ludwigshafen *W Germ* 6B3
Ludwigslust *E Germ* 6C2
Luebo *Zaïre* 20C4
Luema, R *Zaïre* 20C4
Luembe, R *Angola* 21C4
Luena *Angola* 21B5
Luene, R *Angola* 21C5
Lufkin *USA* 25D3
Lugano *Switz* 10B1
Lugela *Mozam* 21D5
Lugenda, R *Mozam* 21D5
Lugo *Spain* 9A1
Lugoj *Rom* 11E1
Lui, R *Angola* 21B4
Luiana *Angola* 21C5
Luiana, R *Angola* 21C5
Luionga, R *Zaïre* 20B3
Luishia *Zaïre* 21C5
Luixi *China* 16C4
Luiza *Zaïre* 21C4
Lukenie, R *Zaïre* 20B4
Lukolela *Zaïre* 20B4
Łuków *Pol* 7E2
Lukuga, R *Zaïre* 20C4
Lukulu *Zambia* 21C5
Luleå *Sweden* 2J5
Lüleburgaz *Turk* 11F2
Lullaillaco, Mt *Chile* 28E8
Lulonga, R *Zaïre* 20C3
Lumbala *Angola* 21C5
Lumberton *USA* 25F3
Lumeje *Angola* 21C5
Lumsden *NZ* 32A3
Lund *Sweden* 2G7
Lundazi *Zambia* 21D5
Lundi, R *Zim* 21D6
Lundy, I *Eng* 5C6
Lüneburg *W Germ* 6C2
Lunga, R *Zambia* 21C5
Lungue Bungo, R *Angola* 21B5
Luninec *USSR* 7F2
Luobomo *Congo* 20B4
Luoyang *China* 16E3
Luozi *Zaïre* 20B4
Lupane *Zim* 21C5
Lupilichi *Mozam* 21D5
Luque *Par* 27E3
Lurgan *N Ire* 5B4
Lurio, R *Mozam* 21D5
Lusaka *Zambia* 21C5
Lusambo *Zaïre* 20C4
Lushnjë *Alb* 11D2
Lushoto *Tanz* 20D4
Lushui *China* 16C4
Luton *Eng* 5E6
Luuq *Somalia* 20E3
Luvua, R *Zaïre* 21C4
Luwegu, R *Tanz* 21D4
Luwingu *Zambia* 21D5
Luxembourg *Lux* 8D2
Luxembourg, Grand Duchy *Lux* 8D2
Luxor *Egypt* 19C2
Luzern *Switz* 10B1
L'vov *USSR* 7E3
Lybster *Scot* 4D2
Lycksele *Sweden* 2H6
Lydenburg *S Africa* 21C6
Lyell,Mt *USA* 24B3
Lyme B *Eng* 5D6
Lyme Regis *Eng* 5D6
Lynchburg *USA* 25F3
Lynx L *Can* 22H3
Lyon *France* 8C2
Lyons, R *Aust* 30A3
Lyttelton *NZ* 32B2
Lyubeshov *USSR* 7F2

M

Maastricht *Belg* 6B2
Mabaruma *Guyana* 29G2
Mablethorpe *Eng* 5F5
Mabote *Mozam* 21D6
Mabrita *USSR* 7E2
M'adel *USSR* 7F2
McAlester *USA* 24D3
McAllen *USA* 24D4
Macaloge *Mozam* 21D5
Macapá *Brazil* 29H3
Macas *Ecuador* 28C4
Macaú *Brazil* 29L5
Macau, Dependency *China* 16E4
M'Bari, R *CAR* 20C3
Macclesfield *Eng* 5D5
McClintock B *Can* 23K1
McClintock Chan *Can* 22H2
McClure Str *Can* 22G2
McCook *USA* 24C2
Macculloch,C *Can* 23L2
McDame *Can* 22F4
Macdonnell Ranges, Mts *Aust* 30C3
Macedo de Cavaleiros *Port* 9A1
Maceió *Brazil* 29L5
Macenta *Guinea* 18B4
Macerata *Italy* 10C2
McGrath *USA* 22C3
Machaíla *Mozam* 21D6
Machakos *Kenya* 20D4
Machala *Ecuador* 28C4
Machaze *Mozam* 21D6
Machiques *Ven* 28D1
Machu-Picchu, Hist Site *Peru* 28D6
Macia *Mozam* 21D6
Mackay *Aust* 30D3
Mackay,L *Aust* 30B3
McKean, I *Phoenix Is* 31H1
Mackenzie, R *Can* 22F3
Mackenzie, Region *Can* 22F3
Mackenzie B *Can* 22E3
Mackenzie King I *Can* 22G2
Mackenzie Mts *Can* 22E3
Mackinson Inlet, B *Can* 23L2
McLennan *Can* 22G4
McLeod B *Can* 22G3
McLeod,L *Aust* 30A3
Macmillan, R *Can* 22E3
Macomer *Sardegna* 10B2
Macomia *Mozam* 21D5
Mâcon *France* 8C2
Macon, Georgia *USA* 25E3
Macondo *Angola* 21C5
McTavish Arm, B *Can* 22G3
McVicar Arm, B *Can* 22F3
M'yaróvár *Hung* 6D3
Madadi, Well *Chad* 20C2
Madagascar, I *Indian O* 21E5
Madama *Niger* 20B1
Madang *PNG* 30D1
Madaoua *Niger* 18C3
Madeira, I *Atlantic O* 18A1
Madeira, R *Brazil* 28F5
Madera *Mexico* 26B2
Madimba *Zaïre* 20B4
Madingo Kayes *Congo* 20B4
Madingou *Congo* 20B4
Madison, Indiana *USA* 25E3
Madison, Wisconsin *USA* 25E2
Mado Gashi *Kenya* 20D3
Madras *India* 15F4
Madre de Dios, I *Chile* 27A8
Madre de Dios, R *Bol* 28E6
Madrid *Spain* 9B1
Madridejos *Spain* 9B2
Madurai *India* 15F5
Maevatanana *Madag* 21E5
Maewo, I *Vanuatu* 31F2
Mafia, I *Tanz* 21D4
Mafra *Brazil* 27G3
Magadan *USSR* 13R4
Magargué *Colombia* 28D2
Magdalene *Mexico* 26A1
Magdalen Is *Can* 23M5
Magdeburg *E Germ* 6C2
Magdelena, R *Colombia* 28D2
Magé *Brazil* 29K8
Magherafelt *N Ire* 4B4
Maglie *Italy* 11D2
Magoé *Mozam* 21D5
Maguse River *Can* 23J3
Mahajanga *Madag* 21E5
Mahanoro *Madag* 21E5
Mahavavy, R *Madag* 21E5
Mahéli, I *Comoros* 21E5
Mahenge *Tanz* 21D4
Mahia Pen *NZ* 32C1
Mahón *Spain* 9C2
Maicao *Colombia* 28D1
Maidstone *Eng* 5F6
Maiduguri *Nig* 20B2
Mai-Ndombe, L *Zaïre* 20B4
Maine, State *USA* 25G2
Mainland, I *Scot* 4D2
Maintirano *Madag* 21E5
Mainz *W Germ* 6B2
Maio, I *Cape Verde* 18A4
Maipó, Mt *Arg/Chile* 27C4
Maiquetía *Ven* 28E1
Maitland, New South Wales *Aust* 30E4
Majene *Indon* 30A1
Majes, R *Peru* 28D7
Maji *Eth* 20D3
Makale *Eth* 20D2
Makarska *Yugos* 10D2
Makassar Str *Indon* 17E7
Makeni *Sierra Leone* 18A4
Makgadikgadi, Salt Pan *Botswana* 21C6
Makindu *Kenya* 20D4
Makkovik *Can* 23N4
Makó *Hung* 7E3
Makokou *Gabon* 20B3
Makorako,Mt *NZ* 32C1
Makoua *Congo* 20B3
Makumbi *Zaïre* 20C4
Makurdi *Nig* 18C4
Malacca,Str of *Indon/Malay* 17D6
Málaga *Colombia* 28D2
Malaga *Spain* 9B2
Malaimbandy *Madag* 21E6
Malaita, I *Solomon Is* 31F1
Malakal *Sudan* 20D3
Malang *Indon* 17E7
Malange *Angola* 21B4
Mal Anyuy, R *USSR* 13S3
Mälaren, L *Sweden* 2H7
Malatya *Turk* 14B2
Malawi, Republic *Africa* 21D5
Malaysia, Federation *S E Asia* 17D6
Malbork *Pol* 7D2
Malchin *E Germ* 6C2
Maldives Is *Indian O* 15F5
Maldonado *Urug* 27F4
Malé Karpaty, Upland *Czech* 6D3
Malekula, I *Vanuatu* 31F2
Malema *Mozam* 21D5
Malgomaj, L *Sweden* 2H5
Malha, Well *Sudan* 20C2
Mali, Republic *Africa* 18B3
Malin *USSR* 7F2
Malindi *Kenya* 20E4
Malin Head, Pt *Irish Rep* 3B2
Malkara *Turk* 11F2
Malko Tŭrnovo *Bulg* 11F2
Mallaig *Scot* 4C3
Mallawi *Egypt* 19C2
Mallorca, I *Spain* 9C2
Malm *Nor* 2G6
Malmberget *Sweden* 2J5
Malmesbury *Eng* 5D6
Malmö *Sweden* 2G7
Måloy *Nor* 2F6
Malta, Montana *USA* 24C2
Malta, Chan *Malta/Italy* 10C3
Malta, I *Medit S* 10C3
Malton *Eng* 5E4
Malung *Sweden* 2G6
Malyy Kavkaz, Mts *USSR* 12F5
Mama *USSR* 13N4
Mambasa *Zaïre* 20C3
Mamberamo, R *Indon* 17G7
Mambéré, R *CAR* 20B3
Mamfé *Cam* 20A3
Mamoré, R *Bol* 28E6
Mamou *Guinea* 18A3
Mampikony *Madag* 21E5
Man *Ivory Coast* 18B4
Manabo *Madag* 21E6
Manacapuru *Brazil* 28F4
Manacor *Spain* 9C2
Manado *Indon* 17F6
Managua *Nic* 28A1
Manakara *Madag* 21E6
Manam, I *PNG* 30D1
Mananara *Madag* 21E5
Mananjary *Madag* 21E6
Manapouri *NZ* 32A3
Manapouri,L *NZ* 32A3
Manas *China* 15G1
Manas Hu, L *China* 12K5
Manaus *Brazil* 29G4
Man,Calf of, I *Eng* 5C4
Manchester *Eng* 5D5
Manchester, New Hampshire *USA* 25F2
Manchuria, Hist Region *China* 16F2
Manda *Tanz* 21D5
Mandal *Nor* 2F7
Mandalay *Burma* 15H3
Mandalgovĭ *Mongolia* 16D2
Mandalya Körfezi, B *Turk* 11F3
Mandan *USA* 24C2
Mandera *Eth* 20E3
Mandidzudzure *Zim* 21D5
Mandimba *Mozam* 21D5
Mandritsara *Madag* 21E5
Manduria *Italy* 11D2
Manevichi *USSR* 7F2
Manfredonia *Italy* 10D2
Manga, Desert Region *Niger* 20B2
Mangakino *NZ* 32C1
Mangalia *Rom* 11F2
Mangalmé *Chad* 20C2
Mangalore *India* 15F4
Mangnai *China* 16C3
Mangoche *Malawi* 21D5
Mangoky, R *Madag* 21E6
Mangui *China* 13O4
Manhattan *USA* 24D3
Manhuacu *Brazil* 29K8
Mania, R *Madag* 21E5
Manica *Mozam* 21D5
Manicouagan, R *Can* 23M5
Manicouagan Res *Can* 23M4
Maninian *Ivory Coast* 18B3
Man,Isle of *Irish Sea* 3C3
Manitoba, Province *Can* 22J4
Manitoba,L *Can* 22J4
Manitoulin, I *Can* 23K5
Manizales *Colombia* 28C2
Manja *Madag* 21E6
Manjimup *Aust* 30A4
Mankato *USA* 25D2
Mankono *Ivory Coast* 18B4
Manly *NZ* 32B1
Mannar,G of *India* 15F5
Mannheim *W Germ* 6B3
Mano *Sierra Leone* 18A4
Manokwari *Indon* 30C1
Manono *Zaïre* 21C4
Mansa *Zambia* 21C5
Mansel I *Can* 23K3
Mansfield *Eng* 5E5
Mansfield, Ohio *USA* 25E2
Mansyu Deep *Pacific O* 17G5
Manta *Ecuador* 28B4
Mantaro, R *Peru* 28C6
Mantes *France* 8C2
Mantova *Italy* 10C1
Mantta *Fin* 2J6
Manukau *NZ* 31G4
Manus, I *Pacific O* 17H7
Manzanares *Spain* 9B2
Manzanillo *Cuba* 26E2
Manzanillo *Mexico* 26B3
Manzhouli *USSR* 13N5
Manzini *Swaziland* 21D6
Mao *Chad* 20B2
Mapai *Mozam* 21D6
Mapia, Is *Pacific O* 17G6
Maple Creek *Can* 22H5
Maputo *Mozam* 21D6
Maquela do Zombo *Angola* 20B4
Maquinchao *Arg* 27C6
Marabá *Brazil* 29J5
Maracaibo *Ven* 28D1
Maracay *Ven* 28E1
Marādah *Libya* 19A2
Maradi *Niger* 18C3
Maralal *Kenya* 20D3
Maramasike, I *Solomon Is* 31F1
Maramba *Zambia* 21C5
Maranhõa, State *Brazil* 29J4
Marañón, R *Peru* 28C4
Marathon *Can* 23K5
Marbella *Spain* 9B2
Marble Bar *Aust* 30A3
Marburg *W Germ* 6B2
Marche *Belg* 6B2
Marchena *Spain* 9A2
Mar del Plata *Arg* 27E5
Maré, I *Nouvelle Calédonie* 31F3
Mareb, R *Eth* 20D2
Mareeba *Aust* 17H8
Margate *Eng* 5F6
Marghita *Rom* 11E1
Marianas, Is *Pacific O* 17H5
Maria Van Diemen,C *NZ* 25G4
Mariazell *Austria* 6D3
Maribor *Yugos* 10D1
Maricourt *Can* 23L3
Maridi *Sudan* 20C3
Mariehamn *Fin* 2H6
Marienburg *Suriname* 29H2
Mariestad *Sweden* 2G7
Marilia *Brazil* 27G2
Marimba *Angola* 21B4
Marinette *USA* 25E2
Maringá *Brazil* 27F2
Maringa, R *Zaïre* 20C3
Marion, Indiana *USA* 25E2
Marion, Ohio *USA* 25E2
Marion,L *USA* 25E3
Marion Reef *Aust* 31E2
Marjina Gorki *USSR* 7F2
Marka *Somalia* 20E3
Markaryd *Sweden* 6C1
Market Drayton *Eng* 5D5
Market Harborough *Eng* 5E5
Markovo *USSR* 13S3
Marlborough *Aust* 30D3
Marmande *France* 8C3
Marmara Adi, I *Turk* 11F2
Marmaris *Turk* 11F3
Marmolada, Mt *Italy* 10C1
Maro *Chad* 20B3
Maroantsetra *Madag* 21E5
Marondera *Zim* 21D5
Maroni, R *French Guiana* 29H3
Maroua *Cam* 20B2
Marovoay *Madag* 21E5
Marquesas Keys, Is *USA* 25E4
Marquette *USA* 25E2
Marrakech *Mor* 18B1
Marree *Aust* 30C3
Marromeu *Mozam* 21D5
Marrupa *Mozam* 21D5
Marsabit *Kenya* 20D3
Marsala *Italy* 10C3
Marseille *France* 8D3
Marshall, Texas *USA* 25D3
Martigny *Switz* 8D2
Martigues *France* 8D3
Martin *Czech* 7D3
Martinborough *NZ* 32C2
Martinique, I *France* 28F1
Marton *NZ* 32C2
Martos *Spain* 9B2
Mary *USSR* 12H6
Maryborough, Queensland *Aust* 31E3
Mary Henry,Mt *Can* 22F4
Maryland, State *USA* 25F3
Maryport *Eng* 4D4
Maryville, Missouri *USA* 25D2
Marzuq *Libya* 19A2
Masai Steppe, Upland *Tanz* 20D4
Masaka *Uganda* 20D4
Masasi *Tanz* 21D5
Masaya *Nic* 26D3
Mashhad *Iran* 14D2
Masi-Manimba *Zaïre* 20B4
Masindi *Uganda* 20D3
Masisi *Zaïre* 20C4
Masoala, C *Madag* 21F5
Mason City *USA* 25D2
Mass, R *Neth* 6B2
Massa *Italy* 10C2
Massachusetts, State *USA* 25F2
Massakori *Chad* 20B2
Massangena *Mozam* 21D6
Massawa *Eth* 20D2
Massénya *Chad* 20B2
Massif Central, Mts *France* 8C2
Massif de l'Adamaoua, Mts *Cam* 20B3
Massif de l'Isalo, Upland *Madag* 21E6
Massif des Bongo, Upland *CAR* 20C3
Massif du Pelvoux, Mts *France* 8D2
Massif du Tsaratanana, Mt *Madag* 21E5
Massina, Region *Mali* 18B3
Massinga *Mozam* 21D6
Masterton *NZ* 31G5
Matadi *Zaïre* 20B4
Matagalpa *Nic* 28A1
Matagami *Can* 23L5
Matagorda B *USA* 24D4
Matakana I *NZ* 32C1
Matala *Angola* 21B5
Matam *Sen* 18A3
Matameye *Niger* 18C3
Matamoros *Mexico* 26C2
Ma'tan as Sarra, Well *Libya* 19B2
Matane *Can* 23M5
Matanó *Spain* 9C1
Matanzas *Cuba* 26D2
Mataram *Indon* 30A1
Matarani *Peru* 28D7
Mataura *NZ* 32A3
Matehuala *Mexico* 26B2
Matera *Italy* 10D2
Mátészalka *Hung* 7E3
Matlock *Eng* 5E5
Mato Grosso *Brazil* 29G6
Mato Grosso, State *Brazil* 29G6
Mato Grosso do Sul, State *Brazil* 29G7
Matruh *Egypt* 19B1
Mattagami, R *Can* 23K5
Matterhorn, Mt *Switz/Italy* 10B1
Maturin *Ven* 28F2
Maúa *Mozam* 21D5
Maubeuge *France* 8C1
Maun *Botswana* 21C5
Maunoir,L *Can* 22F3
Mauriac *France* 8C2
Mauritania, Republic *Africa* 18A2
Mauritius, I *Indian O* 21F6
Mavinga *Angola* 21C5
Maya, R *USSR* 13P4
Mayaguana, I *Bahamas* 25F4
Mayahi *Niger* 18C3
Mayama *Congo* 20B4
Maybole *Scot* 4C4
May,C *USA* 25F3
Mayenne *France* 8B2
Maykop *USSR* 12F5
Maymaneh *Afghan* 12H6
Mayo *Can* 22E3
Mayor, Mt *Spain* 9C2
Mayor I *NZ* 32C1
Mayor P Lagerenza *Par* 27D1
Mayotte, I *Indian O* 21E5
Mayumba *Gabon* 20B4
Mazabuka *Zambia* 21C5
Mazara del Vallo *Italy* 10C3
Mazatlán *Mexico* 26B2
Mbabane *Swaziland* 21D6
Mbaïki *CAR* 20B3
Mbala *Zambia* 21D4
Mbalabala *Zim* 21C6
Mbale *Uganda* 20D3
Mbalmayo *Cam* 20B3
Mbam, R *Cam* 20B3
Mbamba Bay *Tanz* 21D5
Mbandaka *Zaïre* 20B3
Mbanza Congo *Angola* 20B4
Mbanza-Ngungu *Zaïre* 20B4
Mbarara *Uganda* 20D4

Mbènza Münster

Mbènza *Congo* 20B3
Mbére, R *Cam* 20B3
Mbeya *Tanz* 21D4
Mbinda *Congo* 20B4
Mbout *Maur* 18A3
Mbuji-Mayi *Zaïre* 20C4
Mbulu *Tanz* 20D4
Mcherrah, Region *Alg* 18B2
Mchinji *Malawi* 21D5
Mead,L *USA* 24B3
Meadow Lake *Can* 22H4
Mealy Mts *Can* 23N4
Meander River *Can* 22G4
Meath *Irish Rep* 5B5
Meaux *France* 8C2
Mecca *S Arabia* 14B3
Mechelen *Belg* 6A2
Mecklenburger Bucht, B *E Germ* 6C2
Meconta *Mozam* 21D5
Mecuburi *Mozam* 21D5
Mecufi *Mozam* 21E5
Mecula *Mozam* 21D5
Medan *Indon* 17C6
Medellín *Colombia* 28C2
Medford *USA* 24A2
Medgidia *Rom* 11F2
Mediaş *Rom* 11E1
Medicine Hat *Can* 22G5
Medinaceli *Spain* 9B1
Medina del Campo *Spain* 9A1
Medina de Rio Seco *Spain* 9A1
Medouneu *Gabon* 20B3
Medvezh'i Ova, I *USSR* 13S2
Medvezh'yegorsk *USSR* 12E3
Meekatharra *Aust* 30A3
Mega *Eth* 20D3
Megalópolis *Greece* 11E3
Mégara *Greece* 11E3
Meiganga *Cam* 20B3
Meissen *E Germ* 6C2
Mejillones *Chile* 28D8
Mekambo *Gabon* 20B3
Meknès *Mor* 18B1
Melbourne *Aust* 30D4
Melbourne *USA* 25E4
Melchor Muźguiz *Mexico* 24C4
Melfi *Chad* 20B2
Melfort *Can* 22H4
Melilla *Sp* 18B1
Melimoyu, Mt *Chile* 27B6
Meliville Bugt, B *Greenland* 23M2
Melo *Urug* 27F4
Melton Mowbray *Eng* 5E5
Melun *France* 8C2
Melville *Can* 22H4
Melville Hills, Mts *Can* 22F3
Melville I *Aust* 30C2
Melville I *Can* 22G2
Melville,L *Can* 23N4
Melville Pen *Can* 23K3
Memba *Mozam* 21E5
Memboro *Indon* 30A1
Memmingen *W Germ* 6C3
Memphis, Tennessee *USA* 25E3
Mena *USSR* 7G2
Menai Str *Wales* 5C5
Ménaka *Mali* 18C3
Mende *France* 8C3
Mendebo, Mts *Eth* 20D3
Mendi *PNG* 30D1
Mendip Hills, Upland *Eng* 5D6
Mendoza *Arg* 27C4
Mendoza, State *Arg* 27C5
Menemen *Turk* 11F3
Menindee *Aust* 30D4
Menongue *Angola* 21B5
Menorca, I *Spain* 9C1
Meppen *W Germ* 6B2
Merano *Italy* 10C1
Merauke *Indon* 30D1
Merced *USA* 24A3
Mercedario, Mt *Chile* 27B4
Mercedes *Arg* 27C4
Mercedes, Buenos Aires *Arg* 27E4
Mercedes, Corrientes *Arg* 27E3
Mercedes *Urug* 27E4
Mercury B *NZ* 32C1
Mercury Is *NZ* 32C1
Mercy B *Can* 22F2
Mercy,C *Can* 23M3
Meregh *Somalia* 20E3
Mérida *Mexico* 26D2
Mérida *Spain* 9A2
Mérida *Ven* 28D2
Meridian *USA* 25E3
Merowe *Sudan* 20D2
Merredin *Aust* 30A4
Merrick, Mt *Scot* 4C4
Mers el Kebir *Alg* 9B2
Mersey, R *Eng* 5D5
Merseyside, Metropolitan County *Eng* 5D5
Merthyr Tydfil *Wales* 5D6
Mertola *Port* 9A2
Meru, Mt *Tanz* 20D4
Mesa *USA* 24B3
Meshra Er Req *Sudan* 20C3
Mesolóngion *Greece* 11E3
Messalo, R *Mozam* 21D5
Messina *Italy* 10D3
Messíni *Greece* 11E3
Messiniakós Kólpos, G *Greece* 11E3
Mesta, R *Bulg* 11E2
Mestre *Italy* 10C1
Meta, R *Colombia* 28D3
Meta, R *Ven* 28E2
Meta Incognito Pen *Can* 23L3
Metán *Arg* 27D3
Metangula *Mozam* 21D5
Metaponto *Italy* 10D2
Methil *Scot* 4D3
Methven *NZ* 32B2
Metz *France* 8D2
Meuse, R *France* 8D2
Mexicali *Mexico* 26A1
Mexico, Federal Republic *Central America* 26B2
México *Mexico* 26C3
Mexico,G of *C America* 26C2
Mezen' *USSR* 12F3
Mezha, R *USSR* 7G1
Miami, Florida *USA* 25E4
Miami Beach *USA* 25E4
Miandrivazo *Madag* 21E5
Michalovce *Czech* 7E3
Michigan, State *USA* 25E2
Michigan,L *USA* 25E2
Michigan,L *USA* 25E2
Michipicoten I *Can* 23K5
Michunnsk *USSR* 12F4
Michurin *Bulg* 11F2
Middlesboro *USA* 25E3
Middlesbrough *Eng* 5E4
Mid Glamorgan, County *Wales* 5D6
Midland *Can* 23L5
Midland, Texas *USA* 24C3
Midongy Atsimo *Madag* 21E6
Midžor, Mt *Yugos* 11E2
Mielec *Pol* 7E2
Miercurea-Ciuc *Rom* 11F1
Mieres *Spain* 9A1
Mikhayiovka *USSR* 12F4
Mikhaylovgrad *Bulg* 11E2
Mikhaylovskiy *USSR* 12J4
Mikkeli *Fin* 2K6
Míkonos, I *Greece* 11F3
Mikulov *Czech* 6D3
Mikumi *Tanz* 21D4
Milagro *Ecuador* 28C4
Milange *Mozam* 21D5
Milano *Italy* 10B1
Mildura *Aust* 30D4
Miles *Aust* 30E3
Miles City *USA* 24C2
Milford Haven *Wales* 5C6
Milford Haven, Sd *Wales* 5C6
Milford Sd *NZ* 32A2
Miliana *Alg* 9C2
Mil'Kovo *USSR* 13R4
Millau *France* 8C3
Milne Land, I *Greenland* 23Q2
Mílos, I *Greece* 11E3
Milparinka *Aust* 30D3
Milton *NZ* 32A3
Milwaukee *USA* 25E2
Mina, R *Alg* 9C2
Minas *Urug* 27E4
Minas Gerais, State *Brazil* 29J7
Minatitlan *Mexico* 26C3
Minch,Little, Sd *Scot* 4B3
Minch,North, Sd *Scot* 4B2
Minch,The, Sd *Scot* 3B2
Mindanao, I *Phil* 17F6
Minden *W Germ* 6B2
Mindoro, I *Phil* 17F5
Minehead *Eng* 5D6
Mineiros *Brazil* 29H7
Minna *Nig* 18C4
Minneapolis *USA* 25D2
Minnedosa *Can* 22J4
Minnesota, State *USA* 25D2
Miño, R *Spain* 9A1
Minot *USA* 24C2
Minsk *USSR* 12D4
Minsk Mazowiecki *Pol* 7E2
Minto Inlet, B *Can* 22G2
Minto,L *Can* 23L4
Minusinsk *USSR* 16C1
Miquelon *Can* 23N5
Miramar *Arg* 27E5
Miranda de Ebro *Spain* 9B1
Mirik,C *Maur* 18A3
Mirnoye *USSR* 13K3
Mirnyy *USSR* 13N3
Mironovka *USSR* 7G3
Mirtoan S *Greece* 11E3
Misima, I *Solomon Is* 31E2
Misiones, State *Arg* 27F3
Miskolc *Hung* 7E3
Misoöl, I *Indon* 17G7
Misrātah *Libya* 19A1
Missinaibi, R *Can* 23K5
Mississippi, State *USA* 25D3
Mississippi, R *USA* 25D3
Missoula *USA* 24B2
Missouri, State *USA* 25D3
Missouri, R *USA* 25D2
Mistassini,L *Can* 25F1
Misti, Mt *Peru* 28D7
Mitchell *USA* 24D2
Mitchell, R *Aust* 30D2
Mitchell,Mt *USA* 25E3
Mitchell River *Aust* 17H8
Mitilíni *Greece* 11F3
Mitre, I *Solomon Is* 31G2
Mitu *Colombia* 28D3
Mitumbar, Mts *Zaïre* 20C4
Mitwaba *Zaïre* 21C4
Mitzic *Gabon* 20B3
Miyake, I *Japan* 16G3
Miyako, I *Japan* 16F4
Mizan Teferi *Eth* 20D3
Mizdah *Libya* 19A1
Mizil *Rom* 11F1
Mjolby *Sweden* 2H7
Mkushi *Zambia* 21C5
Mladá Boleslav *Czech* 6C2
Mława *Pol* 7E2
Mljet, I *Yugos* 11D2
Moa, R *Sierra Leone* 18A4
Moab *USA* 24C3
Moanda *Congo* 20B4
Moanda *Gabon* 20B4
Moba *Zaïre* 21C4
Mobaye *CAR* 20C3
Mobayi *Zaire* 20C3
Moberly *USA* 25D3
Mobile *USA* 25E3
Mobile B *USA* 25E3
Mobridge *USA* 24C2
Moçambique *Mozam* 21E5
Moçâmedes *Angola* 21B5
Mocimboa da Praia *Mozam* 21E5
Mocoa *Colombia* 28C3
Mocuba *Mozam* 21D5
Modena *Italy* 10C2
Modesto *USA* 24A3
Modica *Italy* 10C3
Mödling *Austria* 6D3
Moe *Aust* 30D4
Moffat *Scot* 4D4
Mogilev *USSR* 7G2
Mogincual *Mozam* 21E5
Mogocha *USSR* 16E1
Mogochin *USSR* 12K4
Moguer *Spain* 9A2
Mohaka, R *NZ* 32C1
Mohoro *Tanz* 21D4
Mointy *USSR* 12J5
Mo i Rana *Nor* 2G5
Moissac *France* 8C3
Mojave Desert *USA* 24B3
Mokau, R *NZ* 32B1
Mokolo *Cam* 20B2
Moláoi *Greece* 11E3
Molde *Nor* 2F6
Moldoveanu, Mt *Rom* 11E1
Molfetta *Italy* 10D2
Mollendo *Peru* 28D7
Molounddu *Cam* 20B3
Molson L *Can* 24D1
Molucca S *Indon* 30B1
Moluccas, Is *Indon* 17F7
Moma *Mozam* 21D5
Mombaca *Brazil* 29K5
Mombasa *Kenya* 20D1
Mompono *Zaïre* 20C3
Mon, I *Den* 6C2
Monach, Is *Scot* 4B3
Monaco, Principality *Europe* 8D3
Monadhliath, Mts *Scot* 4C3
Monaghan, County *Irish Rep* 5B4
Monaghan *Irish Rep* 5B4
Monashee Mts *Can* 22G4
Monastereven *Irish Rep* 3B3
Monção *Brazil* 29J4
Monchegorsk *USSR* 2L5
Mönchen-gladbach *W Germ* 6B2
Monclova *Mexico* 26B2
Moncton *Can* 23M5
Mondego, R *Port* 9A1
Mondovi *Italy* 10B2
Monfalcone *Italy* 10C1
Monforte de Lemos *Spain* 9A1
Monga *Zaïre* 20C3
Mongala, R *Zaïre* 20C3
Mongalla *Sudan* 20D3
Mongo *Chad* 20B2
Mongolia, Republic *Asia* 16C2
Mongu *Zambia* 21C5
Mönhhaan *Mongolia* 13N5
Monkoto *Zaïre* 20C4
Monmouth *Eng* 5D6
Monopoli *Italy* 11D2
Monreal del Campo *Spain* 9B1
Monroe *USA* 25D3
Monrovia *Lib* 18A4
Mons *Belg* 6A2
Mönsterås *Sweden* 6D1
Montagne d'Ambre, Mt *Madag* 21E5
Montaigu *France* 8B2
Montallo, Mt *Italy* 10D3
Montana, State *USA* 24B2
Montañas de León, Mts *Spain* 9A1
Montargis *France* 8C2
Montauban *France* 8C3
Montbéliard *France* 8D2
Mont Blanc, Mt *France/Italy* 10B1
Montceau les Mines *France* 8C2
Montceny, Mt *Spain* 9C1
Mont-de-Marsin *France* 8B3
Montdidier *France* 8C2
Monteagudo *Bol* 28F7
Monte Alegre *Brazil* 29H4
Monte Amiata, Mt *Italy* 10C2
Monte Bello Is *Aust* 30A3
Monte Carlo *Italy* 10B2
Monte Cimone, Mt *Italy* 10C2
Monte Cinto, Mt *Corse* 10B2
Monte Corno, Mt *Italy* 10C2
Montecristo, I *Italy* 10C2
Monte Gargano, Mt *Italy* 10D2
Montélimar *France* 8C3
Monte Miletto, Mt *Italy* 10C2
Montemorelos *Mexico* 26C2
Montemor-o-Novo *Port* 9A2
Montenegro, Region *Yugos* 11D2
Monte Pollino, Mt *Italy* 10D3
Montepuez *Mozam* 21D5
Monterey, California *USA* 24A3
Monterey B *USA* 24A3
Montería *Colombia* 28C2
Montero *Bol* 28F7
Monterrey *Mexico* 26B2
Montes Claros *Brazil* 29K7
Montes de Toledo, Mts *Spain* 9B2
Montevideo *Urug* 27E4
Monte Viso, Mt *Italy* 10B2
Montgomery, Alabama *USA* 25E3
Mont Gréboun *Niger* 18C2
Monticello, Utah *USA* 24C3
Monti del Gennargentu, Mt *Sardegna* 10B2
Monti Nebrodi, Mts *Italy* 10C3
Mont-Laurier *Can* 23L5
Montluçon *France* 8C2
Montmagny *Can* 23L5
Montoro *Spain* 9B2
Mont Pelat, Mt *France* 8D3
Montpelier, Vermont *USA* 25F2
Montpellier *France* 8C3
Montréal *Can* 23L5
Montreuil *France* 8C1
Montreux *Switz* 10B1
Montrose, Colorado *USA* 24C3
Montrose *Scot* 3C2
Montrose, Oilfield *N Sea* 4F3
Mont-St-Michel *France* 8B2
Monts des Ouled Nail, Mts *Alg* 9C3
Monts du Hodna, Mts *Alg* 9C2
Monument V *USA* 24B3
Monveda *Zaïre* 20C3
Monywa *Burma* 15H3
Monza *Italy* 10B1
Monze *Zambia* 21C5
Moora *Aust* 30A4
Moore,L *Aust* 30A3
Moorfoot Hills *Scot* 4D4
Moorhead *USA* 24D2
Moose, R *Can* 23K4
Moose Jaw *Can* 22H4
Moosomin *Can* 22H4
Moosonee *Can* 23K4
Mopeia *Mozam* 21D5
Mopti *Mali* 18B3
Moquegua *Peru* 28D7
Mora *Sweden* 2G6
Morada *Brazil* 29L5
Morafenobe *Madag* 21E5
Moramanga *Madag* 21E5
Morava, R *Austria/Czech* 6D3
Morava, R *Yugos* 11E2
Moray Firth, Estuary *Scot* 3C2
Morden *Can* 22J5
Morecambe *Eng* 5D4
Morecambe B *Eng* 5D4
Moree *Aust* 30D3
Morelia *Mexico* 26B3
Moresby I *Can* 22E4
Morkoka, R *USSR* 13N3
Morlaix *France* 8B2
Mornington, I *Aust* 30C2
Morobe *PNG* 30D1
Morocco, Kingdom *Africa* 18B1
Morogoro *Tanz* 21D4
Morombe *Madag* 21E6
Morondava *Madag* 21E6
Moron de la Frontera *Spain* 9A2
Moroni *Comoros* 21E5
Moroto *Uganda* 20D3
Morpeth *Eng* 4E4
Morrinsville *NZ* 32C1
Morrumbala *Mozam* 21D5
Morrumbene *Mozam* 21D6
Mortes, R, Malo Grosso *Brazil* 29H6
Morvern, Pen *Scot* 4C3
Mosel, R *W Germ* 6B2
Mosgiel *NZ* 32B3
Moshi *Tanz* 20D4
Mosjøen *Nor* 2G5
Moskal'vo *USSR* 13Q4
Moskva *USSR* 12E4
Moss *Nor* 2G7
Mossaka *Congo* 20B4
Mossendjo *Congo* 20B4
Mossoró *Brazil* 29L5
Most *Czech* 6C2
Mostar *Yugos* 11D2
Mosty *USSR* 7E2
Mosul *Iraq* 14C2
Motala *Sweden* 2H7
Motherwell *Scot* 4D4
Motilla del Palancar *Spain* 9B2
Motril *Spain* 9B2
Motueka *NZ* 32B2
Motueka, R *NZ* 32B2
Mouila *Gabon* 20B4
Mould Bay *Can* 22G2
Moulins *France* 8C2
Moulmein *Burma* 15H4
Moundou *Chad* 20B3
Mount Aigoual, Mt *France* 8C3
Mount Hagen *PNG* 30D1
Mount Isa *Aust* 30C3
Mount Magnet *Aust* 30A3
Mount Mézenc, Mt *France* 8C3
Mount Morgan *Aust* 30E3
Mounts B *Eng* 5C6
Mourne Mts *N Ire* 5B4
Moussoro *Chad* 20B2
Mouths of the Niger *Nigeria* 18C4
Mouydir, Mts *Alg* 18C2
Mouyondzi *Congo* 20B4
Moyale *Kenya* 20D3
Moyamba *Sierra Leone* 18A4
Moyen Atlas, Mts *Mor* 18B1
Moyero, R *USSR* 13M3
Moyo *Uganda* 20D3
Moyobamba *Peru* 28C5
Mozambique, Republic *Africa* 21D6
Mozambique Chan *Mozam/Madag* 21D6
Mozyr, R *USSR* 2K8
Mpanda *Tanz* 20D4
Mpika *Zambia* 21D5
Mporokosa *Zambia* 21D4
Mposhi *Zambia* 21C5
Mpulungu *Zambia* 21D4
Mpwapwa *Tanz* 20D4
Mstislavl' *USSR* 7G2
Mtwara *Tanz* 21E5
Mubende *Uganda* 20D3
Muchinga, Mts *Zambia* 21D5
Muck, I *Scot* 4B3
Mucusso *Angola* 21C5
Mueda *Mozam* 21D5
Mueo *Nouvelle Calédonie* 31F3
Mufulira *Zambia* 21C5
Mugodzhary, Mts *USSR* 12G5
Mühldorf *W Germ* 6C3
Muhlhausen *E Germ* 6C2
Muhos *Fin* 2K6
Muine Bheag *Irish Rep* 5B5
Mujimbeji *Zambia* 21C5
Mukachevo *USSR* 7E3
Muko-jima, I *Japan* 16H4
Mulde, R *E Germ* 6C2
Mulgrave I *Aust* 17H8
Mulhacén, Mt *Spain* 9B2
Mulhouse *France* 8D2
Mull, I *Scot* 4C3
Mullewa *Aust* 30A3
Mullingar *Irish Rep* 5B5
Mull of Kintyre, Pt *Scot* 4C4
Mull of Oa, C *Scot* 4B4
Mulobezi *Zambia* 21C5
Multan *India* 15F2
Mumbwa *Zambia* 21C5
München *W Germ* 6C3
Münden *W Germ* 6B2
Mungbere *Zaïre* 20C3
Muñoz Gomero,Pen *Chile* 27B8
Münster *W Germ* 6B2

Nugssuag **Patta**

Nugssuag, Pen *Greenland* **23N2**
Nûgussuag, I *Greenland* **23N2**
Nui, I *Tuvalu* **31G1**
Nukufetau, I *Tuvalu* **31G1**
Nukulaelae, I *Tuvalu* **31G1**
Nukunon, I *Tokelau Is* **31H1**
Nukus *USSR* **12G5**
Nullarbor Plain *Aust* **30B4**
Numatinna, R *Sudan* **20C3**
Numfoor, I *Indon* **17G7**
Nuoro *Sardegna* **10B2**
Nurmes *Fin* **2K6**
Nürnberg *W Germ* **6C3**
Nutak *Can* **23M4**
Nuyukjuak *Can* **23L3**
Nyahururu Falls *Kenya* **20D3**
Nyai *USA* **22C3**
Nyaingentanglha Shan, Mts *China* **16C3**
Nyakabindi *Tanz* **20D4**
Nyala *Sudan* **20C2**
Nyamlell *Sudan* **20C3**
Nyanda *Zim* **21D6**
Nyanga, R *Gabon* **20B4**
Nyasa L *Malawi/Mozam* **21D5**
Nyborg *Den* **2G7**
Nybro *Sweden* **2H7**
Nyda *USSR* **12J3**
Nyeboes Land, Region *Can* **23M1**
Nyeri *Kenya* **20D4**
Nyimba *Zambia* **21D5**
Nyingchi *China* **15H3**
Nyíregyháza *Hung* **7E3**
Nyiru,Mt *Kenya* **20D3**
Nykarleby *Fin* **2J6**
Nykøbing *Den* **2F7**
Nykøbing *Den* **2G8**
Nyköping *Sweden* **2H7**
Nynäshamn *Sweden* **2H7**
Nyong, R *Cam* **20B3**
Nyons *France* **8D3**
Nysa *Pol* **6D2**
Nyukzha, R *USSR* **16F1**
Nyurba *USSR* **13N3**
Nzega *Tanz* **20D4**
Nzérékore *Guinea* **18B4**

O

Oaggsimiut *Greenland* **23O3**
Oahe Res *USA* **24C2**
Oakland *USA* **24A3**
Oamaru *NZ* **32B3**
Oaxaca *Mexico* **26C3**
Ob', R *USSR* **12J3**
Oban *NZ* **32A3**
Oban *Scot* **4C3**
Obidos *Brazil* **29G4**
Obo *CAR* **20C3**
Obock *Djibouti* **20E2**
Oborniki *Pol* **6D2**
Obskava Guba, B *USSR* **12J2**
Obuasi *Ghana* **18B4**
Ocana *Colombia* **28D2**
Ocaña *Spain* **9B2**
Ocean Falls *Can* **22F4**
Ochil Hills *Scot* **4D3**
Oda *Ghana* **18B4**
Ódáðahraun, Region *Iceland* **2B2**
Odda *Nor* **2F6**
Odemira *Port* **9A2**
Ödemiş *Turk* **11F3**
Odense *Den* **2G7**
Oder, R *Pol/E Germ* **6C2**
Odessa *USSR* **12E5**
Odienné *Ivory Coast* **18B4**
Odra, R *Pol* **7D2**
Oeiras *Brazil* **29K5**
Ofanto, R *Italy* **10D2**
Offaly, County *Irish Rep* **5B5**
Offenbach *W Germ* **6B2**
Ogaden, Region *Eth* **20E3**
Ogasawara Gunto, Is *Japan* **16H4**
Ogbomosho *Nig* **18C4**
Ogden *USA* **24B2**
Ogilvie Mts *Can* **22E3**
Ogooué, R *Gabon* **20A4**
Ogre *USSR* **7E1**
Oguilet Khenachich, Well *Mali* **18B2**
Ogulin *Yugos* **10D1**
Ohai *NZ* **32A3**
Ohakune *NZ* **32C1**
Ohanet *Alg* **18C2**
Ohau,L *NZ* **32A2**
Ohio, State *USA* **25E2**
Ohopoho *Namibia* **21B5**
Ohre, R *Czech* **6C2**
Ohrid *Yugos* **11E2**
Ohridsko Jezero, L *Yugos/Alb* **11E2**
Ohura *NZ* **32B1**
Oiapoque *French Guiana* **29H3**
Oijiaojing *China* **16C2**
Oilian Shan, Mts *China* **13L6**
Oise, R *France* **8C2**
Ojinaga *Mexico* **26B2**
Ojos del Salado, Mt *Arg* **27C3**
Okavango, R *Namibia/Angola* **21B5**
Okavango Delta, Marsh *Botswana* **21C5**
Okhotsk *USSR* **13Q4**
Okhotsk,S of *USSR* **13Q4**
Okinawa, I *Japan* **16F4**
Okinawa gunto, Arch *Japan* **16F4**
Oklahoma, State *USA* **24D3**
Oklahoma City *USA* **24D3**
Okondja *Gabon* **20B4**
Okoyo *Congo* **20B4**
Oktyabr'skiy, Kamchatka *USSR* **16J1**
Olafsvik *Iceland* **2A2**
Öland, I *Sweden* **2H7**
Olavarría *Arg* **27D5**
Olbia *Sardegna* **10B2**
Oldenburg, Niedersachsen *W Germ* **6B2**
Oldenburg, Schleswig-Holstein *W Germ* **6C2**
Oldham *Eng* **5D5**
Old Head of Kinsale, C *Scot* **3B3**
Olekma, R *USSR* **13O4**
Olekminsk *USSR* **13N3**
Olenek *USSR* **13N3**
Olenek, R *USSR* **13O2**
Olevsk *USSR* **7F2**
Ólimbos, Mt *Greece* **11E2**
Olinda *Brazil* **29M5**
Olivares, Mt *Arg* **27C4**
Ollagüe *Chile* **27C2**
Ollagüe, Mt *Bol* **27C2**
Olochi *USSR* **16F1**
Olofstrom *Sweden* **2G7**
Olombo *Congo* **20B4**
Olomouc *Czech* **6D3**
Oloron ste Marie *France* **8B3**
Olovyannaya *USSR* **16E1**
Olsztyn *Pol* **7E2**
Oltul, R *Rom* **11E2**
Omagh *N Ire* **4B4**
Omaha *USA* **24D2**
Oman, Sultanate *Arabian Pen* **14E2**
Oman, G of *UAE* **14D3**
Omboué *Gabon* **20A4**
Omdurman *Sudan* **20D2**
Ommanney B *Can* **22H2**
Omo, R *Eth* **20D3**
Omolay, R *USSR* **13P3**
Omolon, R *USSR* **13R3**
Omsk *USSR* **12J4**
Oncócua *Angola* **21B5**
Ondangua *Namibia* **21B5**
Ondava, R *Czech* **7E3**
Öndörhaan *Molgolia* **16E2**
One and Half Degree Chan *Indian O* **15F5**
Onega *USSR* **12E3**
Onekotan, I *USSR* **16J2**
Onema *Zaïre* **20C4**
Onezhskoye Ozero, L *USSR* **12E3**
Ongiva *Angola* **21B5**
Onilahy, R *Madag* **21E6**
Onitsha *Nig* **18C4**
Onjüül *Mongolia* **16D2**
Onotoa, I *Kiribati* **31G1**
Onslow *Aust* **30A3**
Ontario, Province *Can* **23J4**
Ontario,L *USA/Can* **25F2**
Onteniente *Spain* **9B2**
Ontong Java Atoll *Solomom Is* **31E1**
Oodnadatta *Aust* **30C3**
Ooldea *Aust* **30C4**
Oostende *Belg* **6A2**
Opala *USSR* **13R4**
Opala *Zaïre* **20C4**
Opava *Czech* **7D3**
Opochka *USSR* **7F1**
Opole *Pol* **7D2**
Opotiki *NZ* **32C1**
Oppdal *Nor* **2F6**
Opunake *NZ* **32B1**
Oradea *Rom* **11E1**
Oraefajökull, Mts *Iceland* **2B2**
Oran *Alg* **18B1**
Orán *Arg* **27D2**
Orange *France* **8C3**
Orange, R *S Africa* **21C6**
Orange Free State, Prov *S Africa* **21C6**
Oranienburg *E Germ* **6C2**
Orăstie *Rom* **11E1**
Oravita *Rom* **11E1**
Orbetello *Italy* **10C2**
Ord, R *Aust* **30B2**
Ord,Mt *Aust* **30B2**
Ordos, Desert *China* **13M6**
Örebro *Sweden* **2H7**
Oregon, State *USA* **24A2**
Oregrund *Sweden* **2H6**
Orense *Spain* **9A1**
Oresund, Str *Den/Sweden* **6C1**
Oreti, R *NZ* **32A3**
Orgeyev *USSR* **7F3**
Orhaneli, R *Turk* **11F3**
Orhon Gol, R *Mongolia* **16D2**
Orihuela *Spain* **9B2**
Orinoco, R *Ven* **28F2**
Oristano *Sardegna* **10B3**
Orivesi, L *Fin* **2K6**
Oriximina *Brazil* **29G4**
Orizaba *Mexico* **26C3**
Orkney, I *Scot* **4D2**
Orlando *USA* **25E4**
Orléanais, Region *France* **8C2**
Orléans *France* **8C2**
Orlik *USSR* **13L4**
Orne, R *France* **8B2**
Örnsköldsvik *Sweden* **2H6**
Orocué *Colombia* **28D3**
Orosháza *Hung* **7E3**
Orotukan *USSR* **13R3**
Orsha *USSR* **7G2**
Orsk *USSR* **12G4**
Ørsta *Nor* **2F6**
Orthez *France* **8B3**
Ortigueira *Spain* **9A1**
Ortles, Mt *Italy* **8E2**
Oruro *Bol* **28E7**
Ōsaka *Japan* **16G3**
Osa,Pen de *Costa Rica* **26D4**
Osbrov Stolbovoy, I *USSR* **13P2**
Oshogbo *Nig* **18C4**
Oshosh *USA* **23K5**
Oshwe *Zaïre* **20B4**
Osijek *Yugos* **11D1**
Osinniki *USSR* **12K5**
Osipovichi *USSR* **7F2**
Oslo *Nor* **2G6**
Osnabrück *W Germ* **6B2**
Osório *Brazil* **27F3**
Osorno *Chile* **27B6**
Osorno *Spain* **9B1**
Ossa,Mt *Aust* **30D5**
Ossora *USSR* **13S4**
Østerdalen, V *Nor* **2G6**
Östersund *Sweden* **2G6**
Östhammär *Sweden* **2H6**
Ostia *Italy* **10C2**
Ostrava *Czech* **7D3**
Ostróda *Pol* **7D2**
Ostroleka *Pol* **7E2**
Ostrova De-Longa, I *USSR* **13R2**
Ostrova Petra, I *USSR* **13N2**
Ostrov Balyy, I *USSR* **12J2**
Ostrov Begicheva, I *USSR* **13N2**
Ostrov Bel'kovskiy, I *USSR* **13P2**
Ostrov Bennetta, I *USSR* **13R2**
Ostrov Beringa, I *USSR* **13S4**
Ostrov Bolshavik, I *USSR* **13M2**
Ostrov Bol'shoy Lyakhovskiy, I *USSR* **13Q2**
Ostrov Faddeyevskiy, I *USSR* **13Q2**
Ostrov Green Bell, I *Barents S* **12H1**
Ostrov Hurup, I *USSR* **13Q5**
Ostrov Karaginskiy, I *USSR* **13S4**
Ostrov Komsomolets, I *USSR* **13L1**
Ostrov Kotel'nyy, I *USSR* **13P2**
Ostrov Malvy Lyalchovskiy, I *USSR* **13Q2**
Ostrov Malyy Taymyr, I *USSR* **13M2**
Ostrov Mechdusharskiy, I *Barents S* **12G2**
Ostrov Mednyy, I *USSR* **13S4**
Ostrov Novaya Sibir, I *USSR* **13R2**
Ostrov Oktyabrskay Revolyutsii, I *USSR* **13L2**
Ostrov Pioner, I *USSR* **13K2**
Ostrov Rudol'fa, I *Barents S* **12G1**
Ostrov Russkiy, I *USSR* **13L2**
Ostrov Shmidta, I *USSR* **13L1**
Ostrov Ushakova, I *USSR* **12J1**
Ostrov Vaygach, I *USSR* **12G2**
Ostrov Vrangelya, I *USSR* **13T2**
Ostrów *Pol* **7D2**
Ostrowiec *Pol* **7E2**
Ostrów Mazowiecka *Pol* **7E2**
Osuna *Spain* **9A2**
Oswestry *Eng* **5D5**
Oświęcim *Pol* **7D3**
Otago Pen *NZ* **32B3**
Otaki *NZ* **32C2**
Otavalo *Ecuador* **28C3**
Otavi *Namibia* **21B5**
Óthris, Mt *Greece* **11E3**
Otish Mts *Can* **25F1**
Otjiwarongo *Namibia* **21B6**
Otorohanga *NZ* **32C1**
Otranto *Italy* **11D2**
Otranto,Str of, Chan *Italy/Alb* **11D2**
Otta *Nor* **2F6**
Otta, R *Nor* **2F7**
Ottawa *Can* **23L5**
Ottawa Is *Can* **23K4**
Otter Rapids *Can* **23K4**
Otto Fjord *Can* **23K1**
Otusco *Peru* **28C5**
Otwock *Pol* **7E2**
Ouadane *Maur* **18A2**
Ouadda *CAR* **20C3**
Ouaddai, Desert Region *Chad* **20C2**
Ouaka *CAR* **20C3**
Oualam *Niger* **18C3**
Ouallen *Alg* **18C2**
Ouanda Djallé *CAR* **20C3**
Ouarane, Region *Maur* **18A2**
Ouargla *Alg* **18C1**
Ouarra, R *CAR* **20C3**
Ouarzazate *Mor* **18B1**
Ouassel, R *Alg* **9C2**
Oubangui, R *Congo* **20B3**
Oued Tlēlat *Alg* **9B2**
Ouesso *Congo* **20B3**
Ouham, R *Chad* **20B3**
Oujda *Alg* **18B1**
Oulainen *Fin* **2J6**
Oulu *Fin* **2K5**
Oulu, R *Fin* **2K6**
Oulujärvi, L *Fin* **2K6**
Oum Chalouba *Chad* **20C2**
Oum Hadjer *Chad* **20B2**
Oum Haouach, Watercourse *Chad* **20C2**
Ounas, R *Fin* **2K5**
Ounianga Kebir *Chad* **20C2**
Ouricurí *Brazil* **29K5**
Ouse, R *Eng* **5E4**
Ouse, R *Eng* **5F5**
Outer Hebrides, Is *Is* **3B2**
Outjo *Namibia* **21B6**
Outokumpu *Fin* **2K6**
Ovamboland, Region *Namibia* **21B5**
Övertorneå *Sweden* **2J5**
Oviedo *Spain* **9A1**
Øvre Årdal *Nor* **2F6**
Ovsyanka *USSR* **13O4**
Owaka *NZ* **32A3**
Owen Stanley Range, Mts *PNG* **30D1**
Oxampampa *Peru* **28C6**
Oxelösund *Sweden* **2H7**
Oxford, County *Eng* **5E6**
Oxford *Eng* **5E6**
Oyen *Gabon* **20B3**
Oykel, R *Scot* **4C3**
Oymyakon *USSR* **13Q3**
Ozarichi *USSR* **7F2**
Ozark Plat *USA* **25D3**
Ózd *Hung* **7E3**
Ozero Alakol, L *USSR* **12K5**
Ozero Balkhash, L *USSR* **12J5**
Ozero Baykal, L *USSR* **13M4**
Ozero Chany, L *USSR* **12J4**
Ozero Evoron, L *USSR* **13P4**
Ozero Imandra, L *USSR* **2L5**
Ozero Issyk Kul', L *USSR* **15F1**
Ozero Kovdozero, L *USSR* **2L5**
Ozero Taymyr, L *USSR* **13M2**
Ozero Tengiz, L *USSR* **12H4**
Ozero Zaysan *USSR* **12K5**

P

Pabbay, I *Scot* **4B3**
Pabianice *Pol* **7D2**
Pabrade *USSR* **7F2**
Pacasmayo *Peru* **28C5**
Pachuca *Mexico* **26C2**
Padang *Indon* **17D7**
Paderborn *W Germ* **6B2**
Padlei *Can* **22J3**
Padova *Italy* **10C1**
Padre I *USA* **24D4**
Padstow *Eng* **5C6**
Padunskoye More, L *USSR* **2L5**
Paeroa *NZ* **32C1**
Pag, I *Yugos* **10C2**
Pagalu, I *Eq Guinea* **18C4**
Pagan, I *Pacific O* **17H5**
Pago Mission *Aust* **17F8**
Pagondhas *Greece* **11F3**
Pahiatua *NZ* **32C2**
Päijänne, L *Fin* **2K6**
Paisley *Scot* **4C4**
Paita *Peru* **28B5**
Pajala *Sweden* **2J5**
Pakistan, Republic *Asia* **14E3**
Pakrac *Yugos* **10D1**
Paks *Hung* **11D1**
Pakwach *Uganda* **20D3**
Pala *Chad* **20B3**
Palagruža, I *Yugos* **10D2**
Palana *USSR* **13R4**
Palau Is *Pacific O* **17G6**
Palawan, I *Phil* **17E6**
Paldiski *USSR* **2J7**
Palembang *Indon* **17D7**
Palencia *Spain* **9B1**
Palermo *Italy* **10C3**
Pallastunturi, Mt *Fin* **2J5**
Palliser B *NZ* **32B2**
Palliser,C *NZ* **32C2**
Palma *Mozam* **21E5**
Palma de Mallorca *Spain* **9C2**
Palmares *Brazil* **29L5**
Palmas,C *Lib* **18B4**
Palmeira dos Indos *Brazil* **29L5**
Palmerston *NZ* **32B3**
Palmerston North *NZ* **32C2**
Palmi *Italy* **10D3**
Palmira *Colombia* **28C3**
Palm Is *Aust* **30D2**
Palm Springs *USA* **24B3**
Paloích *Sudan* **20D2**
Pamiers *France* **8C3**
Pamir, Mts *China* **15F2**
Pampas, Region *Arg* **27D5**
Pamplona *Colombia* **28D2**
Pamplona *Spain* **9B1**
Panagyurishte *Bulg* **11E2**
Panamá *Panama* **28C2**
Panama, Republic *C America* **28B2**
Pancevo *Yugos* **11E2**
Panevežys *USSR* **7E1**
Panfilov *USSR* **12K5**
Pangani *Tanz* **20D4**
Pangani, R *Tanz* **20D4**
Pangi *Zaïre* **20C4**
Pangnirtung *Can* **23M3**
Pantelleria, I *Medit S* **10C3**
Paola *Italy* **10D3**
Papa *Hung* **6D3**
Papakura *NZ* **32B1**
Papa Stour, I *Scot* **4E1**
Papatoetoe *NZ* **32B1**
Papa Westray, I *Scot* **4D2**
Papua,G of *PNG* **30D1**
Papua New Guinea, Republic *S E Asia* **30D1**
Para, State *Brazil* **29H4**
Pará, R *Brazil* **29J4**
Paraburdoo *Aust* **30A3**
Paracas,Pen de *Peru* **28C6**
Paracin *Yugos* **11E2**
Paraguá, R *Bol* **28F6**
Paragua, R *Ven* **28F2**
Paraguai, R *Brazil* **29G7**
Paraguay, Republic *S America* **27E2**
Paraguay, R *Par* **27E2**
Paraiba, State *Brazil* **29L5**
Parakou *Benin* **18C4**
Paramaribo *Suriname* **29G2**
Paramushir, I *USSR* **16J1**
Paraná *Arg* **27D4**
Paraná, State *Brazil* **27F2**
Paraná, R *Arg* **27E4**
Paranã, R *Brazil* **29J6**
Paraparaumu *NZ* **32B2**
Pardubice *Czech* **6D2**
Parece Vela, Reef *Pacific O* **16G4**
Parent *Can* **25F2**
Parepare *Indon* **30A1**
Paria,Pen de *Ven* **28F1**
Paris *France* **8C2**
Parma *Italy* **10C2**
Parnaiba *Brazil* **29K4**
Parnaiba, R *Brazil* **29K4**
Párnon Óros, Mts *Greece* **11E3**
Páros, I *Greece* **11F3**
Parras *Mexico* **24C4**
Parry B *Can* **23K3**
Parry Is *Can* **22G2**
Parry Sd *Can* **23L5**
Parsberg *W Germ* **6C3**
Parsnip, R *Can* **22F4**
Parthenay *France* **8B2**
Partinico *Italy* **10C3**
Paru, R *Brazil* **29H4**
Pasadena *USA* **24B3**
Paşcani *Rom* **11F1**
Pasewalk *W Germ* **2G8**
Pasley,C *Aust* **30B4**
Paso de los Toros *Urug* **27E4**
Paso Limay *Arg* **27B6**
Passau *W Germ* **6C3**
Passo de los Libres *Arg* **27E3**
Pastaza, R *Peru* **28C4**
Pas,The *Can* **22H4**
Pasto *Colombia* **28C3**
Pasvalys *USSR* **7E1**
Patagonia, Region *Arg* **27B8**
Patea *NZ* **32B1**
Patea, R *NZ* **32B2**
Paterno *Italy* **10C3**
Paterson Inlet, B *NZ* **32A3**
Pativilca *Peru* **28C6**
Pátmos, I *Greece* **11F3**
Patna *India* **15G3**
Patos *Brazil* **29L5**
Pátrai *Greece* **11E3**
Patta, I *Kenya* **20E4**

Qattāra Depression — Salina

Qattāra Depression *Egypt* 19B2
Qena *Egypt* 19C2
Qilian Shan *China* 16C3
Qingdao *China* 16F3
Qinghai Hu, L *China* 16C3
Qing Zang, Upland *China* 15G2
Qiqihar *China* 16F2
Qitai *China* 13K5
Qom *Iran* 14D2
Qôrnoq *Greenland* 23N3
Quagadougou *U Volta* 18B3
Qu' Appelle, R *Can* 22H4
Quardho *Somalia* 19D4
Québec *Can* 23L5
Quebec, Province *Can* 23L4
Quedas do Iguaçu *Brazil/Arg* 27F3
Queen Charlotte Is *Can* 22E4
Queen Elizabeth Is *Can* 22H1
Queen Maud G *Can* 22H3
Queens Ch *Aust* 17F8
Queensland, State *Aust* 30D3
Queenstown *NZ* 32A3
Quela *Angola* 21B4
Quelimane *Mozam* 21D5
Querétaro *Mexico* 26B2
Quetta *Pak* 15E2
Quezaltenango *Guatemala* 26C3
Quezon City *Phil* 17F5
Quibala *Angola* 21B5
Quibaxe *Angola* 21B4
Quibdó *Colombia* 28C2
Quiberon *France* 8B2
Quicama Nat Pk *Angola* 21B4
Quillabamba *Peru* 28D6
Quillacollo *Bol* 28E7
Quillan *France* 8C3
Quill L *Can* 22H4
Quimbele *Angola* 21B4
Quimper *France* 8B2
Quimperlé *France* 8B2
Quintanar de la Orden *Spain* 9B2
Quirima *Angola* 21B5
Quissanga *Mozam* 21E5
Quissico *Mozam* 21D6
Quito *Ecuador* 28C4
Quixadá *Brazil* 29L4
Qutdligssat *Greenland* 23N3

R

Raahe *Fin* 2J6
Raasay, I *Scot* 4B3
Raasay,Sound of, Chan *Scot* 4B3
Rab, I *Yugos* 10C2
Rába, R *Hung* 6D3
Rabat *Mor* 18B1
Rabaul *PNG* 30E1
Race,C *Can* 23N5
Rachel, Mt *W Germ* 6C3
Rădăuţi *Rom* 7F3
Radom *Pol* 7E2
Radomsko *Pol* 7D2
Radomyshl' *USSR* 7F2
Radviliškis *USSR* 7E1
Rae *Can* 22G3
Rae Isthmus *Can* 23K3
Rae L *Can* 22G3
Raetihi *NZ* 32C1
Rafai *CAR* 20C3
Raga *Sudan* 20C3
Raguba *Libya* 19A2
Ragusa *Italy* 10C3
Rakaia, R *NZ* 32B2
Raka Zangbo, R *China* 15G3
Rakhov *USSR* 7E3
Rakov *USSR* 7F2
Raleigh *USA* 25F3
Ramapo Deep *Pacific Oc* 16H3
Ramsey *Eng* 5C4
Ramsey I *Wales* 5C6
Ramsgate *Eng* 5F6
Ramu, R *PNG* 30D1
Rancagua *Chile* 27B4
Randers *Den* 2F7
Ranfurly *NZ* 32B3
Rangiora *NZ* 32B2
Rangitaiki, R *NZ* 32C1
Rangitate, R *NZ* 32B2
Rangitikei, R *NZ* 32C1
Rangoon *Burma* 15H4
Ranier,Mt, Mt *USA* 24A2
Ranklin Inlet *Can* 23J3
Rany L *Can* 23J5
Raoul, I *NZ* 31H3
Raper,C *Can* 23M3
Rashad *Sudan* 20D2
Ras Khanzira, C *Somalia* 20E2
Ras Nouadhibou, C *Maur* 18A2
Rasshua, I *USSR* 16J2
Rastatt *W Germ* 6B3
Ras Xaafuun, C *Somalia* 19E3
Ratherow *E Germ* 6C2
Rathlin, I *N Ire* 4B4
Ratno *USSR* 7E2
Rättvik *Sweden* 2H6
Raukumara Range, Mts *NZ* 32C1
Rauma *Fin* 2J6
Rava Russkaya *USSR* 7E2
Ravensburg *W Germ* 6B3
Ravenshoe *Aust* 30D2
Ravno *USSR* 7F2
Rawalpindi *India* 15F2
Rawicz *Pol* 6D2
Rawlinna *Aust* 30B4
Rawlins *USA* 24C2
Rawson *Arg* 27D6
Ray,C *Can* 23N5
Razdel'naya *USSR* 7G3
Razgrad *Bulg* 11F2
Razim, L *Rom* 11F2
Reading *Eng* 5E6
Read Island *Can* 22G3
Rebiana, Well *Libya* 19B2
Rebiana Sand Sea *Libya* 19B2
Reboly *USSR* 2L6
Recherche,Arch of the, *Is Aust* 30B4
Rechitsa *USSR* 7G2
Recife *Brazil* 29M5
Récifs D'Entrecasteaux *Nouvelle Calédonie* 31F2
Red Basin *China* 16D3
Redcar *Eng* 5E4
Red Deer *Can* 22G4
Red L *USA* 25D2
Red Lake *Can* 23J4
Redon *France* 8B2
Red Sea *Africa/Arabian Pen* 14B3
Reefton *NZ* 32B2
Regensburg *W Germ* 6C3
Reggane *Alg* 18C2
Reggio di Calabria *Italy* 10D3
Reghin *Rom* 11E1
Regina *Can* 22H4
Reicito *Ven* 28E1
Reigate *Eng* 5E6
Reims *France* 8C2
Reindeer L *Can* 22H4
Reinosa *Spain* 9B1
Reliance *Can* 22H3
Rena *Nor* 2G6
Rendsburg *W Germ* 6B2
Reni *USSR* 7F3
Renk *Sudan* 20D2
Renland, Pen *Greenland* 23Q2
Rennell, I *Solomon Is* 31F2
Rennes *France* 8B2
Reno *USA* 24B3
Repki *USSR* 7G2
Republic of Ireland *NW Europe* 3B3
Repulse Bay *Can* 23K3
Réservoire Cabonga, Res *Can* 23L5
Réservoire Gouin, Res *Can* 23L5
Réservoire Manicouagan, Res *Can* 25G1
Resistencia *Arg* 27E3
Resita *Rom* 11E1
Resolute *Can* 23J2
Resolution I *NZ* 32A3
Resolution Island *Can* 23M3
Réthimnon *Greece* 11E3
Reus *Spain* 9C1
Revelstoke *Can* 22G4
Revillagigedo, Is *Mexico* 26A3
Reykjavik *Iceland* 2A2
Reynosa *Mexico* 26C2
Rezé *France* 8B2
Rezekne *USSR* 7F1
Rhein, R *W Europe* 6B2
Rheine *W Germ* 6B2
Rheinland Pfalz, Region *W Germ* 8D2
Rhône, R *France* 8C3
Rhyl *Wales* 5D5
Riachão do Jacuipe *Brazil* 29L6
Ria de Arosa, B *Spain* 9A1
Ria de Betanzos, B *Spain* 9A1
Ria de Corcubion, B *Spain* 9A1
Ria de Lage, B *Spain* 9A1
Ria de Sta Marta, B *Spain* 9A1
Ria de Vigo, B *Spain* 9A1
Ribadeo *Spain* 9A1
Ribauè *Mozam* 21D5
Ribble, R *Eng* 5D5
Ribeirão *Brazil* 29J8
Riberalta *Bol* 28E6
Richmond *NZ* 32B2
Richmond, Queensland *Aust* 30D3
Richmond *USA* 25F3
Richmond Range, Mts *NZ* 32B2
Riesa *E Germ* 6C2
Riesco, I *Chile* 27B8
Rieti *Italy* 10C2
Rif, Mts *Mor* 9B2
Rif, Mts *Mor* 18B1
Riga *USSR* 7E1
Rigolet *Can* 23N4
Riihimaki *Fin* 2J6
Rijeka *Yugos* 10C1
Rimbo *Sweden* 2H7
Rîmnicu Sărat *Rom* 11F1
Rîmnicu Vîlcea *Rom* 11E1
Rimouski *Can* 25G2
Ringkøbing *Den* 2F7
Rio Benito *Eq Guinea* 20A3
Rio Branco *Brazil* 28E5
Rio Bravo del Norte, R *USA/Mexico* 26B1
Riochacha *Colombia* 28D1
Rio de Jacuipe *Brazil* 29L6
Rio de Janeiro *Brazil* 29K8
Rio Gallegos *Arg* 27C8
Rio Grande *Arg* 27C8
Rio Grande *Brazil* 27F4
Rio Grande, R *Nicaragua* 26D3
Rio Grande, R *USA/ Mexico* 26B2
Rio Grande do Norte, State *Brazil* 29L5
Riom *France* 8C2
Riombamba *Ecuador* 28C4
Rio Mulatos *Bol* 28E7
Rio Pardo *Brazil* 27F3
Rio Theodore Roosevelt, R *Brazil* 28F6
Rio Turbio *Arg* 27B8
Ripon *Eng* 5E4
Risør *Nor* 2F7
Ritenberk *Greenland* 23N2
Rivas *Nic* 28A1
River Cess *Lib* 18B4
Riversdale *NZ* 32A3
Riverside *USA* 24B3
Riverton *NZ* 32A3
Rivière aux Feuilles, R *Can* 23L4
Rivière de la Baleine, R *Can* 23M4
Rivière du Petit Mècatina, R *Can* 23M4
Riyadh *S Arabia* 14C3
Rjukan *Nor* 2F7
Roanes Pen *Can* 23K2
Roanne *France* 8C2
Robertsfors *Sweden* 2J6
Robertsport *Lib* 18A4
Roberval *Can* 23L5
Roca Partida, I *Mexico* 26A3
Rocas, I *Brazil* 29M4
Rochdale *Eng* 5D5
Rochefort *France* 8B2
Rocher River *Can* 22G3
Rochester *Eng* 5F6
Rochester *USA* 23L5
Rochester *USA* 25F2
Rockhampton *Aust* 30E3
Rocks Pt *NZ* 32B2
Rocky Mts *Can/USA* 24B1
Rødbyhavn *Den* 2G8
Rodez *France* 8C3
Ródhos *Greece* 11F3
Ródhos, I *Greece* 11F3
Rodi Garganico *Italy* 10D2
Rodopi Planina, Mts *Bulg* 11E2
Roebourne *Aust* 30A3
Roes Welcome Sd *Can* 23K3
Rogachev *USSR* 7F2
Roja *USSR* 7E1
Roma *Italy* 10C2
Roman *Rom* 11F1
Romania, Republic *E Europe* 11E1
Romans sur Isère *France* 8D2
Romilly-sur-Seine *France* 8C2
Rømø, I *Den* 6B1
Romoratin *France* 8C2
Ronda *Spain* 9A2
Rondônia *Brazil* 28F6
Rondônia, State *Brazil* 28F6
Rønne *Denmark* 2G7
Ronneby *Sweden* 2H7
Roof Butte, Mt *USA* 24C3
Roper, R *Aust* 30C2
Roraima, State *Brazil* 28F3
Roraime, Mt *Ven* 28F2
Røros *Nor* 2G6
Rørvik *Nor* 2G6
Ros', R *USSR* 7G3
Rosario *Arg* 27D4
Rosário *Brazil* 29K4
Roscoff *France* 8B2
Roscommon *Irish Rep* 3B3
Roscrea *Irish Rep* 5B5
Rosenheim *W Germ* 6C3
Rosiorii de Verde *Rom* 11E2
Roskilde *Den* 2G7
Ross *NZ* 32B2
Rossan, Pt *Irish Rep* 3B3
Rossano *Italy* 10D3
Rossel, I *Solomon Is* 31E2
Rosslare *Irish Rep* 5B5
Ross,Mt *NZ* 32C2
Rosso *Maur* 18A3
Ross-on-Wye *Eng* 5D6
Ross River *Can* 22E3
Rostock *E Germ* 6C2
Rostov-na-Donu *USSR* 12F5
Rota *Pacific O* 17H5
Rotenburg, Niedersachsen *W Germ* 6B2
Rotherham *Eng* 5E5
Rothesay *Scot* 4C4
Rotoiti,L *NZ* 32B2
Rotoroa,L *NZ* 32B2
Rotorua *NZ* 32C1
Rotorua,L *NZ* 32C1
Rotterdam *Neth* 6A2
Rotuma, I *Fiji* 31G2
Rouen *France* 8C2
Rough, Gasfield *N Sea* 5F5
Round I *Mauritius* 21F6
Rousay, I *Scot* 4D2
Roussillon, Region *France* 8C3
Rovaniemi *Fin* 2K5
Rovinj *Yugos* 10C1
Rowley I *Can* 23L3
Rowley Shoals *Aust* 30A2
Roxburgh *NZ* 32A3
Royal Canal *Irish Rep* 5B5
Royal Leamington Spa *Eng* 5E5
Royal Tunbridge Wells *Eng* 5F6
Royan *France* 8B2
Royston *Eng* 5E5
Rožňava *Czech* 7E3
Ruaha Nat Pk *Tanz* 21D4
Ruahine Range, Mts *NZ* 32C1
Ruapehu,Mt *NZ* 32C1
Rub' al, Desert *S Arabia* 14C4
Rubha Hunish *Scot* 4B3
Rubtsoysk *USSR* 12K4
Rudnya *USSR* 7G2
Rudoka Planina, Mt *Yugos* 11E2
Rudolf,L *Kenya/Eth* 20D3
Ruffec *France* 8C2
Rufiji, R *Tanz* 21D4
Rufisque *Sen* 18A3
Rufunsa *Zambia* 21C5
Rugby *Eng* 5E5
Rügen, I *E Germ* 2G8
Ruhr, R *W Germ* 6B2
Rujen, Mt *Bulg/Yugos* 11E2
Rukwa, L *Tanz* 21D4
Rum, I *Scot* 4B3
Ruma *Yugos* 11D1
Rumbek *Sudan* 20C3
Rum Jungle *Aust* 30C2
Rumphi *Malawi* 21D5
Runanga *NZ* 32B2
Runaway,C *NZ* 32C1
Rundu *Namibia* 21B5
Rungwa *Tanz* 21D4
Rungwa, R *Tanz* 21D4
Rungwe, Mt *Tanz* 21D4
Ruoqiang *China* 15G2
Ruo Shui, R *China* 16D2
Rupea *Rom* 11F1
Rupert, R *Can* 23L4
Rurrenabaque *Bol* 28E6
Rusape *Zim* 21D5
Ruse *Bulg* 11F2
Russell *NZ* 32B1
Rutana *Burundi* 20C4
Ruvuma, R *Tanz/Mozam* 21E5
Ruwenzori Range, Mts *Uganda/Zaïre* 20D3
Ruya, R *Zim* 21D5
Ružomberok *Czech* 7D3
Rwanda, Republic *Africa* 20C4
Ryazan' *USSR* 12E4
Rybnitsa *USSR* 7F3
Ryde *Eng* 5E6
Rye *Eng* 5F6
Ryskany *USSR* 7F3
Ryūkyū Retto, Arch *Japan* 16F4
Rzeszów *Pol* 7E2

S

Saale, R *E Germ* 6C2
Saarbrücken *W Germ* 6B3
Saaremaa, I *USSR* 2J7
Šabac *Yugos* 11D2
Sabadell *Spain* 9C1
Sabah, State *Malay* 17E6
Sabaya *Bol* 28E7
Sabhā *Libya* 19A2
Sabi, R *Zim* 21D6
Sabinas *Mexico* 26B2
Sabinas Hidalgo *Mexico* 26B2
Sable,C *Can* 23M5
Sable I *Can* 23M5
Sachigo, R *Can* 25D1
Sachs Harbour *Can* 22F2
Sacramento *USA* 24A3
Sacramento, Mts *USA* 24C3
Sadanski *Bulg* 11E2
Sado, R *Port* 9A2
Saffle *Sweden* 2G7
Safi *Mor* 18B1
Safonovo *USSR* 7G1
Saglek B *Can* 23M4
Saglouc *Can* 23L3
Saguenay, R *Can* 23L5
Saguia el Hamra, Watercourse *Mor* 18A2
Sagunto *Spain* 9B2
Sahagún *Spain* 9A1
Sahara, Desert *N Africa* 18B2
Saibai I *Aust* 30D1
Saida *Alg* 18C1
Saidia *Mor* 9B2
Saigon *Viet* 17D5
Saihan Tal *China* 16E2
Saimaa, L *Fin* 2K6
St Abb's Head, Pt *Scot* 4D4
St Albans *Eng* 5E6
St Albans Head, C *Eng* 5D6
St Amand-Mont Rond *France* 8C2
St André, C *Madag* 21E5
St Andrews *Scot* 4D3
St Anthony *Can* 23N4
St Austell *Eng* 5C6
St Bees Head, Pt *Eng* 5D4
St Brides B *Wales* 5C6
St-Brieuc *France* 8B2
St Catherines *Can* 23L5
St Catherines Pt *Eng* 5E6
St Chamond *France* 8C2
St Claude *France* 8D2
St Davids Head, Pt *Wales* 5C6
St Denis *Réunion* 21F6
Saintes *France* 8B2
St Étienne *France* 8C2
St-Gaudens *France* 8C3
St Georges Chan *Irish Rep/Wales* 5B5
St Georges Chan *PNG* 31E1
St Govans Head, Pt *Wales* 5C6
St Helens *Eng* 5D5
St Helier *Jersey* 8B2
St-Hyacinthe *Can* 23L5
St Ives *Eng* 5C6
St Jean-d'Angely *France* 8B2
Saint John *Can* 23M5
St John's *Can* 23N5
St Joseph,L *Can* 23J4
St-Junien *France* 8C2
St Kilda, I *Scot* 4A3
St Lawrence, R *Can* 23M5
Saint Lawrence,G of *Can* 23M5
St Lô *France* 8B2
St Louis *Sen* 18A3
St Louis *USA* 25D3
St Lucia, I *Caribbean* 28F1
St Magnus, B *Scot* 4E1
St Malo *France* 8B2
Ste Marie, C *Madag* 21E6
St Mary,Mt *PNG* 30D1
St Marys, I *UK* 5B7
Saint Mathias Group, Is *PNG* 30E1
St-Nazaire *France* 8B2
St Paul *USA* 25D2
St Paul, R *Lib* 18A4
St Petersburg *USA* 25E4
St Pierre, I *Can* 23N5
St Pölten *Austria* 6D3
St Raphaël *France* 8D3
St Sébastien, C *Madag* 21E5
St Vincent, C *Madag* 21E6
St Vincent, I *Caribbean* 28F1
Saipan, I *Pacific O* 17H5
Sajama, Mt *Bol* 28E7
Sakai *Japan* 16G3
Sakami,L *Can* 25F1
Sakania *Zaïre* 21C5
Sakaraha *Madag* 21E6
Sakasleja *USSR* 7E1
Sakhalin, I *USSR* 13Q4
Sakishima gunto, Is *Japan* 16F4
Sal, I *Cape Verde* 18A4
Sala *Sweden* 2H7
Salado, R, Sante Fe *Arg* 27D3
Salal *Chad* 20B2
Salamanca *Spain* 9A1
Salamat, R *Chad* 20B3
Salamaua *PNG* 17H7
Salangen *Nor* 2H5
Salar de Arizaro *Arg* 27C2
Salar de Atacama, Salt Pan *Chile* 27C2
Salar de Coipasa, Salt Pan *Bol* 28E7
Salar de Uyuni, Salt Pan *Bol* 28E8
Salawati, I *Indon* 30C1
Salbris *France* 8C2
Saldus *USSR* 7E1
Salem *USA* 24A2
Salen *Sweden* 2G6
Salerno *Italy* 10C2
Salford *Eng* 5D5
Salgótarjan *Hung* 7D3
Salgueiro *Brazil* 29L5
Salihli *Turk* 11F3
Salima *Malawi* 21D5
Salina, I *Italy* 10C3

Salina de Arizato **Simrishamn**

Salina de Arizato *Arg* **28E8**
Salinópolis *Brazil* **29J4**
Salisbury *Eng* **5E6**
Salisbury I *Can* **23L3**
Salisbury Plain *Eng* **5E6**
Salla *Fin* **2K5**
Salmi *USSR* **2L6**
Salo *Fin* **2J6**
Salon-de-Provence *France* **8D3**
Salonta *Rom* **11E1**
Salpausselka, Region *Fin* **2K6**
Salta *Arg* **27C2**
Salta, State *Arg* **27C2**
Saltillo *Mexico* **26B2**
Salt Lake City *USA* **24B2**
Salto Angostura, Waterfall *Colombia* **28D3**
Salto del Angel, Waterfall *Ven* **28F2**
Salto del Guaira, Waterfall *Brazil* **27E2**
Salto Grande, Waterfall *Colombia* **28D4**
Salvador *Brazil* **29L6**
Salzburg *Austria* **6C3**
Salzgitter *W Germ* **6C2**
Salzwedel *E Germ* **6C2**
Samagaltay *USSR* **16C1**
Samarai *PNG* **30E2**
Samarinda *Indon* **17E7**
Samarkand *USSR* **14E2**
Sambava *Madag* **21F5**
Sambor *USSR* **7E3**
Same *Tanz* **20D4**
Samfya *Zambia* **21C5**
Samoan Is *Pacific O* **31H2**
Sámos, I *Greece* **11F3**
Samothráki, I *Greece* **11F2**
Samsø, I *Den* **6C1**
Samsun *Turk* **14B1**
San, R *Pol* **7E2**
Şan' a' *Yemen* **14C4**
Sanaga, R *Cam* **20B3**
San Agustín *Arg* **27C4**
San Andrés Tuxtla *Mexico* **26C3**
San Antioco *Sardegna* **10B3**
San Antioco, I *Medit S* **10B3**
San Antonio *USA* **24D4**
San Antonio Abad *Spain* **9C2**
San Antonio,C *Cuba* **26D2**
San Benedicto, I *Mexico* **26A3**
San Bernardino *USA* **24B3**
San Bernardo *Chile* **27B4**
San Carlos *Nic* **28B1**
San Carlos de Bariloche *Arg* **27B6**
San-chung *Taiwan* **16F4**
San Cristóbal *Mexico* **26C3**
San Cristóbal *Ven* **28D2**
San Cristobal, I *Solomon Is* **31F2**
Sancti Spíritus *Cuba* **26E2**
Sanday, I *Scot* **4D2**
Sandnes *Nor* **2F7**
Sandnessjøen *Nor* **2G5**
Sandø *Faroes* **2D3**
Sandoa *Zaïre* **21C4**
Sandomierz *Pol* **7E2**
Sandstone *Aust* **30A3**
Sandviken *Sweden* **2H6**
Sandy L *Can* **23J4**
San Felipe, Baja Cal *Mexico* **24B3**
San Feliu de Guixols *Spain* **9C1**
San Fernando *Spain* **9A2**
San Fernando *Ven* **28E2**
Sanford *USA* **25E4**
San Francisco *USA* **24A3**
San Francisco del Oro *Mexico* **26B2**
Sangar *USSR* **13O3**
Sangha, R *Congo* **20B3**
Sangmélima *Cam* **20B3**
San Gorgonio Mt *USA* **24B3**
Sangre de Cristo, Mts *USA* **24C3**
San Ignacio *Arg* **27E3**
San Jacinto *Colombia* **28D2**
San João del Rei *Brazil* **27H2**
San José *Costa Rica* **28B1**
San José *Guatemala* **26C3**
San Jose *USA* **24A3**
San José, I *Mexico* **24B4**
San José de Chiquitos *Bol* **28F7**
San José do Rio Prêto *Brazil* **27G2**
San Joseé del Cabo *Mexico* **26B2**
San Juan *Arg* **27C4**
San Juan *Ven* **28E2**
San Juan, Mts *USA* **24C3**
San Juan, R *Nicaragua/Costa Rica* **26D3**
San Juan Bautista *Par* **27E3**
San Juan del Norte *Nic* **26D3**
San Juan del Sur *Nicaragua* **26D3**
San Julián *Arg* **27C7**
Sankuru, R *Zaïre* **20C4**
San Lorenzo *Colombia* **28C3**
San Luis Potosi *Mexico* **26B2**
Sanluri *Sardegna* **10B3**
San Maigualida, Mts *Ven* **28E2**
San Matias *Brazil* **29G7**
San Miguel *El Salvador* **26D3**
San Miguel de Tucumán *Arg* **27C3**
San Nicolas, I *USA* **24B3**
Sanniquellie *Lib* **18B4**
Sanok *Pol* **7E3**
San Pablo *Phil* **17F5**
San Pédro *Ivory Coast* **18B4**
San Pedro, Jujuy *Arg* **27D2**
San Pedro *Par* **27E2**
San Pedro de los Colonias *Mexico* **24C4**
San Pedro Sula *Honduras* **26D3**
San Pietro, I *Medit S* **10B3**
San Quintin *Mexico* **26A1**
San Salvador *El Sal* **26D3**
San Salvador de Jujuy *Arg* **27C2**
San Sebastian *Spain* **9B1**
San Severo *Italy* **10D2**
Santa *Vanuatu* **31F2**
Santa Ana *Bol* **28E7**
Santa Ana *Guatemala* **26C3**
Santa Barbara *Mexico* **26B2**
Santa Barbara *USA* **24B3**
Santa Catalina *USA* **24B3**
Santa Catarina, State *Brazil* **27F3**
Santa Cruz *Arg* **27C8**
Santa Cruz *Bol* **28F7**
Santa Cruz, State *Arg* **27B7**
Santa Cruz, Is *Solomon Is* **31F2**
Santa Cruz de la Palma *Canary Is* **18A2**
Santa Cruz de Tenerife *Canary Is* **18A2**
Santa Cruz do Cuando *Angola* **21C5**
Santa Elena *Ven* **28F3**
Santa Fe *Arg* **27D4**
Santa Fe *USA* **24C3**
Santa Inés, I *Chile* **27B8**
Santa Isabel, I *Solomon Is* **31E1**
Santa Luzia, I *Cape Verde* **18A4**
Santa Maria, I *Açores* **18A1**
Santa Marta *Colombia* **28D1**
Santander *Colombia* **28C3**
Santander *Spain* **9B1**
Santañy *Spain* **9C2**
Santa Quitéria *Brazil* **29K4**
Santarem *Brazil* **29H4**
Santarém *Port* **9A2**
Santa Rosa *Honduras* **26D3**
Santa Rosalía *Mexico* **26A2**
Santa Talhada *Brazil* **29L5**
Santa Teresa di Gallura *Sardegna* **10B2**
Santiago *Chile* **27B4**
Santiago *Panama* **28B2**
Santiago, R *Peru* **28C4**
Santiago de Compostela *Spain* **9A1**
Santiago del Estero, State *Arg* **27D3**
Santo Antão, I *Cape Verde* **18A4**
Santos *Brazil* **27G2**
San Valentin, Mt *Chile* **27B7**
Sanza Pomba *Angola* **21B4**
São Félix, Mato Grosso *Brazil* **29H5**
São Francisco, R *Brazil* **29L5**
São Francisco do Sul *Brazil* **27G3**
Sao Hill *Tanz* **21D4**
São Jorge, I *Açores* **18A1**
São Luis *Brazil* **29K4**
São Miguel, I *Açores* **18A1**
Saône, R *France* **8C2**
São Nicolau, I *Cape Verde* **18A4**
São Paulo *Brazil* **29J8**
São Raimundo Nonato *Brazil* **29K5**
São Tiago, I *Cape Verde* **18A4**
São Tomé, I *W Africa* **18C4**
São Tomé and Principe, Republic *W Africa* **18C4**
Saoura, Watercourse *Alg* **18B2**
São Vicente *Brazil* **29J8**
São Vincente, I *Cape Verde* **18A4**
Sápai *Greece* **11F2**
Sapporo *Japan* **16H2**
Sapri *Italy* **10D2**
Saquenay, R *Can* **25F2**
Sarafa *USSR* **11F1**
Sarajevo *Yugos* **11D2**
Sarala *USSR* **13K4**
Sarandë *Alb* **11E3**
Saratov *USSR* **12F4**
Sarawak, State *Malay* **17E6**
Sardalais *Libya* **19A2**
Sardegna, I *Medit S* **10B2**
Sarektjåkkå, Mt *Sweden* **2H5**
Sarh *Chad* **20B3**
Sarigan, I *Pacific O* **17H5**
Sarina *Aust* **30D3**
Sarir *Libya* **19B2**
Sarir Tibesti, Desert *Libya* **19A2**
Sark, I *UK* **8B2**
Sarmi *Indon* **17G7**
Sarmiento *Arg* **27C7**
Särna *Sweden* **2G6**
Sarny *USSR* **7F2**
Saroaq *Greenland* **23N2**
Saronikós Kólpos, G *Greece* **11E3**
Saros Körfezi, B *Turk* **11F2**
Sarpsborg *Nor* **2G7**
Sarrion *Spain* **9B1**
Sartène *Corse* **10B2**
Sarthe, R *France* **8B2**
Sarysu, R *USSR* **12H5**
Saskatchewan, Province *Can* **22H4**
Saskatchewan, R *Can* **22H4**
Saskatoon *Can* **22H4**
Saskylakh *USSR* **13N2**
Sassandra *Ivory Coast* **18B4**
Sassandra, R *Ivory Coast* **18B4**
Sassari *Sardegna* **10B2**
Sassnitz *E Germ* **6C2**
Satellite B *Can* **22G2**
Säter *Sweden* **2H6**
Satu Mare *Rom* **11E1**
Sauda *Nor* **2F7**
Saudi Arabia, Kingdom *Arabian Pen* **14C3**
Sauðárkrókur *Iceland* **2B1**
Sault Sainte Marie *Can* **23K5**
Saumlaki *Indon* **17G7**
Saumur *France* **8B2**
Saurimo *Angola* **21C4**
Sava, R *Yugos* **11D2**
Saval'i, I *Western Samoa* **31H2**
Savannah *USA* **25F3**
Savant Lake *Can* **23J4**
Save, R *Mozam* **21D6**
Savoie, Region *France* **8D2**
Savonlinna *Fin* **2K6**
Savukoski *Fin* **2K5**
Sawknah *Libya* **19A2**
Sawu, I *Indon* **30B2**
Saynshand *Mongolia* **16D2**
Sázava, R *Czech* **6C3**
Sbisseb, R *Alg* **9C2**
Scafell Pike, Mt *Eng* **5D4**
Scalloway *Scot* **4E1**
Scapa Flow, Sd *Scot* **4D2**
Scarborough *Eng* **5E4**
Scarp, I *Scot* **4B2**
Schaffhausen *Switz* **10B1**
Scharding *Austria* **6C3**
Schefferville *Can* **23M4**
Schleswig *W Germ* **6B2**
Schleswig Holstein, State *W Germ* **6B2**
Schouten Is *PNG* **30D1**
Schreiber *Can* **23K5**
Schwabische Alb, Upland *W Germ* **6B3**
Schwarzwald, Upland *W Germ* **6B3**
Schweinfurt *W Germ* **6C2**
Schwerin *E Germ* **6C2**
Sciacca *Italy* **10C3**
Scilly Isles, Is *UK* **5B7**
Scoresby Sd *Greenland* **23Q2**
Scotland, Country *U K* **4C3**
Scott Inlet, B *Can* **23L2**
Scott Reef *Timor S* **30B2**
Scranton *USA* **25F2**
Seal, R *Can* **22J4**
Seattle *USA* **24A2**
Sebez *USSR* **7F1**
Secretary I *NZ* **32A3**
Seddonville *NZ* **32B2**
Sédhiou *Sen* **18A3**
Sefton,Mt *NZ* **32B2**
Segorbe *Spain* **9B2**
Ségou *Mali* **18B3**
Segovia *Spain* **9B1**
Segre, R *Spain* **9C1**
Séguéla *Ivory Coast* **18B4**
Segura, R *Spain* **9B2**
Seinäjoki *Fin* **2J6**
Seine, R *France* **8C2**
Sekenke *Tanz* **20D4**
Sekondi *Ghana* **18B4**
Selaru, I *Indon* **17G7**
Selat Dampier, Str *Indon* **17G7**
Selby *Eng* **5E5**
Selçuk *Turk* **11F3**
Selennyakh, R *USSR* **13Q3**
Selfoss *Iceland* **23Q3**
Selima Oasis *Sudan* **20C1**
Selizharovo *USSR* **7G1**
Selkirk *Can* **22J4**
Selkirk *Scot* **4D4**
Selkirk Mts *Can* **22G4**
Selouane *Mor* **9B2**
Selvas, Region *Brazil* **28D5**
Selwyn *Aust* **30D3**
Selwyn Mts *Can* **22E3**
Semarang *Indon* **17D7**
Semipalatinsk *USSR* **12K4**
Sena Madureira *Brazil* **28E5**
Senanga *Zambia* **21C5**
Sendai *Japan* **16H3**
Senegal, Republic *Africa* **18A3**
Sénégal, R *Maur Sen* **18A3**
Senhor do Bonfim *Brazil* **29L6**
Senigallia *Italy* **10C2**
Senj *Yugos* **10D2**
Senkaku Gunto, Is *Japan* **16F4**
Senlis *France* **8C2**
Sennar *Sudan* **20D2**
Senneterre *Can* **23L5**
Senta *Yugos* **11D1**
Sentery *Zaïre* **20C4**
Separation Pt *NZ* **32B2**
Sept-Iles *Can* **23M4**
Séquédine *Niger* **20B1**
Seram, I *Indon* **17F7**
Serbia, Region *Yugos* **11D2**
Serengeti Nat Pk *Tanz* **20D4**
Serenje *Zambia* **21D5**
Seret, R *USSR* **7F3**
Sergino *USSR* **12H3**
Sergipe, State *Brazil* **29L6**
Sérifos, I *Greece* **11E3**
Serir Calanscio, Desert *Libya* **19B2**
Serov *USSR* **12H4**
Serpa *Port* **9A2**
Serra da Estrela, Mts *Port* **9A1**
Serra do Cachimbo, Mts *Brazil* **29G5**
Serra do Chifre *Brazil* **29K7**
Serra do Navio *Brazil* **29H3**
Serra dos Caiabis, Mts *Brazil* **29G6**
Serra dos Parecis, Mts *Brazil* **28F6**
Serra Formosa, Mts *Brazil* **29G6**
Sérrai *Greece* **11E2**
Serrana Bank, Is *Caribbean* **26D3**
Serrana de Cuenca, Mts *Spain* **9B1**
Serra Pacaraima, Mts *Brazil/Ven* **28F3**
Serra Parima, Mts *Brazil* **28F3**
Serra Tumucumaque *Brazil* **29H3**
Serrinha *Brazil* **29L6**
Serrmilik *Greenland* **23P3**
Sesfontein *Namibia* **21B5**
Sesheke *Zambia* **21C5**
Sète *France* **8C3**
Sétif *Alg* **18C1**
Settle *Eng* **5D4**
Settler *Can* **22G4**
Sêtúbal *Port* **9A2**
Severn, R *Can* **23K4**
Severn, R *Eng* **5D5**
Severnaya Zemlya, I *USSR* **13M1**
Severo-Baykalskoye Nagorye, Mts *USSR* **13M4**
Severo Sos'va, R *USSR* **12H3**
Sevilla *Spain* **9A2**
Sevlievo *Bulg* **11F2**
Sewa, R *Sierra Leone* **18A4**
Seychelles, Is *Indian O* **21E4**
Seyðisfjörður *Iceland* **2C1**
Seyðisfjörður *Iceland* **2C1**
Seymohan *USSR* **13R3**
Sfax *Tunisia* **18D1**
Sfîntu Gheorghe *Rom* **11F1**
's-Gravenhage *Neth* **6A2**
Shabunda *Zaïre* **20C4**
Shache *China* **15F2**
Shaftesbury *Eng* **5D6**
Shag Rocks, Is *South Georgia* **27J8**
Shambe *Sudan* **20D3**
Shanghai *China* **16F3**
Shangombo *Zambia* **21C5**
Shannon, R *Irish Rep* **3B3**
Shantarskiye Ostrova, I *USSR* **16G1**
Shapinsay, I *Scot* **4D2**
Shark B *Aust* **30A3**
Shashamanna *Eth* **20D3**
Shashone Mts *USA* **24B3**
Shay Gap *Aust* **30B3**
Shchuchinsk *USSR* **12J4**
Shebshi, Mts *Nig* **20B3**
Sheep Haven, Estuary *Irish Rep* **4B4**
Sheerness *Eng* **5F6**
Sheffield *Eng* **5E5**
Shelter Pt *NZ* **32A3**
Shenyang *China* **16F2**
Shepetovka *USSR* **7F2**
Sherard,C *Can* **23K2**
Sherborne *Eng* **5D6**
Sherbro I *Sierra Leone* **18A4**
Sheridan *USA* **24C2**
s-Hertogenbosh *Neth* **6B2**
Shetland, Is *Scot* **3C1**
Shiashkotan, I *USSR* **16J2**
Shibeli, R *Eth* **20E3**
Shibin el Kom *Egypt* **19C1**
Shijiazhuang *China* **16E3**
Shilka *USSR* **16E1**
Shilka, R *USSR* **16E1**
Shinyanga *Tanz* **20D4**
Shīrāz *Iran* **14D3**
Shishmaret *USA* **22B3**
Shiwa Ngandu *Zambia* **21D5**
Shkodër *Alb* **11D2**
Shkov *USSR* **7G2**
Shreveport *USA* **25D3**
Shrewsbury *Eng* **5D5**
Shropshire, County *Eng* **5D5**
Shule He *China* **16C2**
Shumen *Bulg* **11F2**
Shurugwi *Zim* **21C5**
Šiauliai *USSR* **7E1**
Sibay *USSR* **12G4**
Šibenik *Yugos* **10D2**
Sibiti *Congo* **20B4**
Sibiti, R *Tanz* **20D4**
Sibiu *Rom* **11E1**
Sibut *CAR* **20B3**
Sicilia, I *Medit S* **10C3**
Sicilian, Chan *Italy/Tunisia* **10C3**
Sicuani *Peru* **28D6**
Sidi Barrani *Egypt* **19B1**
Sidi-bel-Abbès *Alg* **18C1**
Sidlaw Hills *Scot* **4D3**
Siedlce *Pol* **7E2**
Siegen *W Germ* **6B2**
Siena *Italy* **10C2**
Sierpc *Pol* **7D2**
Sierra de Albarracin, Mts *Spain* **9B1**
Sierra de Alcaraz, Mts *Spain* **9B2**
Sierra de Gredos, Mts *Spain* **9A1**
Sierra de Guadalupe, Mts *Spain* **9A2**
Sierra de Guadarrama, Mts *Spain* **9B1**
Sierra de Guara, Mts *Spain* **9B1**
Sierra de Gudar, Mts *Spain* **9B1**
Sierra del Codi, Mts *Spain* **9C1**
Sierra de los Alamitos, Mts *Mexico* **26B2**
Sierra de los Filabres *Spain* **9B2**
Sierra de Ronda, Mts *Spain* **9A2**
Sierra de Segura, Mts *Spain* **9B2**
Sierra de Urbion, Mts *Spain* **9B1**
Sierra Leone, Republic *Africa* **18A4**
Sierra Leone,C *Sierra Leone* **18A4**
Sierra Madre del Sur, Mts *Mexico* **26B3**
Sierra Madre Occidental, Mts *Mexico* **26B2**
Sierra Madre Oriental, Mts *Mexico* **26B2**
Sierra Mojada *Mexico* **24C4**
Sierra Morena, Mts *Spain* **9A2**
Sierra Nevada, Mts *Spain* **9B2**
Sierra Nevada, Mts *USA* **24A3**
Sierra Nevada de santa Marta, Mts *Colombia* **28D1**
Sífnos, I *Greece* **11E3**
Sighet *Rom* **7E3**
Sighisoara *Rom* **11E1**
Siglufjörður *Iceland* **2B1**
Siguatepeque *Honduras* **28A1**
Sigüenza *Spain* **9B1**
Siguiri *Guinea* **18B3**
Sikai Hu, L *China* **16C3**
Sikasso *Mali* **18B3**
Síkinos, I *Greece* **11F3**
Sikionía *Greece* **11E3**
Siktyakh *USSR* **13O2**
Sil, R *Spain* **9A1**
Silet *Alg* **18C2**
Siling Co, L *China* **15G2**
Silistra *Bulg* **11F2**
Silkeborg *Den* **2F7**
Siltou, Well *Chad* **20B2**
Šilute *USSR* **7E1**
Simav *Turk* **11F3**
Simav, R *Turk* **11F3**
Sími, I *Greece* **11F3**
Simplon, Mt *Switz* **8D2**
Simpson,C *USA* **22C3**
Simpson Desert *Aust* **30C3**
Simpson Pen *Can* **23K3**
Simrishamn *Sweden* **2G7**

Simushir **Tanga**

Simushir, I *USSR* **16J2**
Sinadogo *Somalia* **20E3**
Sinai, Pen *Egypt* **14B3**
Sincelejo *Colombia* **28C2**
Sindirği *Turk* **11F3**
Sines *Port* **9A2**
Singa *Sudan* **20D2**
Singapore, Republic *SE Asia* **17D6**
Singida *Tanz* **20D4**
Siniscola *Sardgena* **10B2**
Sinkiang, Autonomous Region **15F1**
Sinnamary *French Guiana* **29H2**
Sintana *Rom* **11E1**
Sintra *Port* **9A2**
Sinú, R *Colombia* **28C2**
Siofok *Hung* **7D3**
Siracusa *Italy* **10D3**
Sir Edward Pellew Group Is *Aust* **30C2**
Siret, R *Rom* **11F1**
Síros, I *Greece* **11E3**
Sirt *Libya* **19A1**
Sirte Desert *Libya* **19A1**
Sirte,G of *Libya* **19A1**
Sisak *Yugos* **10D1**
Sisteron *France* **8D3**
Sistig Khem *USSR* **13L4**
Sitía *Greece* **11F3**
Sitka *USA* **22E4**
Sivas *Turk* **14B2**
Siwa *Egypt* **19B2**
Sjaelland, I *Den* **6C1**
Skagen *Den* **2G7**
Skagerrak, Str *Nor/Den* **2F7**
Skagway *USA* **22E4**
Skara *Sweden* **2G7**
Skarzysko-Kamlenna *Pol* **7E2**
Skeena, R *Can* **22F4**
Skeenjek, R *USA* **22D3**
Skegness *Eng* **5F5**
Skellefteå *Sweden* **2J6**
Skíathos, I *Greece* **11E3**
Skidegate *Can* **22E4**
Skiemiewice *Pol* **7E2**
Skien *Nor* **2F7**
Skikda *Alg* **18C1**
Skipton *Eng* **5E5**
Skíros, I *Greece* **11E3**
Skive *Den* **2F7**
Skjern *Den* **6B1**
Skjoldungen *Greenland* **23O3**
Skópelos, I *Greece* **11E3**
Skopje *Yugos* **11E2**
Skövde *Sweden* **2G7**
Skovorodino *USSR* **13O4**
Skwentna *USA* **22C3**
Skwierzyna *Pol* **6D2**
Skye, I *Scot* **3B2**
Slagelse *Den* **2G7**
Slaney, R *Irish Rep* **5B5**
Slatina *Rom* **11E2**
Slav Brod *Yugos* **11D1**
Slave, R *Can* **22G3**
Slavgorod, Belorusskoya *USSR* **7G2**
Slavgorod, Rossiyskaya *USSR* **12J4**
Slavuta *USSR* **7F2**
Sławno *Pol* **6D2**
Sleat,Sound of, Chan *Scot* **4C3**
Slieve Bloom, Mts *Irish Rep* **5B5**
Sligo *Irish Rep* **3B3**
Sligo, B *Irish Rep* **3B3**
Sliven *Bulg* **11F2**
Slobozia *Rom* **11F2**
Slonim *USSR* **7F2**
Slough *Eng* **5E6**
Slovensko, Region *Czech* **7D3**
Slubice *Pol* **6C2**
Sluch', R *USSR* **7F2**
Słupsk *Pol* **6D2**
Slutsk *USSR* **7F2**
Slutsk, R *USSR* **7F2**
Slyne Head, Pt *Irish Rep* **3A3**
Slyudvanka *USSR* **13M4**
Smallwood Res *Can* **23M4**
Smara *Mor* **18A2**
Smederevo *Yugos* **11E2**
Smederevska Palanka *Yugos* **11E2**
Smith I *Can* **23L3**
Smøla, I *Nor* **2F6**
Smólikas, Mt *Greece* **11E2**
Smolyan *Bulg* **11E2**
Smorgon' *USSR* **7F2**
Snaefell, Mt *Eng* **5C4**
Snaefell, Mt *Iceland* **2B2**
Snake River Canyon *USA* **24B2**
Snares, Is *NZ* **31F5**
Sneek *Neth* **6B2**
Sněžka, Mt *Pol/Czech* **6D2**
Snøhetta, Mt *Nor* **2F6**
Snowdon, Mt *Wales* **5C5**
Snowdonia Nat Pk *Wales* **5C5**
Snowdrift *Can* **22G3**
Snow Lake *Can* **22H4**
Sobat, R *Sudan* **20D3**
Sobral *Brazil* **29K4**
Sochaczew *Pol* **7E2**
Socorro, I *Mexico* **26A3**
Sodankylä *Fin* **2K5**
Soddo *Eth* **20D3**
Soderhamn *Sweden* **2H6**
Södertälje *Sweden* **2H7**
Sodiri *Sudan* **20C2**
Sofala *Mozam* **21D5**
Sofiya *Bulg* **11E2**
Sofu Gan, I *Japan* **16H4**
Sogamoso *Colombia* **28D2**
Sognefjorden, Inlet *Nor* **2F6**
Sog Xian *China* **15H2**
Sohano *PNG* **31E1**
Sokodé *Togo* **18C4**
Sokołka *Pol* **7E2**
Sokolo *Mali* **18B3**
Søkongens Øy, I *Greenland* **23Q3**
Sokota *Eth* **20D2**
Sokoto *Nig* **18C3**
Solander I *NZ* **32A3**
Solent, Sd *Eng* **5E6**
Soligorsk *USSR* **7F2**
Solimões *Peru* **28D4**
Sol'Itesk *USSR* **12G4**
Sollefteå *Sweden* **2H6**
Solomon Is *Pacific O* **31E1**
Soltau *W Germ* **2F8**
Solway Firth, Estuary *Scot/Eng* **4D4**
Solwezi *Zambia* **21C5**
Soma *Turk* **11F3**
Somalia, Republic *E Africa* **14C5**
Sombor *Yugos* **11D1**
Somerset *Aust* **30D2**
Somerset, County *Eng* **5D6**
Somerset I *Can* **23J2**
Somes, R *Rom* **11E1**
Somoto *Nic* **28A1**
Sønderborg *Den* **2F8**
Søndre Strømfjord *Greenland* **23N3**
Søndre Upernavik *Greenland* **23N2**
Sondrio *Italy* **8D2**
Songea *Tanz* **21D5**
Sonora, R *Mexico* **26A2**
Sonoran Desert *USA* **24B3**
Sonsonate *El Salvador* **26D3**
Sonsorol, I *Pacific O* **17G6**
Soo Canals *USA/Can* **25E2**
Sopot *Pol* **7D2**
Sopron *Hung* **6D3**
Sora *Italy* **10C2**
Soria *Spain* **9B1**
Sørkjosen *Nor* **2J5**
Sørksop, I *Barents S* **12C2**
Sorocaba *Brazil* **29J8**
Soroki *USSR* **7F3**
Sorol, I *Pacific O* **17H6**
Sorong *Indon* **17G7**
Soroti *Uganda* **20D3**
Sørøya, I *Nor* **2J4**
Sorrento *Italy* **10C2**
Sorsatunturi, Mt *Fin* **2K5**
Sorsele *Sweden* **2H5**
Sosnowiec *Pol* **7D2**
Sos'va *USSR* **12H4**
Souanké *Congo* **20B3**
Soubré *Ivory Coast* **18B4**
Souillac *France* **8C3**
Souk *Alg* **18C1**
Söul *S Korea* **16F3**
Soummam, R *Alg* **9C2**
Sousa *Brazil* **29L5**
Sousse *Tunisia* **18D1**
South Africa, Republic *Africa* **21C7**
Southampton *Eng* **5E6**
Southampton I *Can* **23K3**
South Aulatsivik I *Can* **23M4**
South Australia, State *Aust* **30C3**
South Carolina, State *USA* **25E3**
South China S *S E Asia* **17E5**
South Dakota, State *USA* **24C2**
South Downs *Eng* **5E6**
Southen Alps, Mts *NZ* **32A2**
Southend-on-Sea *Eng* **5F6**
Southern Alps, Mts *NZ* **31F5**
Southern Cross *Aust* **30A4**
Southern Indian L *Can* **22J4**
South Foreland, Pt *Eng* **5F6**
South Georgia, I *UK* **27J8**
South Glamorgan, County *Wales* **5D6**
South Henik L *Can* **22J3**
South I *NZ* **32A2**
South Korea, Republic *SE Asia* **16F3**
South Nahanni, R *Can* **22F3**
Southport *Eng* **5D5**
South Ronaldsay, I *Scot* **4D2**
South Saskatchewan, R *Can* **22H4**
South Shields *Eng* **4E4**
South Taranaki Bight, B *NZ* **32B1**
South Uist, I *Scot* **4B3**
South West C *Aust* **30D5**
South Yemen, Republic *Arabian Pen* **14D3**
South Yorkshire, County *Eng* **5E5**
Sovetsk, R.S.F.SR *USSR* **7E1**
Soyo Congo *Angola* **21B4**
Sozh, R *USSR* **7G2**
Spain, Kingdom **9**
Spalding *Eng* **5E5**
Spartí *Greece* **11E3**
Spence Bay *Can* **23J3**
Spencer I *Can* **23L3**
Spenser Mts *NZ* **32B2**
Sperrin, Mts *N Ire* **4B4**
Spey, R *Scot* **4D3**
Speyer *W Germ* **6B3**
Spirit River *Can* **22G4**
Spitsbergen, I *Barents S* **12C2**
Spittal *Austria* **6C3**
Spjelkavik *Nor* **2F6**
Split *Yugos* **10D2**
Spokane *USA* **24B2**
Sporádhes, Is *Greece* **11F3**
Spratly, Is *S China Sea* **17E6**
Spree, R *E Germ* **6C2**
Springfield *USA* **25D3**
Springfield *USA* **25F2**
Springs *S Africa* **21C6**
Spurn Head, C *Eng* **5F5**
Sredhekolymsk *USSR* **13R3**
Sredinnyy Khrebet, Mts *USSR* **13S4**
Sredne Sibirskoye Ploskogorve, Tableand *USSR* **13M3**
Sretensk *USSR* **16E1**
Sri Lanka, Republic *S Asia* **15G5**
Srinagar *India* **15F2**
Sroda *Pol* **6D2**
Sta Ana *USA* **24B3**
Stack Skerry, I *Scot* **4C2**
Stade *W Germ* **6B2**
Staffa, I *Scot* **4B3**
Stafford, County *Eng* **5D5**
Stafford *Eng* **5D5**
Stallworthy,C *Can* **23J1**
Stalowa Wola *Pol* **7E2**
Stanke Dimitrov *Bulg* **11E2**
Stanley *Falkland Is* **27E8**
Stann Creek *Belize* **26D3**
Stanovoy Khrebet, Mts *USSR* **16F1**
Stanton Banks, Sand-bank *Scot* **4B3**
Starachowice *Pol* **7E2**
Stara Planiná, Mts *Bulg* **11E2**
Stara Zagora *Bulg* **11F2**
Stargard *Pol* **6D2**
Starnberg *W Germ* **6C3**
Starogard Gdanski *Pol* **7D2**
Starokonstantinov *USSR* **7F3**
Start Pt *Eng* **5D6**
Stavanger *Nor* **2F7**
Steenstrups Gletscher, Gl *Greenland* **23N2**
Stefansson I *Can* **22H2**
Steinkjer *Nor* **2G6**
Stendal *E Germ* **6C2**
Stephens,C *NZ* **32B2**
Stephenville *Can* **23N5**
Stevens Village *USA* **22D3**
Stewart I *NZ* **32A3**
Stewart Is *Solomon Is* **31F1**
Stewart River *Can* **22E3**
Steyr *Austria* **6C3**
Stirling *Scot* **4D3**
Stjørdal *Nor* **2G6**
Stockerau *Austria* **6D3**
Stockholm *Sweden* **2H7**
Stockport *Eng* **5D5**
Stockton *Eng* **5E4**
Stockton *USA* **24A3**
Stoke-on-Trent *Eng* **5D5**
Stokkseyri *Iceland* **2A2**
Stokmarknes *Nor* **2G5**
Stolbtsy *USSR* **2K8**
Stolin *USSR* **7F2**
Stonehaven *Scot* **4D3**
Storavan, L *Sweden* **2H5**
Støren *Nor* **2G6**
Stornoway *Scot* **4B2**
Storozhinets *USSR* **7F3**
Storsjon, L *Sweden* **2G6**
Storuman *Sweden* **2H5**
Stowmarket *Eng* **5F5**
Strablane *N Ire* **4B4**
Stralsund *E Germ* **6C2**
Stranda *Nor* **2F6**
Strangford Lough, L *Irish Rep* **5C4**
Strängnäs *Sweden* **2H7**
Stranraer *Scot* **4C4**
Strasbourg *France* **8D2**
Stratford *NZ* **32B1**
Stratford-on-Avon *Eng* **5E5**
Strathclyde, Region *Scot* **4C4**
Stretto de Messina, Str *Italy/Sicily* **10D3**
Stromboli, I *Italy* **10D3**
Stromness *Scot* **4D2**
Strømø *Faroes* **2D3**
Stromsund *Sweden* **2H6**
Ströms Vattudal, L *Sweden* **2G6**
Stronsay, I *Scot* **4D2**
Stroud *Eng* **5D6**
Struma, R *Bulg* **11E2**
Strumble Head, Pt *Wales* **5C5**
Strumica *Yugos* **11E2**
Stryy *USSR* **7E3**
Stryy, R *USSR* **7E3**
Stura, R *Italy* **10B2**
Sturt Creek, R *Aust* **30B2**
Stuttgart *W Germ* **6B3**
Stykkishólmur *Iceland* **2A1**
Styr, R *USSR* **7F2**
Subotica *Yugos* **11D1**
Sucre *Bol* **28E7**
Sudan, Republic *Africa* **20C2**
Sudbury *Can* **23K5**
Sudbury *Eng* **5F5**
Sudd, Swamp *Sudan* **20C3**
Suddie *Guyana* **29G2**
Sue, R *Sudan* **20C3**
Suerdrup Is *Can* **22H2**
Suez *Egypt* **19C1**
Suez Canal *Egypt* **19C1**
Suez,G of *Egypt* **19C2**
Suffolk, County *Eng* **5F5**
Sugoy, R *USSR* **13R3**
Sühbaatar *Mongolia* **16D1**
Suir, R *Irish Rep* **3B3**
Sukkertoppen *Greenland* **23N3**
Sukkertoppen, L *Greenland* **23N3**
Sukkozero *USSR* **2L6**
Sukses *Namibia* **21B6**
Sulaiman Ra, Mts *Pak* **15E3**
Sula Sgeir, I *Scot* **4B2**
Sulawesi, I *Indon* **17E7**
Sule Skerry, I *Scot* **4C2**
Sulina *Rom* **11F1**
Sulitjelma *Nor* **2H5**
Sullana *Peru* **28B4**
Sulmona *Italy* **10C2**
Sulu S *Philip* **17E6**
Sumampa *Arg* **27D3**
Sumatera, I *Indon* **17C6**
Sumba, I *Indon* **17E7**
Sumbawa, I *Indon* **17E7**
Sumbawanga *Tanz* **21D4**
Sumburgh Head, Pt *Scot* **4E2**
Sumisu, I *Japan* **16H3**
Summit Lake *Can* **22F4**
Sumner,L *NZ* **32B2**
Sunderland *Eng* **4E4**
Sundsvall *Sweden* **2H6**
Suntar *USSR* **13N3**
Sunyani *Ghana* **18B4**
Suonenjoki *Fin* **2K6**
Superior,L *USA/Can* **24E2**
Supiori, I *Indon* **17G7**
Surabaya *Indon* **17E7**
Surakarta *Indon* **17E7**
Suriname, Republic **29G3**
Surrey, County *Eng* **5E6**
Surtsey, I *Iceland* **2A2**
Suva *Fiji* **25G2**
Suva *Fiji* **31G2**
Suwałki *Pol* **7F2**
Suzhou *China* **16F3**
Svalbard, Is *Barents S* **12C2**
Svalyava *USSR* **7E3**
Svartenhuk Halvø, Region *Greenland* **23N2**
Svartisen, Mt *Nor* **2G5**
Sveg *Sweden* **2G6**
Svendborg *Den* **2G7**
Sverdlovsk *USSR* **12H4**
Sverdrup Chan *Can* **23J1**
Svetlogorsk *USSR* **7E2**
Svetogorsk *Fin* **2K6**
Svetozarevo *Yugos* **11E2**
Svilengrad *Bulg* **11F2**
Svir' *USSR* **7F2**
Švitavy *Czech* **6D3**
Svolvaer *Nor* **2G5**
Swain Reefs *Aust* **31E3**
Swains, I *American Samoa* **31H2**
Swale, R *Eng* **5E4**
Swan, I *Honduras* **26D3**
Swanage *Eng* **5E6**
Swan River *Can* **22H4**
Swansea *Wales* **5D6**
Swansea B *Wales* **5D6**
Swaziland, Kingdom *Africa* **21D6**
Sweden, Kingdom *N Europe* **2G7**
Świdnica *Pol* **6D2**
Swidwin *Pol* **6D2**
Swiebodzin *Pol* **6D2**
Swiecie *Pol* **7D2**
Swift Current *Can* **22H4**
Swindon *Eng* **5E6**
Świnoujście *Pol* **6C2**
Switzerland, Federal Republic *Europe* **8D2**
Swords *Irish Rep* **5B5**
Syderø *Faroes* **2D3**
Sydney *Aust* **30E4**
Sydney *Can* **23M5**
Syktyukar *USSR* **12G3**
Sylarna, Mt *Sweden* **2G6**
Sylt, I *W Germ* **6B1**
Syracuse *USA* **25F2**
Syrdal'ya, R *USSR* **12H5**
Syria, Republic *S W Asia* **14B2**
Szczecin *Pol* **6C2**
Szczecinek *Pol* **6D2**
Szczytno *Pol* **7E2**
Szeged *Hung* **7E3**
Székesfehérvar *Hung* **7D3**
Szekszard *Hung* **7D3**
Szolnok *Hung* **7D3**
Szombathely *Hung* **6D3**
Szprotawa *Pol* **6D2**

T

Tabar Is *PNG* **30E1**
Tabatinga *Brazil* **28E4**
Tabelbala *Alg* **18B2**
Table Mt *S Africa* **21B7**
Tábor *Czech* **6C3**
Tabora *Tanz* **20D4**
Tabou *Ivory Coast* **18B4**
Tabriz *Iran* **14C2**
Tacheng *China* **15G1**
Tacna *Peru* **28D7**
Tacoma *USA* **24A2**
Tadjoura *Djibouti* **20E2**
Tadzhikskaya SSR, Republic *USSR* **15E2**
Taegu *S Korea* **16F3**
Taejŏn *S Korea* **16F3**
Tafalla *Spain* **9B1**
Tafasaset, Watercourse *Alg* **18C2**
Taff, R *Wales* **5D6**
Tagant, Region *Maur* **18A3**
Taguenout Hagguerete, Well *Maur* **18B2**
Tagula, I *Solomon Is* **31E2**
Tahat, Mt *Alg* **18C2**
Tahoua *Niger* **18C3**
Taiani *Can* **23J3**
Taieri, R *NZ* **32B3**
Taihape *NZ* **32C1**
Tain *Scot* **4C3**
T' ai-pei *Taiwan* **16F4**
Taitao,Pen de *Chile* **27B7**
Taivalkoski *Fin* **2K5**
Taiwan, Republic *China* **16F4**
Taiyuan *China* **16E3**
Ta' izz *Yemen* **14C4**
Tajo, R *Spain* **9B1**
Takaka *NZ* **32B2**
Takapuna *NZ* **32B1**
Takjvak L *Can* **22G3**
Takkaze, R *Eth* **20D2**
Takoradi *Ghana* **18B4**
Talabanya *Hung* **7D3**
Talara *Peru* **28B4**
Talasea *PNG* **30E1**
Talavera de la Reina *Spain* **9B2**
Talcahuano *Chile* **27B5**
Taldy Kurgan *USSR* **15F1**
Talek, Desert, Region *Niger* **18C3**
Tali Post *Sudan* **20D3**
Tallahassee *USA* **25E3**
Tal'menka *USSR* **16B1**
Talpaki *USSR* **7E2**
Taltal *Chile* **27B3**
Tamale *Ghana* **18B4**
Tamanrasset *Alg* **18C2**
Tamanrasset, Watercourse *Alg* **18C2**
Tambacounda *Sen* **18A3**
Tambre, R *Spain* **9A1**
Tambura *Sudan* **20C3**
Tamchaket *Maur* **18A3**
Tamega, R *Port* **9A1**
Tamis, R *Rom* **11E1**
Tampa *USA* **25E4**
Tampere *Fin* **2J6**
Tamsagbulag *Mongolia* **16E2**
Tamworth *Eng* **5E5**
Tana *Nor* **2K4**
Tana, L *Eth* **20D2**
Tana, R *Kenya* **20E4**
Tana, R *Nor/Fin* **2K5**
Tanafjord, Inlet *Nor* **2K4**
Tanahmerah *Indon* **17H7**
Tandaho *Eth* **20E2**
Tandjung d'Urville, C *Indon* **17G7**
Tandjung Vals, C *Indon* **17G7**
Taneatua *NZ* **32C1**
Tanezrouft, Desert Region *Alg* **18B2**
Tanga *Tanz* **20D4**

Tanga Is **Tyrone**

Tanga Is *PNG* 31E1
Tanganyika,L *Tanz/Zaïre* 20C4
Tanger *Mor* 18B1
Tanggula Shan, Mts *China* 15H2
Tangra Yumco, L *China* 15G2
Tangshan *China* 16E3
Tanguy *USSR* 16D1
Tanjung Priok *Indon* 17D7
Tanjung Selatan, Pt *Indon* 30A1
Tanna, I *Vanuatu* 31F2
Tannu Ola, Mts *USSR* 16C1
Tanout *Niger* 18C3
Tanta *Egypt* 19C1
Tan-Tan *Mor* 18A2
Tanunak *USA* 22B3
Tanzania, Republic *Africa* 20D4
Taolañaro *Madag* 21E6
Tapachula *Mexico* 26C3
Tapajós, R *Brazil* 29G4
Tapanui *NZ* 32A3
Tapauá, R *Brazil* 28E5
Tapuaeniku, Mt *NZ* 32B2
Tapurucuara *Brazil* 28F4
Tara *USSR* 12J4
Tara, R *USSR* 12J4
Tara, R *Yugos* 11D2
Tarabuco *Bol* 28F7
Taradale *NZ* 32C1
Tarancón *Spain* 9B1
Taransay, I *Scot* 4B3
Taranto *Italy* 10D2
Tarapoto *Peru* 28C5
Tarare *France* 8C2
Tararua Range, Mts *NZ* 32C2
Tarat *Alg* 18C2
Tarawera *NZ* 32C1
Tarazona *Spain* 9B1
Tarbat Ness, Pen *Scot* 4D3
Tarbert, Strathclyde *Scot* 4C4
Tarbert, Western Isles *Scot* 4B3
Tarbes *France* 8B3
Tarcoola *Aust* 30C4
Tarfaya *Mor* 18A2
Tarhūnah *Libya* 19A1
Tarija *Bol* 28F8
Tarime *Tanz* 20D4
Tarim He, R *China* 15G1
Tarim Pendi, Basin *China* 15G2
Tarma *Peru* 28C6
Tarn, R *France* 8C3
Tarnobrzeg *Pol* 7E2
Tarnów *Pol* 7E3
Taroom *Aust* 30D3
Tarragona *Spain* 9C1
Tarrasa *Spain* 9C1
Tartan, Oilfield *N Sea* 4E2
Tashauz *USSR* 14D1
Tashkent *USSR* 15E1
Tashtagol *USSR* 12K4
Tashtyp *USSR* 13L4
Tasiussaq *Greenland* 23N2
Tasker, Well *Niger* 20B2
Tasman B *NZ* 32B2
Tasmania, I *Aust* 30D5
Tasman Mts *NZ* 32B2
Tasman S *NZ Aust* 31E4
Tassili du Hoggar, Desert, Region *Alg* 18C3
Tassili N'jjer, Desert, Region *Alg* 18C2
Tata *Mor* 18B2
Tatarsk *USSR* 12J4
Tatry, Mts *Pol/Czech* 7D3
Ta'u, I *American Samoa* 31H2
Tauá *Brazil* 29K5
Taumarunui *NZ* 32C1
Taunton *Eng* 5D6
Taupo *NZ* 32C1
Taupo,L *NZ* 32C1
Taurage *USSR* 7E1
Tauranga *NZ* 32C1
Tauranga Harbour, B *NZ* 32C1
Tauroa Pt *NZ* 32B1
Taveuni, I *Fiji* 31H2
Tavira *Port* 9A2
Tavistock *Eng* 5C6
Tawa *NZ* 32B2
Taweisha *Sudan* 20C2
Tay, R *Scot* 4D3
Taymura, R *USSR* 13L3
Tayshet *USSR* 13L4
Tayshir *Mongolia* 16C2
Tayside, Region *Scot* 4D3
Tazerbo, Region *Libya* 19B2
Tazovskiy *USSR* 12J3
Tbilisi *USSR* 12F5
Tchibanga *Gabon* 20B4
Tchigai,Plat du *Niger* 20B1
Tchin Tabaradene *Niger* 18C3
Tcholliré *Cam* 20B3
Tczew *Pol* 7D2
Te Anau *NZ* 32A3
Te Anua,L *NZ* 32A3
Te Aroha *NZ* 32C1
Te Awamutu *NZ* 32C1
Tecuci *Rom* 11F1
Tedzhen *USSR* 14E2
Tedzhen, R *USSR* 12H6
Tees, R *Eng* 5E4
Tefé *Brazil* 28F4
Tegucigalpa *Honduras* 26D3
Tehek L *Can* 22J3
Tehrān *Iran* 14D2
Tehuantepec *Mexico* 26C3
Teifi, R *Wales* 5C5
Tejo, R *Port* 9A2
Tekapo,L *NZ* 32B2
Tekeli *USSR* 15F1
Tekir Dağlari, Mts *Turk* 11F2
Te Kuiti *NZ* 32C1
Tela *Honduras* 26D3
Tel Aviv *Israel* 14B2
Teles Pires, R *Brazil* 29G5
Teli *USSR* 13K4
Tělok Flamingo, B *Indon* 17G7
Telšiai *USSR* 7E1
Teluk Berau, B *Indon* 17G7
Teluk Cendrawasih, B *Indon* 17G7
Temir *USSR* 12G5
Temirtau *USSR* 12J4
Templemore *Irish Rep* 5B5
Temuco *Chile* 27B5
Temuka *NZ* 32B2
Tena *Ecuador* 28C4
Tenby *Wales* 5C6
Ténéré, Desert Region *Niger* 20B2
Tenerife, I *Canary Is* 18A2
Tenke *Zaïre* 21C5
Tennant Creek *Aust* 30C2
Tennessee, State *USA* 25E3
Tenosique *Mexico* 26C3
Tepehuanes *Mexico* 26B2
Tepic *Mexico* 26B2
Teplice *Czech* 6C2
Te Puke *NZ* 32C1
Ter, R *Spain* 9C1
Téra *Niger* 18C3
Teramo *Italy* 10C2
Terceira, I *Açores* 18A1
Terebovlya *USSR* 7F3
Teresina *Brazil* 29K5
Termez *USSR* 14E2
Termoli *Italy* 10C2
Terni *Italy* 10C2
Ternopol *USSR* 7F3
Terracina *Italy* 10C2
Terrafirma *S Africa* 21C6
Terschelling, I *Neth* 6B2
Teruel *Spain* 9B1
Teshekpuk *USA* 22C2
Tesiyn Gol, Mts *Mongolia* 16C2
Tessalit *Mali* 18C2
Tessaoua *Niger* 18C3
Tete *Mozam* 21D5
Teterev, R *USSR* 7F2
Tetouan *Mor* 18B1
Teuco, R *Arg* 28F8
Teuco, R *Par* 27D2
Tevere, R *Italy* 10C2
Teviot, R *Scot* 4D4
Tevriz *USSR* 12J4
Te Waewae B *NZ* 32A3
Texas, State *USA* 24C3
Texel, I *Neth* 6A2
Thailand, Kingdom *SE Asia* 17D5
Thailand,G of *Thai* 17D5
Thames *NZ* 32C1
Thames, R *Eng* 5F6
Thar, Desert *India* 15F3
Thásos, I *Greece* 11E2
The Dalles *USA* 22F5
Thelon, R *Can* 22H3
Theodore *Aust* 30E3
Thermaïkós Kólpos, G *Greece* 11E2
Thesiger B *Can* 22F2
Thessaloníki *Greece* 11E2
Thetford *Eng* 5F5
Thicket Portage *Can* 22J4
Thiers *France* 8C2
Thiès *Sen* 18A3
Thika *Kenya* 20D4
Thimphu *Bhutan* 15G3
Thionville *France* 8D2
Thíra, I *Greece* 11F3
Thirsk *Eng* 5E4
Thisted *Den* 2F7
Thívai *Greece* 11E3
Thiviers *France* 8C2
Thomastown *Irish Rep* 5B5
Thom Bay *Can* 23J2
Thompson *Can* 22J4
Thompson Landing *Can* 22G3
Thomson, R *Aust* 30D3
Thornhill *Scot* 4D4
Thouars *France* 8B2
Three Kings Is *NZ* 25G4
Thule *Greenland* 23M2
Thunder Bay *Can* 23K5
Thuringer Wald, Upland *E Germ* 6C2
Thurles *Irish Rep* 5B5
Thursday I *Aust* 17H8
Thurso *Scot* 4D2
Tianjin *China* 16E3
Tiān Shan, Mts *C Asia* 15G1
Tibesti, Mountain Region *Chad* 20B1
Tibet, Autonomous Region *China* 15G2
Tiburón, I *Mexico* 26A2
Tichitt *Maur* 18B3
Tichla *Mor* 18A2
Ticul *Mexico* 26D2
Tidjikja *Maur* 18A3
Tierp *Sweden* 2H6
Tierra del Fuego, Territory *Arg* 27C8
Tigil *USSR* 13R4
Tigre, R *Peru* 28C4
Tigre, R *Ven* 28F2
Tigris, R *Iraq* 14C2
Tijuana *Mexico* 26A1
Tikopia, I *Solomon Is* 31F2
Tiksi *USSR* 13O2
Tilbury *Eng* 5F6
Tilcara *Arg* 27C2
Tillabéri *Niger* 18C3
Tillia *Niger* 18C3
Tílos, I *Greece* 11F3
Timaru *NZ* 32B2
Timbákion *Greece* 11E3
Timbédra *Maur* 18B3
Timétrine Monts, Mts *Mali* 18B3
Timia *Niger* 18C3
Timimoun *Alg* 18C2
Timişoara *Rom* 11E1
Timor, I *Indon* 30B1
Timor S *Aust/Indon* 30B2
Tindouf *Alg* 18B2
Tinfouchy *Alg* 18B2
Tin Fouye *Alg* 18C2
Tingmiarmiut *Greenland* 23O3
Tingo Maria *Peru* 28C5
Tingrela *Ivory Coast* 18B3
Tinian, I *Pacific O* 17H5
Tínos, I *Greece* 11F3
Tintagel Head, Pt *Eng* 5C6
Tin Tarabine, Watercourse *Alg* 18C2
Tin Zaouaten *Alg* 18C2
Tipperary, County *Irish Rep* 5B5
Tipperary *Irish Rep* 3B3
Tiranë *Alb* 11D2
Tire *Turk* 11F3
Tiree, I *Scot* 4B3
Tîrgovişte *Rom* 11F2
Tîrgu Jiu *Rom* 11E1
Tîrgu Mureş *Rom* 11E1
Tiris, Region *Mor* 18A2
Tîrnăveni *Rom* 11E1
Tírnavos *Greece* 11E3
Tirso, R *Sardegna* 10B2
Tisza, R *Hung* 7E3
Titograd *Yugos* 11D2
Titovo Užice *Yugos* 11D2
Titov Veles *Yugos* 11E2
Titule *Zaïre* 20C3
Tiverton *Eng* 5D6
Tivoli *Italy* 10C2
Tiyeglow *Somalia* 20E3
Tizimin *Mexico* 26D2
Tiznit *Mor* 18B2
Tlemcen *Alg* 18B1
Toamasina *Madag* 21E5
Tobago, I *Caribbean* 28F1
Tobermory *Scot* 4B3
Tobi, I *Pacific O* 17G6
Tobol, R *USSR* 12H4
Tobol'sk *USSR* 12H4
Tocantins, R *Brazil* 29J4
Tocopilla *Chile* 27B2
Tocorpuri *Bol* 27C2
Tocuyo, R *Ven* 28E1
Todos Santos *Mexico* 24B4
Tofua, I *Tonga* 31H2
Togo, Republic *Africa* 18C4
Tokara Retto, Arch *Japan* 16F4
Tokelau, Is *Pacific O* 31H1
Tokmak *USSR* 15F1
Tokomaru Bay *NZ* 32C1
Tokuno, I *Japan* 16F4
Tōkyō *Japan* 16H3
Tolaga Bay *NZ* 32C1
Toledo *Brazil* 29H8
Toledo *Spain* 9B2
Toledo *USA* 25E2
Toliara *Madag* 21E6
Tolima *Colombia* 28C2
Tolocin *USSR* 7F2
Tolosa *Spain* 9B1
Tomar *Port* 9A2
Tomaszów Mazowiecka *Pol* 7E2
Tomboco *Angola* 21B4
Tombouctou *Mali* 18B3
Tomelloso *Spain* 9B2
Tomkinson Range, Mts *Aust* 30B3
Tommot *USSR* 13O4
Tomorrit, Mt *Alb* 11E2
Tomsk *USSR* 12K4
Tonalá *Mexico* 26C3
Tonga, Is *Pacific O* 31H3
Tongatapu, I *Tonga* 31H3
Tongatapu Group, Is *Tonga* 31H3
Tonga Trench *Pacific O* 31H3
Tongtian He, R *China* 16C3
Tongue *Scot* 4C2
Tonhil *Mongolia* 13L5
Tonich *Mexico* 24C4
Tonj *Sudan* 20C3
Toowoomba *Aust* 30E3
Topeka *USA* 24D3
Topolobampo *Mexico* 24C4
Torbali *Turk* 11F3
Torbay *Eng* 5D6
Tordesillas *Spain* 9A1
Torgau *E Germ* 6C2
Tori *Eth* 20D3
Tori, I *Japan* 16H3
Torino *Italy* 10B1
Torit *Sudan* 20D3
Tormes, R *Spain* 9A1
Torne, L *Sweden* 2J5
Torneträsk *Sweden* 2H5
Torngat, Mts *Can* 23M4
Tornio *Fin* 2J5
Toronto *Can* 23L5
Tororo *Uganda* 20D3
Torrão *Port* 9A2
Torreblanca *Spain* 9C1
Torre del Greco *Italy* 10C2
Torrelavega *Spain* 9B1
Torremolinos *Spain* 9B2
Torreón *Mexico* 26B2
Torres Is *Vanuatu* 31F2
Torres Str *Aust* 30D2
Torres Vedras *Port* 9A2
Torshavn *Faroes* 2D3
Tortosa *Spain* 9C1
Toruń *Pol* 7D2
Tory, I *Irish Rep* 3B2
Tosno *USSR* 2L7
Totana *Spain* 9B2
Totnes *Eng* 5D6
Totness *Suriname* 29G2
Touba *Ivory Coast* 18B4
Touba *Sen* 18A3
Toubkal, Mt *Mor* 18B1
Touggourt *Alg* 18C1
Tougué *Guinea* 18A3
Toulon *France* 8D3
Toulouse *France* 8C3
Toumodi *Ivory Coast* 18B4
Tourcoing *France* 8C1
Tourine *Maur* 18A2
Tours *France* 8C2
Townsville *Aust* 30D2
Towy, R *Wales* 5D6
Tralee *Irish Rep* 3B3
Tramore *Irish Rep* 5B5
Tranås *Sweden* 2H7
Trangan, I *Indon* 17G7
Transvaal, Prov *S Africa* 21C6
Trapani *Italy* 10C3
Trarza, Region *Maur* 18A3
Travemünde *W Germ* 6C2
Travers,Mt *NZ* 32B2
Třebíč *Czech* 6D3
Trebinje *Yugos* 11D2
Trebon *Czech* 6C3
Trelew *Arg* 27C6
Trelleborg *Sweden* 2G7
Tremadog B *Wales* 5C5
Trenčin *Czech* 7D3
Trent, R *Eng* 5E5
Trenton *USA* 25F2
Trepassey *Can* 23N5
Três Lagoas *Brazil* 27F2
Trier *W Germ* 6B3
Trieste *Italy* 10C1
Trim *Irish Rep* 5B5
Trinidad *Bol* 28F6
Trinidad, I *Caribbean* 28F1
Trinidad & Tobago, Republic *Caribbean* 28F1
Trinity, R *USA* 24D3
Trinity B *Can* 23N5
Tripoli *Libya* 19A1
Trípolis *Greece* 11E3
Trnava *Czech* 7D3
Trobriand Is *PNG* 30E1
Trois Riviéres *Can* 23L5
Troitsk *USSR* 12H4
Trollhättan *Sweden* 2G7
Trollheimen, Mt *Nor* 2F6
Tromsø *Nor* 2H5
Trondheim *Nor* 2G6
Trondheimfjord, Inlet *Nor* 2G6
Troon *Scot* 4C4
Troudenni *Mali* 18B2
Trout L, Ontario *Can* 23J4
Troyan *Bulg* 11E2
Troyes *France* 8C2
Trujillo *Honduras* 26D3
Trujillo *Peru* 28C5
Trujillo *Spain* 9A2
Trujillo *Ven* 28D2
Truro *Can* 23M5
Truro *Eng* 5C6
Trust Territories of the Pacific Is *Pacific O* 17G6
Tsagaan Nuur, L *Mongolia* 16C2
Tsagan-Tologoy *USSR* 16C1
Tsaratanana *Madag* 21E5
Tsau *Botswana* 21C6
Tsavo *Kenya* 20D4
Tsavo Nat Pk *Kenya* 20D4
Tselinograd *USSR* 12J4
Tseterleg *Mongolia* 16D2
Tsetserleg *Mongolia* 16C2
Tshela *Zaïre* 20B4
Tshibala *Zaïre* 21C4
Tshikapa *Zaïre* 20C4
Tshuapa, R *Zaïre* 20C4
Tsihombe *Madag* 21E6
Tsiroanomandidy *Madag* 21E5
Tsna, R *USSR* 7F2
Tsumeb *Namibia* 21B5
Tsumis *Namibia* 21B6
Tua, R *Port* 9A1
Tuatapere *NZ* 32A3
Tubarão *Brazil* 27G3
Tübingen *W Germ* 6B3
Tubruq *Libya* 19B1
Tucson *USA* 24B3
Tucumán, State *Arg* 27C3
Tucupita *Ven* 28F2
Tudela *Spain* 9B1
Tugur *USSR* 13P4
Tukums *USSR* 7E1
Tukuyu *Tanz* 21D4
Tula *USSR* 12E4
Tulcán *Colombia* 28C3
Tul'chin *USSR* 7F3
Tuli *Zim* 21C6
Tullarnore *Irish Rep* 5B5
Tulle *France* 8C2
Tullow *Irish Rep* 5B5
Tuluá *Colombia* 28C3
Tulun *USSR* 13M4
Tumaco *Colombia* 28C3
Tumany *USSR* 13R3
Tumbes *Ecuador* 28B4
Tunduma *Zambia* 21D4
Tunduru *Tanz* 21D5
Tundzha, R *Bulg* 11F2
Tung-Chiang *Taiwan* 16F4
Tungnafellsjökull, Mts *Iceland* 2B2
Tunguska, R *USSR* 13M3
Tunis *Tunisia* 18D1
Tunisia, Republic *N Africa* 19C1
Tunja *Colombia* 28D2
Tupik *USSR* 7G1
Tupiza *Bol* 28E8
Tupungato, Mt *Arg* 27C4
Tura *USSR* 13M3
Turan *USSR* 13L4
Turbo *Colombia* 28C2
Turda *Rom* 11E1
Turfan Depression *China* 12K5
Turgay *USSR* 12H4
Turgen Uul, Mt *Mongolia* 13L5
Türi *USSR* 2K7
Turia, R *Spain* 9B2
Turkestan, Region *C Asia* 14E1
Turkestan *USSR* 15E1
Turkey, Republic *W Asia* 14A2
Turkmenskaya, SSR, Republic *USSR* 14D1
Turku *Fin* 2J6
Turkwel, R *Kenya* 20D3
Turnagain,C *NZ* 32C2
Turneffe I *Belize* 26D3
Turnu Măgurele *Rom* 11E2
Turnu-Severin *Rom* 11E2
Turpan *China* 13K5
Turtkul' *USSR* 14E1
Turukhansk *USSR* 13K3
Turuntayevo *USSR* 16D1
Tur'ya, R *USSR* 7E2
Tuscaloosa *USA* 25E3
Tutrakan *Bulg* 11F2
Tuttlingen *W Germ* 6B3
Tutulia, I *American Samoa* 31H2
Tuul Gol, R *Mongolia* 16D2
Tuvalu, Is *Pacific O* 31G1
Tuvinskaya ASSR, Republic *USSR* 13L4
Tuxtla Gutiérrez *Mexico* 26C3
Túy *Spain* 9A1
Tuzla *Yugos* 11D2
Tweed, R *Scot/Eng* 4D4
Tweedsmuir Hills *Scot* 4D4
Twillingate *Can* 23N5
Twins,The, Mt *NZ* 32B2
Tygda *USSR* 13O4
Tynda *USSR* 16F1
Tyne, R *Eng* 4E4
Tyne and Wear, Metropolitan County *Eng* 4E4
Tynemouth *Eng* 4E4
Tynset *Nor* 2G6
Tyrone, County *N Ire* 4B4

Tyrrhenian S | Welland

Tyrrhenian S *Italy* **10C2**
Tyumen' *USSR* **12H4**
Tyung, R *USSR* **13O3**
Tywyn *Wales* **5C5**
Tzouméрka, Mt *Greece* **11E3**

U

Uarsciek *Somalia* **20E3**
Ubangi, R *CAR* **20B3**
Ubeda *Spain* **9B2**
Ubekendt Ejland, I *Greenland* **23N2**
Uberaba *Brazil* **29J7**
Uberlândia *Brazil* **29J7**
Ubort, R *USSR* **7F2**
Ubundi *Zaïre* **20C4**
Ucayali, R *Peru* **28D5**
Uchur, R *USSR* **13P4**
Uda, R *USSR* **16C1**
Uddevalla *Sweden* **2G7**
Uddjaur, L *Sweden* **2H5**
Udine *Italy* **10C1**
Udskaya Guba, B *USSR* **13P4**
Udzha *USSR* **13N2**
Uele, R *Zaïre* **20C3**
Uelen *USSR* **13U3**
Uelzen *W Germ* **6C2**
Uere, R *Zaïre* **20C3**
Ufa *USSR* **12G4**
Ugab, R *Namibia* **21B6**
Ugaila, R *Tanz* **20D4**
Uganda, Republic *Africa* **20D3**
Uig *Scot* **4B3**
Uige *Angola* **21B4**
Ujfehértó *Hung* **7E3**
Ujiji *Tanz* **20C4**
Ujina *Chile* **27C2**
Ujung Pandang *Indon* **30A1**
Ukerewe, I *Tanz* **20D4**
Ukiah *USA* **24A3**
Ukmerge *USSR* **7E1**
Ukrainskaya SSR, Republic *USSR* **12D5**
Ulaanbaatar *Mongolia* **16D2**
Ulaangom *Mongolia* **16C2**
Ulan Ude *USSR* **16D1**
Ulan Ul Hu, L *China* **16C3**
Ul'beya, R *USSR* **13Q3**
Ulcinj *Yugos* **11D2**
Uldz *Mongolia* **16E2**
Uliastay *Mongolia* **16C2**
Ulla *USSR* **7F1**
Ullapool *Scot* **4C3**
Ullsfjorden, Inlet *Nor* **2H5**
Ullswater, L *Eng* **5D4**
Ulm *W Germ* **6C3**
Ulster, Region *N Ire* **5B4**
Ulungur He, R *China* **12K5**
Ulungur Hu, L *China* **12K5**
Ulva, I *Scot* **4B3**
Ulverston *Eng* **5D4**
Ulya, R *USSR* **13Q4**
Ulyanovka *USSR* **7G3**
Umanak *Greenland* **23N2**
Umba, R *Tanz* **20D4**
Umboi I *PNG* **30D1**
Ume, R *Sweden* **2H6**
Umea *Sweden* **2J6**
Umm Bell *Sudan* **20C2**
Umm Hagar *Eth* **20D2**
Umm Keddada *Sudan* **20C2**
Umm Ruwaba *Sudan* **20D2**
Umnaiti, R *Zim* **21C5**
Una, R *Yugos* **10D1**
Ungava B *Can* **23M4**
União de Vitória *Brazil* **27F3**
United Arab Emirates *Arabian Pen* **14D3**
United States of America *N America* **24B3**
United States Range, Mts *Can* **23K1**
Unst, I *Scot* **4E1**
Upata *Ven* **28F2**
Upemba Nat Pk *Zaïre* **21C4**
Upernavik *Greenland* **23N2**
Upolu, I *Western Samoa* **31H2**
Upper Hutt *NZ* **32C2**
Upper Laugh Erne, L *N Ire* **5B4**
Upper Seal,L *Can* **23L4**
Upper Volta, Republic *Africa* **18B3**
Uppsala *Sweden* **2H7**
Uralskiy Khrebet, Mts *USSR* **12G4**
Uranium City *Can* **22H4**
Urapunga *Aust* **17G8**
Ure, R *Eng* **5D4**
Urgench *USSR* **14E1**
Urla *Turk* **11F3**
Uroševac *Yugos* **11E2**
Uruaçu *Brazil* **29J6**
Uruapan *Mexico* **26C3**
Uruguay, Republic *S America* **27E4**
Uruguay, R *Urug* **27E4**
Ürümqi *China* **15G1**
Urup, I *USSR* **16J2**
Urziceni *Rom* **11F2**
Usa *China* **15G1**
Ushashi *Tanz* **20D4**
Ush Tobe *USSR* **12J5**
Ushuaia *Arg* **27C8**
Ushumun *USSR* **13O4**
Usk, R *Wales* **5D6**
Üsküdar *Turk* **14A1**
Usol'ye Sibirskoye *USSR* **13M4**
Ust'Belaya *USSR* **13T3**
Ust'Bol'sheretsk *USSR* **13R4**
Ustica, I *Italy* **10C3**
Ústí nad Labem *Czech* **6C2**
Ust'Ishim *USSR* **12J4**
Ustka *Pol* **6D2**
Ust'Kamchatsk *USSR* **13S4**
Ust'-Kamenogorsk *USSR* **12K5**
Ust Karabula *USSR* **13L4**
Ust'-Kut *USSR* **13M4**
Ust'Maya *USSR* **13P3**
Ust'Nera *USSR* **13Q3**
Ust'Nyukzha *USSR* **13N4**
Ust'Ordynskiy *USSR* **13M4**
Ust'Umal'ta *USSR* **13P4**
Usumacinta, R *Guatemala/Mexico* **26C3**
Usvyaty *USSR* **7G1**
Utah, State *USA* **24B3**
Utena *USSR* **7F1**
Utiel *Spain* **9B2**
Utrecht *Neth* **6B2**
Utrera *Spain* **9A2**
Utsjoki *Fin* **2K5**
Uusikaupunki *Fin* **2J6**
Uval *USSR* **12H4**
Uvéa, I *Nouvelle Calédonie* **31F3**
Uvinza *Tanz* **20C4**
Uvira *Zaïre* **20C4**
Uvkusigssat *Greenland* **23N2**
Uvs Nuur, L *China* **16C1**
Uyandina *USSR* **13Q3**
Uyar *USSR* **13L4**
Uyuni *Bol* **28E8**
Uzbekskaya, S.S.R., Republic *USSR* **14E1**
Uzerche *France* **8C2**
Uzh, R *USSR* **7F2**
Uzhgorod *USSR* **7E3**

V

Vaasa *Fin* **2J6**
Vác *Hung* **7D3**
Vacaria *Brazil* **27F3**
Vadodara *India* **15F3**
Vadsø *Nor* **2K4**
Va Gesell *Arg* **27E5**
Vågø *Faroes* **2D3**
Váh, R *Czech* **7D3**
Vaitupu, I *Tuvalu* **31G1**
Valcheta *Arg* **27C6**
Val de la Pascua *Ven* **28E2**
Valdepeñas *Spain* **9B2**
Valence *France* **8C3**
Valencia, Region *Spain* **9B2**
Valencia *Spain* **9B2**
Valencia *Ven* **28E1**
Valencia de Alcantara *Spain* **9A2**
Valenciennes *France* **8C1**
Valera *Ven* **28D2**
Valga *USSR* **2K7**
Valjevo *Yugos* **11D2**
Valkeakoski *Fin* **2J6**
Valladolid *Mexico* **26D2**
Valladolid *Spain* **9B1**
Valledupar *Colombia* **28D1**
Vallée de l'Azaouak, V *Niger* **18C3**
Vallée Tilemis, V *Mali* **18C3**
Valle Grande *Bol* **28F7**
Valls *Spain* **9C1**
Valmiera *USSR* **7F1**
Valognes *France* **8B2**
Valparaíso *Chile* **27B4**
Valverde del Camino *Spain* **9A2**
Vammala *Fin* **2J6**
Vanavara *USSR* **13M3**
Vancouver *Can* **22F5**
Vancouver I *Can* **22F5**
Van Diemen,C *Aust* **17G8**
Van Diemen G *Aust* **30C2**
Vänern, L *Sweden* **2G7**
Vänersborg *Sweden* **2G7**
Vangaindrano *Madag* **21E6**
Vanikoro, I *Solomon Is* **31F2**
Vankarem *USSR* **13U3**
Vännäs *Sweden* **2H6**
Vannes *France* **8B2**
Vansittart I *Can* **23K3**
Vanua Lava, I *Vanuatu* **31F2**
Vanua Levu, I *Fiji* **31G2**
Vanuatu, Is *Pacific O* **31F2**
Väränasi *India* **15G3**
Varangerfjord, Inlet *Nor* **2K4**
Varangerhalvøya, Pen *Nor* **2L4**
Varazdin *Yugos* **10D1**
Varberg *Sweden* **2G7**
Varde *Den* **2F7**
Vardø *Nor* **2L4**
Varéna *USSR* **7E2**
Varkaus *Fin* **2K6**
Varna *Bulg* **11F2**
Värnamo *Sweden* **2G7**
Vascongadas, Region *Spain* **9B1**
Västerås *Sweden* **2H7**
Västervik *Sweden* **2H7**
Vasto *Italy* **10C2**
Vatnajökull, Mts *Iceland* **2B2**
Vatneyri *Iceland* **2A1**
Vatra Dornei *Rom* **11F1**
Vättern, L *Sweden* **2G7**
Vaupés, R *Colombia* **28D3**
Vava'u Group, Is *Tonga* **31H2**
Växjö *Sweden* **2G7**
Vega, I *Nor* **2G5**
Vejer de la Frontera *Spain* **9A2**
Vejle *Den* **2F7**
Velebit, Mts *Yugos* **10D2**
Velenje *Yugos* **10D1**
Velikaya, R, Rossiyskaya *USSR* **13T3**
Velikaya, R, RSFSR *USSR* **7F1**
Velikaya, R *USSR* **2K7**
Velikiye-Luki *USSR* **12E4**
Veliko Tŭrnovo *Bulg* **11F2**
Vélingara *Sen* **18A3**
Velizh *USSR* **7G1**
Vella Lavella, I *Solomon Is* **31E1**
Venado Tuerto *Arg* **27D4**
Vendôme *France* **8C2**
Venezia *Italy* **10C1**
Venezuela, Republic *S America* **28E2**
Venlo *Neth* **6B2**
Venta, R *USSR* **7E1**
Ventspils *USSR* **7E1**
Ventuari, R *Ven* **28E3**
Vera *Spain* **9B2**
Veracruz *Mexico* **26C3**
Verdon, R *France* **8D3**
Vereeniging *S Africa* **21C6**
Vereshchagino *USSR* **12K3**
Verga,C *Guinea* **18A3**
Verin *Spain* **9A1**
Verissimo Sarmento *Angola* **21C4**
Verkh Angara, R *USSR* **13N4**
Verkheimbatskoye *USSR* **13K3**
Verkhnevilyuysk *USSR* **13O3**
Verkhoyansk *USSR* **13P3**
Verkhoyanskiy Khrebet, Mts *USSR* **13O3**
Vermont, State *USA* **25F2**
Verola *Greece* **11E2**
Verona *Italy* **10C1**
Versailles *France* **8C2**
Veselinovo *USSR* **7G3**
Vesoul *France* **8D2**
Vesterålen, Is *Nor* **2G5**
Vestfjorden, Inlet *Nor* **2G5**
Vestmannaeyjar *Iceland* **2A2**
Vesuvio, Mt *Italy* **10C2**
Veszprém *Hung* **7D3**
Vetlanda *Sweden* **2H7**
Viana do Castelo *Port* **9A1**
Viborg *Den* **2F7**
Vibo Valentia *Italy* **10D3**
Vicenza *Italy* **10C1**
Vich *Spain* **9C1**
Vichada, R *Colombia* **28E3**
Vichy *France* **8C2**
Victor Harbor *Aust* **30C4**
Victoria *Can* **22F5**
Victoria *Hong Kong* **16E4**
Victoria, R *Aust* **30C2**
Victoria, State *Aust* **30D4**
Victoria Falls *Zambia/Zim* **21C5**
Victoria I *Can* **22G2**
Victoria,L *C Africa* **20D4**
Victoria,Mt *PNG* **17H7**
Victoria Nile, R *Uganda* **20D3**
Victoria Range, Mts *NZ* **32B2**
Victoria River Downs *Aust* **30C2**
Victoria Str *Can* **22H3**
Videle *Rom* **11F2**
Vidin *Bulg* **11E2**
Vidzy *USSR* **7F1**
Viedma *Arg* **27D6**
Viella *Spain* **9C1**
Vienne *France* **8C2**
Vienne, R *France* **8C2**
Vientiane *Laos* **17D5**
Vierzon *France* **8C2**
Vieste *Italy* **10D2**
Vietnam, Republic *S E Asia* **17D5**
Vignemale, Mt *France* **8B3**
Vigo *Spain* **9A1**
Vijayawāda *India* **15G4**
Vijosë, R *Alb* **11D2**
Vik *Iceland* **2B2**
Vikhren, Mt *Bulg* **11E2**
Viking North, Gasfield *N Sea* **5G5**
Viking South, Gasfield *N Sea* **5G5**
Vikna, I *Nor* **2G6**
Vila da Maganja *Mozam* **21D5**
Vila Machado *Mozam* **21D5**
Vilanculos *Mozam* **21D6**
Vila Nova de Gaia *Port* **9A1**
Vila Real *Port* **9A1**
Vila Vasco da Gama *Mozam* **21D5**
Vileyka *USSR* **7F2**
Vilhelmina *Sweden* **2H6**
Vilhena *Brazil* **29G6**
Vilkovo *USSR* **7F3**
Villaba *Spain* **9A1**
Villach *Austria* **10C1**
Villahermosa *Mexico* **26C3**
Villa Montes *Bol* **28F8**
Villanueva de la Serena *Spain* **9A2**
Villanueva-y-Geltrú *Spain* **9C1**
Villarreal *Spain* **9B2**
Villarrica *Par* **27E3**
Villarrobledo *Spain* **9B2**
Villavicencio *Colombia* **28D3**
Villefranche *France* **8C2**
Ville-Marie *Can* **23L5**
Villena *Spain* **9B2**
Villeneuve-sur-Lot *France* **8C3**
Villeurbanne *France* **8C2**
Vilnius *USSR* **7F2**
Vilyuy *USSR* **13N3**
Vilyuysk *USSR* **13O3**
Viña del Mar *Chile* **27B4**
Vinaroz *Spain* **9C1**
Vindel, R *Sweden* **2H5**
Vinkovci *Yugos* **11D1**
Vinnitsa *USSR* **7F3**
Virei *Angola* **21B5**
Virginia, State *USA* **25F3**
Virovitica *Yugos* **10D1**
Vis, I *Yugos* **10D2**
Visby *Sweden* **2H7**
Viscount Melville Sd *Can* **22H2**
Višegrad *Yugos* **11D2**
Viseu *Port* **9A1**
Vishākhapatnam *India* **15G4**
Vitavia, R *Czech* **6C3**
Vitebsk *USSR* **7G1**
Viterbo *Italy* **10C2**
Vitigudino *Spain* **9A1**
Viti Levu, I *Fiji* **25G2**
Vitim, R *USSR* **13N4**
Vitória *Brazil* **29L8**
Vitoria *Spain* **9B1**
Vitória da Conquista *Brazil* **29K6**
Vitré *France* **8B2**
Vittangi *Sweden* **2J5**
Vittoria *Italy* **10C3**
Vityaz Depth *Pacific O* **16J2**
Vivero *Spain* **9A1**
Vivi, R *USSR* **13L3**
Vizhne-Angarsk *USSR* **13N4**
Vladeasa, Mt *Rom* **11E1**
Vladimir *USSR* **12F4**
Vladimir Volynskiy *USSR* **7E2**
Vladivostok *USSR* **13P5**
Vlieland, I *Neth* **6A2**
Vlissingen *Neth* **8C1**
Vlorë *Alb* **11D2**
Vöcklabruck *Austria* **6C3**
Vohibinany *Madag* **21E5**
Vohimarina *Madag* **21F5**
Voi *Kenya* **20D4**
Voinjama *Lib* **18B4**
Voiron *France* **8D2**
Volcán Lullaillaco, Mt *Chile* **28E8**
Volcán Puraće, Mt *Colombia* **28C3**
Volga, R *USSR* **12F5**
Volgograd *USSR* **12F5**
Volkovysk *USSR* **7E2**
Volochanka *USSR* **13L2**
Vólos *Greece* **11E3**
Volta Redonda *Brazil* **29K8**
Vopnafjörður *Iceland* **23R3**
Vordingborg *Den* **6C1**
Vorkuta *USSR* **12H3**
Vorma, R *Nor* **2G6**
Voronezh *USSR* **12E4**
Voron'ya, R *USSR* **2M5**
Võru *USSR* **2K7**
Vosges, Mts *France* **8D2**
Voss *Nor* **2F6**
Vostochnyy Sayan, Mts *USSR* **13L4**
Vranje *Yugos* **11E2**
Vratsa *Bulg* **11E2**
Vrbas *Yugos* **11D1**
Vrbas, R *Yugos* **10D2**
Vrbovsko *Yugos* **10C1**
Vreed en Hoop *Guyana* **29G2**
Vršac *Yugos* **11E1**
Vrtoče *Yugos* **10D2**
Vukovar *Yugos* **11D1**
Vulcano, I *Italy* **10C3**
Vuollerim *Sweden* **2J5**
Vyrnwy, R *Wales* **5D5**
Vyškov *Czech* **6D3**

W

Wa *Ghana* **18B3**
Wabach *USA* **25E3**
Wabasca, R *Can* **22G4**
Wabowden *Can* **22J4**
Wabush *Can* **23M4**
Waddān *Libya* **19A2**
Waddington,Mt *Can* **22F4**
Wadi el Milk, Watercourse *Sudan* **20C2**
Wadi Halfa *Sudan* **19C2**
Wadi Howa, Watercourse *Sudan* **20C2**
Wadi Ibra, Watercourse *Sudan* **20C2**
Wad Medani *Sudan* **20D2**
Wager B *Can* **23K3**
Wager Bay *Can* **23J3**
Wagin *Aust* **30A4**
Waha *Libya* **19A2**
Waiau *NZ* **32B2**
Waiau, R *NZ* **32A3**
Waiau, R *NZ* **32B2**
Waigeo, I *Indon* **17G6**
Waihi *NZ* **32C1**
Waikaremoana,L *NZ* **32C1**
Waikato, R *NZ* **32C1**
Waikouaiti *NZ* **32B3**
Waimakariri, R *NZ* **32B2**
Waimate *NZ* **32B2**
Waingapu *Indon* **30B1**
Waipara *NZ* **32B2**
Waipukurau *NZ* **32C2**
Wairarapa,L *NZ* **32C2**
Wairau, R *NZ* **32B2**
Wairoa *NZ* **32C1**
Wairoa, R *NZ* **32C1**
Waitaki, R *NZ* **32B2**
Waitara *NZ* **32B1**
Waitomo *NZ* **32C1**
Waiuku *NZ* **32B1**
Wajir *Kenya* **20E3**
Wakatipu,L *NZ* **32A3**
Wakefield *Eng* **5E5**
Wakkanai *China* **16H2**
Walbrzych *Pol* **6D2**
Walcz *Pol* **6D2**
Waldia *Eth* **20E2**
Wales, Country *U K* **5D5**
Wales I *Can* **23K3**
Walikale *Zaïre* **20C4**
Walouru *NZ* **32C1**
Walsall *Eng* **5E5**
Walsenburgh *USA* **24C3**
Walvis Bay *Namibia* **21B6**
Wamba, R *Zaïre* **20B4**
Wanaka *NZ* **32A2**
Wanaka,L *NZ* **32A2**
Wanganui *NZ* **32B1**
Wanganui, R *NZ* **32C1**
Wanle Weyne *Somalia* **20E3**
Warder *Eth* **20E3**
Ward,Mt *NZ* **32A3**
Warmbad *S Africa* **21C6**
Warnemünde *E Germ* **6C2**
Warrego, R *Aust* **30D3**
Warrenpoint *N Ire* **5B4**
Warrington *Eng* **5D5**
Warszawa *Pol* **7E2**
Warta, R *Pol* **7D2**
Warwick, County *Eng* **5E5**
Warwick *Eng* **5E5**
Washburn L *Can* **22H2**
Washington, District of Columbia *USA* **25F3**
Washington, State *USA* **24A2**
Washington Land *Greenland* **23M1**
Wash,The *Eng* **5F5**
Waterford, County *Irish Rep* **5B5**
Waterford *Irish Rep* **3B3**
Waterford Harbour *Irish Rep* **5B5**
Waterways *Can* **22G4**
Watford *Eng* **5E6**
Watkins Bjerge, Mt *Greenland* **23Q3**
Watrous *Can* **24C1**
Watsa *Zaïre* **20C3**
Watson Lake *Can* **22F3**
Wau *PNG* **17H7**
Wau *Sudan* **20C3**
Waua *Can* **23K5**
Wave Hill *Aust* **30C2**
Waveney, R *Eng* **5F5**
Wāw Al Kabīr *Libya* **19A2**
Wāw an Nāmūs, Well *Libya* **19A2**
Weald,The, Upland *Eng* **5F6**
Wear, R *Eng* **4E4**
Weddell I *Falkland Is* **27D8**
Weiden *W Germ* **6C3**
Weipa *Aust* **30D2**
Weissenfels *E Germ* **6C2**
Welkom *S Africa* **21C6**
Welland, R *Eng* **5E5**

Name	Ref
Wellesley Is *Aust*	30C2
Wellingborough *Eng*	5E5
Wellington *NZ*	32B2
Wellington Chan *Can*	23J2
Wells *Eng*	5D6
Wellsford *NZ*	32B1
Wells,L *Aust*	30B3
Wels *Austria*	6C3
Welshpool *Wales*	5D5
Werra, R *E Germ*	6C2
Wesel *W Germ*	6B2
Weser, R *W Germ*	6B2
Wesleyville *Can*	23N5
Wessel Is *Aust*	30C2
West Bromwich *Eng*	5E5
Westerland *W Germ*	6B2
Western Australia, State *Aust*	30B3
Western Ghats, Mts *India*	15F4
Western Isles *Scot*	4B3
Western Sahara, Region *Mor*	18A2
Western Samoa, Is *Pacific O*	31H2
West Falkland, I *Falkland Is*	27D8
West Germany, Federal Republic *Europe*	6B2
West Glamorgan, County *Wales*	5D6
Westmeath, County *Irish Rep*	5B5
West Midlands, County *Eng*	5E5
Westminster *Eng*	5E6
Weston-super-Mare *Eng*	5D6
West Palm Beach *USA*	25E4
Westport *NZ*	32B2
Westray, I *Scot*	3C2
West Sole, Gasfield *N Sea*	5F5
West Sussex *Eng*	5E6
West Virginia, State *USA*	25E3
West Yorkshire, County *Eng*	5E5
Wete *Tanz*	20D4
Wewak *PNG*	30D1
Wexford, County *Irish Rep*	5B5
Wexford *Irish Rep*	5B5
Weyburn *Can*	22H5
Weymouth *Eng*	5D6
Whakatane *NZ*	32C1
Whakatane, R *NZ*	32C1
Whalsay, I *Scot*	4E1
Whangarei *NZ*	32B1
Wharfe, R *Eng*	5E5
Whataroa *NZ*	32B2
Whitby *Eng*	5E4
White B *Can*	23N4
White Coomb, Mt *Scot*	3C2
Whitegull L *Can*	23M4
Whitehaven *Eng*	5D4
Whitehorse *Can*	22E3
White I *NZ*	32C1
White Nile, R *Sudan*	20D2
White River *Can*	23K5
Whithorn *Scot*	4C4
Wholdia L *Can*	22H3
Whyalla *Aust*	30C4
Wichita *USA*	24D3
Wick *Scot*	4D2
Wicklow, County *Irish Rep*	5B5
Wicklow *Irish Rep*	5B5
Wicklow, Mts *Irish Rep*	5B5
Wielun *Pol*	7D2
Wien *Austria*	6D3
Wiener Neustadt *Austria*	6D3
Wieprz, R *Pol*	7E2
Wiesbaden *W Germ*	6B2
Wigan *Eng*	5D5
Wigtown *Scot*	4C4
Wigtown B *Scot*	4C4
Wilhelm,Mt *PNG*	30D1
Wilhelmshaven *W Germ*	6B2
Williams Lake *Can*	22F4
Willis Group, Is *Aust*	30E2
Wilmington *USA*	25F3
Wilson *USA*	25F3
Wilson,C *Can*	23K3
Wiltshire, County *Eng*	5E6
Wiluna *Aust*	30B3
Winchester *Eng*	5E6
Windermere *Eng*	5D4
Windhoek *Namibia*	21B6
Windorah *Aust*	30D3
Windsor *Eng*	5E6
Windsor, Nova Scotia *Can*	23M5
Winisk, R *Can*	23K4
Winisk L *Can*	23K4
Winneba *Ghana*	18B4
Winnipeg *Can*	22J4
Winnipeg,L *Can*	22J4
Winnipegosis *Can*	22J4
Winona *USA*	23J5
Winston-Salem *USA*	25E3
Winton *Aust*	30D3
Winton *NZ*	32A3
Wisbech *Eng*	5F5
Wisconsin, State *USA*	25E2
Wisconsin Rapids *USA*	23K5
Wisla, R *Pol*	7D2
Wismar *E Germ*	6C2
Witagron *Suriname*	29G2
Witchita Falls *USA*	24D3
Witham, R *Eng*	5E5
Withernsea *Eng*	5F5
Witney *Eng*	5E6
Wittenberge *E Germ*	6C2
Wittenoom *Aust*	30A3
Wladyslawowo *Pol*	7D2
Wloclawek *Pol*	7D2
Wlodawa *Pol*	7E2
Wokam *Indon*	17G7
Woking *Eng*	5E6
Woleai, I *Pacific O*	17H6
Wolfsberg *Austria*	6C3
Wolfsburg *W Germ*	6C2
Wollaston Lake *Can*	22H4
Wollaston Pen *Can*	22G3
Wollongong *Aust*	30E4
Wolow *Pol*	6D2
Wolverhampton *Eng*	5D5
Wonthaggi *Aust*	30D4
Woodlark, I *PNG*	31E1
Woodroffe,Mt *Aust*	30C3
Woodville *NZ*	32C2
Woomera *Aust*	30C4
Woomera *Aust*	30C4
Worcester *Eng*	5D5
Worcester *USA*	25F2
Workington *Eng*	5D4
Worms *W Germ*	6B3
Worms Head, Pt *Wales*	5C6
Worthing *Eng*	5E6
Wrangell Mts *USA*	22D3
Wrath,C *Scot*	3B2
Wrexham *Wales*	5D5
Wrigley *Can*	22F3
Wroclaw *Pol*	6D2
Wrzesnia *Pol*	7D2
Wuhan *China*	16E3
Wuppertal *W Germ*	6B2
Würzburg *W Germ*	6B3
Wurzen *E Germ*	6C2
Wuvulu, I *Pacific O*	17H7
Wuxi *China*	16F3
Wye, R *Eng*	5D6
Wylye, R *Eng*	5D6
Wymondham *Eng*	5F5
Wyndham *Aust*	30B2
Wynniatt B *Can*	22G2
Wyoming, State *USA*	24C2

X

Xai Xai *Mozam*	21D6
Xangongo *Angola*	21B5
Xánthi *Greece*	11E2
Xiaguan *China*	16C4
Xi' an *China*	16D3
Xingu, R *Brazil*	29H4
Xingxingxia *China*	16C2
Xuddur *Somalia*	20E3
Xuzhou *China*	16E3

Y

Yabassi *Cam*	20B3
Yablonovyy Khrebet, Mts *USSR*	16D1
Yacuiba *Bol*	28F8
Yafran *Libya*	19A1
Yagotin *USSR*	7G2
Yahuma *Zaïre*	20C3
Yakoma *Zaïre*	20C3
Yakutsk *USSR*	13O3
Yakutskaya ASSR, Republic *USSR*	13N3
Yalinga *CAR*	20C3
Yalong, R *China*	16C3
Yalova *Turk*	11F2
Yamarovka *USSR*	16E1
Yambio *Sudan*	20C3
Yambol *Bulg*	11F2
Yamsk *USSR*	13R4
Yana, R *USSR*	13P3
Yangambi *Zaïre*	20C3
Yankskiy Zaliv, B *USSR*	13P2
Yanqqi *China*	15G1
Yaoundé *Cam*	20B3
Yapen, I *Indon*	17G7
Yap Is *Pacific O*	17G6
Yaqui, R *Mexico*	26B2
Yari, R *Colombia*	28D3
Yarkant He, R *China*	15F2
Yarmouth *Can*	23M5
Yaroslavl' *USSR*	12E4
Yartsevo *USSR*	13L3
Yarumal *Colombia*	28C2
Yasawa Group, Is *Fiji*	25G2
Yasinya *USSR*	7E3
Yathkyed L *Can*	22J3
Yatolema *Zaïre*	20C3
Yavari *Peru*	28D4
Yazd *Iran*	14D2
Yedintsy *USSR*	7F3
Yei *Sudan*	20D3
Yell, I *Scot*	3C1
Yellowhead P *Can*	22G4
Yellowhead P *Can*	24B1
Yellowknife *Can*	22G3
Yellow Sea *China/Korea*	16F3
Yellowstone, R *USA*	24C2
Yel'nya *USSR*	7G2
Yel'sk *USSR*	7F2
Yelverton B *Can*	23K1
Yemen, Republic *Arabian Pen*	14D3
Yenisey, R *USSR*	12K3
Yeniseysk *USSR*	13L4
Yeniseyskiy Kryazh, Ridge *USSR*	13L3
Yeniseyskiy Zai, B *USSR*	12J2
Yeo, R *Eng*	5D6
Yeovil *Eng*	5D6
Yerbogachen *USSR*	13M3
Yerevan *USSR*	12F5
Yerofey Pavlovich *USSR*	13O4
Yeropol *USSR*	13S3
Yessey *USSR*	13M3
Yetti *Maur*	18B2
Yiannitsá *Greece*	11E2
Yining *China*	15G1
Yirga Alem *Eth*	20D3
Yirol *Sudan*	20D3
Yirshi *China*	13N5
Yíthion *Greece*	11E3
Ylitornio *Sweden*	2J5
Ylivieska *Fin*	2J6
Yogyakarta *Indon*	17E7
Yokadouma *Cam*	20B3
Yokohama *Japan*	16G3
Yonne, R *France*	8C2
York *Eng*	5E5
York,C *Aust*	30D2
York Factory *Can*	23J4
York Sd *Aust*	17F8
Yorkshire Dales Nat Pk *Eng*	5D4
Yorkshire Moors, Moorland *Eng*	3C3
Yorkshire Wolds, Upland *Eng*	5E4
Yorkton *Can*	22H4
Yorton *Can*	24C1
Youghal *Irish Rep*	3B3
Young Range, Mts *NZ*	32A2
Ystad *Sweden*	2G7
Ystwyth, R *Wales*	5D5
Ythan, R *Scot*	4D3
Yubi,C *Mor*	18A2
Yucatan, Pen *Mexico*	26D3
Yucatan Chan *Mexico/Cuba*	26D2
Yudoma, R *USSR*	13P4
Yugoslavia, Federal Republic *Europe*	11D2
Yukon Territory *Can*	22E3
Yumen *China*	16C3
Yurimaguas *Peru*	28C5
Yushu, Tibet *China*	15H2
Yuzh Bug, R *USSR*	7F3
Yuzhno-Sakhalinsk *USSR*	13Q5

Z

Zaandam *Neth*	6A2
Zabaykal'sk *USSR*	16E2
Zaborozh' ye *USSR*	12E5
Zabreh *Czech*	6D3
Zabrze *Pol*	7D2
Zadar *Yugos*	10D2
Zafra *Spain*	9A2
Zagazig *Egypt*	19C1
Zagora *Mor*	18B1
Zagreb *Yugos*	10D1
Zähedän *Iran*	14E3
Zahrez Chergui, Marshland *Alg*	9C2
Zaïre, Republic *Africa*	20C4
Zaïre, R *Zaïre/Congo*	20B4
Zajecăr *Yugos*	11E2
Zakamensk *USSR*	16D1
Zákinthos, I *Greece*	11E3
Zakopane *Pol*	7D3
Zalaegerszeg *Hung*	6D3
Zalâu *Rom*	11E1
Zalew Szczeciński, Lg *Pol*	6C2
Zalingei *Sudan*	20C2
Zaliv Akademii, B *USSR*	13P4
Zaliv Faddeya, B *USSR*	13M2
Zaliv Shelekhova, B *USSR*	13R3
Zambezi *Zambia*	21C5
Zambezi, R *Zambia*	21C5
Zambia, Republic *Africa*	21C5
Zamboanga *Phil*	17F6
Zambrów *Pol*	7E2
Zamora *Ecuador*	28C4
Zamora *Spain*	9A1
Zamość *Pol*	7E2
Zanaga *Congo*	20B4
Záncara, R *Spain*	9B2
Zanzibar *Tanz*	20D4
Zanzibar, I *Tanz*	20D4
Zaouatanlaz *Alg*	18C2
Zapadnaja Dvina, R *USSR*	2K7
Zapadno Dvina *USSR*	7G1
Zapadno-Sibirskaya Nizmennost', Lowland *USSR*	12H3
Zapadnyy Sayan, Mts *USSR*	13L4
Zaragoza *Spain*	9B1
Zarara *Ven*	28E2
Zarasai *USSR*	7F1
Zaria *Nig*	18C3
Zaruma *Ecuador*	28C4
Zary *Pol*	6D2
Zarzis *Tunisia*	18D1
Zawiercie *Pol*	7D2
Zawilah *Libya*	19A2
Zayarsk *USSR*	13M4
Zaysan *USSR*	12K5
Zayü, Mt *China*	16C4
Zduńska Wola *Pol*	7D2
Zeebrugge *Belg*	6A2
Zegueren, Watercourse *Mali*	18C3
Zeila *Somalia*	20E2
Zeitz *E Germ*	6C2
Zelenogorsk *USSR*	2K6
Zelten *Libya*	19A2
Zemio *CAR*	20C3
Zemlya Aleksandry, I *Barents S*	12F1
Zemlya Frantsa Josifa, Is *Barents S*	12F2
Zemlya Georga, I *Barents S*	12F1
Zemlya Vil'cheka, I *Barents S*	12H1
Zeya *USSR*	13O4
Zeya, Res *USSR*	13O4
Zézere, R *Port*	9A1
Zgierz *Pol*	7D2
Zharkovskiy *USSR*	7G1
Zhashkov *USSR*	7G3
Zhatay *USSR*	13O3
Zhengzhou *China*	16E3
Zhigalovo *USSR*	16D1
Zhigansk *USSR*	13O3
Zhitkovichi *USSR*	7F2
Zhitomir *USSR*	7F2
Zhlobin *USSR*	7G2
Zhmerinka *USSR*	7F3
Zhodino *USSR*	7F2
Zhougdian *China*	16C4
Zhovten' *USSR*	7G3
Ziel,Mt *Aust*	30C3
Zielona Gora *Pol*	6D2
Ziguinchor *Sen*	18A3
Žilina *Czech*	7D3
Zilupe *USSR*	7F1
Zima *USSR*	13M4
Zimbabwe, Republic *Africa*	21C5
Zinder *Niger*	18C3
Zittau *E Germ*	6C2
Zmeinogorsk *USSR*	12K4
Znin *Pol*	7D2
Znoimo *Czech*	6D3
Zolochev *USSR*	7F3
Zolotonosha *USSR*	7G3
Zomba *Malawi*	21D5
Zongo *Zaïre*	20B3
Zorzor *Lib*	18B4
Zouerate *Maur*	18A2
Zrenjanin *Yugos*	11E1
Zújar, R *Spain*	9A2
Zumbo *Mozam*	21D5
Zürich *Switz*	8D2
Zuwārah *Libya*	19A1
Zvenigorodka *USSR*	7G3
Zvishavane *Zim*	21C6
Zvolen *Czech*	7D3
Zvornik *Yugos*	11D2
Zwickau *E Germ*	6C2
Zwolle *Neth*	6B2
Zyrardów *Pol*	7E2
Zyryanka *USSR*	13R3
Zyryanovsk *USSR*	12K5
Żywiec *Pol*	7D3